Arms Control and Disarmament Law

ELEMENTS OF INTERNATIONAL LAW

Elements of International Law represents a fresh approach in the literature of international law. It is a long series of short books. *Elements* adopts an objective, non-argumentative approach to its subject matter, focusing on narrowly defined core topics in international law. Eventually, the series will offer a comprehensive treatment of the whole of the field. In this volume, Stuart Casey-Maslen traces the history of arms control and disarmament in the modern era, addressing the issues surrounding biological and chemical weapons, the non-proliferation of nuclear weapons, and conventional weapon and arms transfer regimes.

Previously published titles in this series

International Law of Taxation
Peter Hongler

Jus Cogens
Dinah Shelton

The International Tribunal for the Law of the Sea
Kriangsak Kittichaisaree

Jus Cogens
Dinah Shelton

International Law in the Russian Legal System
William E. Butler

Arms Control and Disarmament Law

Stuart Casey-Maslen

University of Pretoria

OXFORD

UNIVERSITY PRESS

OXFORD

UNIVERSITY PRESS

Great Clarendon Street, Oxford, OX2 6DP,
United Kingdom

Oxford University Press is a department of the University of Oxford.
It furthers the University's objective of excellence in research, scholarship,
and education by publishing worldwide. Oxford is a registered trade mark of
Oxford University Press in the UK and in certain other countries

© Stuart Casey-Maslen 2021

The moral rights of the author have been asserted

First Edition published in 2021

Impression: 1

Public sector information reproduced under Open Government Licence v3.0
(http://www.nationalarchives.gov.uk/doc/open-government-licence/open-government-licence.htm)

Published in the United States of America by Oxford University Press
198 Madison Avenue, New York, NY 10016, United States of America

British Library Cataloguing in Publication Data

Data available

Library of Congress Control Number: 2021940841

ISBN 978–0–19–886503–2 (hbk.)
ISBN 978–0–19–886504–9 (pbk.)

DOI: 10.1093/law/9780198865032.001.0001

Printed and bound by
CPI Group (UK) Ltd, Croydon, CR0 4YY

Series Editors' Preface

Elements represents a fresh approach to the literature of international law. It is a long series of short books. Following the traditional path of an international law textbook, *Elements*, rather than treating the whole of the field in one heavy volume, focuses on more narrowly-defined subject matters.

There is nothing like *Elements*. It treats particular topics of international law much more extensively and in significantly more depth than traditional international law texts or encyclopaedias. As each book in the *Elements* series has a relatively narrow focus, it provides a comprehensive treatment of a specialized subject matter, in comparison to the more limited treatment of the same subject matter in other general works.

Like a classic textbook, *Elements* aims to provide objective statements of the law. The series does not concern itself with the academic niches filled ably by doctoral theses, nor include works which take an argumentative point of view, already well done by the OUP *Monograph* series. Except in length and integration, *Elements* is for substantive topics comparable to OUP's *Commentary* series on individual treaties. Each book is exhaustively footnoted in respect of international legal practice and scholarship, including treaties, diplomatic practice, decisions by international and municipal courts and arbitral tribunals, resolutions and acts of international organizations, and commentary by the most authoritative jurists.

Elements adopts an objective, non-argumentative approach to its many subject matters and constitutes a reliable go-to source for practicing international lawyers, judges and arbitrators, government and military lawyers, and scholars, teachers, and students engaged in the discipline of international law.

Mark Janis
Douglas Guilfoyle
Stephan Schill
Bruno Simma
Kimberley Trapp

Contents

Table of Cases and Materials   xi
  Treaties   xi
  Directives   xiii
  Soft Law Instruments and Guidelines   xiii
  Cases   xiii
    International Court of Justice   xiii
    European Court of Human Rights   xiv
  United Nations Resolutions   xiv
    General Assembly   xiv
    Security Council   xiv
Glossary of Abbreviations and Acronyms   xv

Introduction   1
  Definition of key terms   1
    Arms and weapons   2
    Weapons of mass destruction   3
    Conventional weapons   3
    Disarmament   5
    Arms control   6
    Non-proliferation   7
  A brief history of arms control and disarmament   7
  The role of multilateral institutions in arms control and
    disarmament   14
    The role of the United Nations   14
      Action in the Security Council   14
      Action in the General Assembly   16
      Special Sessions of the General Assembly on Disarmament 17
    The role of the Conference on Disarmament   18
    The role of treaty-based mechanisms   22

1. Key Components of Arms Control and Disarmament   24
  The general scope of prohibitions   25
  Prohibitions and controls on development and testing   26
  Prohibitions and controls on production   28
  Prohibitions and controls on stockpiling   29
  Prohibitions and controls on transfer   30

Prohibitions and controls on use   31
Assisting or encouraging prohibited activities   32
The inter-relationship between arms control and
    disarmament and *jus ad bellum*   34
The inter-relationship between arms control and
    disarmament and international humanitarian law   36
The inter-relationship between arms control and
    disarmament and international criminal law   37
National implementation of arms control and
    disarmament measures   39
    UN Security Council Resolution 1540   41

2. Biological and Chemical Weapons   43
The negotiation and entry into force of the 1971
    Biological Weapons Convention   43
The content of the 1971 Biological Weapons Convention   45
The negotiation and entry into force of the 1992
    Chemical Weapons Convention   48
The content of the 1992 Chemical Weapons Convention   50
Comparing and contrasting the two treaties   54
Verification and compliance mechanisms   55
    The UN Secretary-General's Mechanism   58
    The OPCW   59
    Australia Group   60

3. Nuclear Weapons and Nuclear Weapon Regimes   63
The development and use of nuclear weapons   65
    Manhattan Project   66
    Nuclear weapons development during the Cold War   68
The NPT   69
    The IAEA   71
    The Nuclear Suppliers Group   73
    Zangger Committee   74
The partial and comprehensive nuclear-test-ban treaties   75
Bilateral nuclear arms control and disarmament treaties   78
    The ABM Treaty   78
    The SALT Treaties   79
    The 1987 Intermediate-Range Nuclear Forces Treaty   80
    The START Treaties   81
        START I and New START   82
        START II   84
        START III   84

Regional nuclear-free zones   85
  Antarctic Treaty   86
  Treaty of Tlatelolco   86
  Treaty of Rarotonga   87
  Treaty of Bangkok   89
  Treaty of Pelindaba   90
  Treaty of Semipalatinsk   91
  The Outer Space Treaty   92
The Treaty on the Prohibition of Nuclear Weapons   94
Current developments   96
  The situation of Iran   97
  The situation of the Democratic People's Republic of Korea   98
  A new kind of nuclear arms race   99

4. Conventional Weapon Regimes   103
The 1997 Anti-Personnel Mine Ban Convention   104
  The negotiation of the 1997 Anti-Personnel Mine Ban
    Convention   106
  The content of the 1997 Anti-Personnel Mine Ban Convention   107
    The prohibition on use   108
    The prohibition on development and production   110
    The prohibition on transfer   111
    The prohibition on assisting prohibited activities   112
    The destruction of stockpiles   113
    Clearance of mined area   115
    Victim assistance   117
    International cooperation and assistance   118
The 2008 Convention on Cluster Munitions   119
The Convention on Certain Conventional Weapons   122
The 1990 Conventional Forces in Europe (CFE) Treaty   124
The 1992 Open Skies Treaty   125
The 1990 Vienna Document   127

5. Arms Transfer Regimes   128
The Arms Trade Treaty   128
  The content of the Arms Trade Treaty   130
  The implementation of the Arms Trade Treaty   137
Regional transfer regimes   139
  The European Union Common Position   139
  The 2006 ECOWAS Convention on Small Arms and Light
    Weapons   141
  The 2010 Kinshasa Convention on Small Arms and
    Light Weapons   141

Politically binding transfer regimes 142
   The Wassenaar Arrangement 143
   Missile Technology Control Regime 144
   The UN Register of Conventional Arms 146
   Data on the arms trade 148

6. Verification of Arms Control and Disarmament Agreements 150
Introduction 150
Thematic areas where verification is especially important 151
   Verification of the prohibitions on development and production 151
      The inspections regime under the Chemical Weapons Convention 152
      Routine inspections 152
      Challenge inspections 153
      Safeguards against the development and production of nuclear weapons 154
   Verification of the prohibition on testing of nuclear weapons 158
   Verification of the prohibition on stockpiling and deployment of weapons 161
   Verification of stockpile destruction 164
   Verification of the prohibition on use 167
      The Open Skies Treaty 167
      Investigating alleged use of a weapon 169

7. The Future of Arms Control and Disarmament 172
Introduction 172
Trends and lessons since 1945 172
Arms control and disarmament and new technologies 175

Index 179

Table of Cases and Materials

TREATIES

1868 Declaration Renouncing the Use, in Time of War, of Explosive
    Projectiles Under 400 Grammes Weight 7–8
1890 General Act on the Slave Trade and Importation into Africa of Firearms,
    Ammunition, and Spirituous Liquors (Brussels General Act) 9
1899 Convention (II) with Respect to the Laws and Customs of War on
    Land and its Annex: Regulations concerning the Laws and Customs
    of War on Land 8–9, 135
1899 Declaration (IV,2) concerning the Use of Asphyxiating or
    Deleterious Gases 8–9, 37–38, 48–49
1899 Declaration (IV,3) concerning the Use of Expanding Bullets 8–9
1907 Convention (IV) with Respect to the Laws and Customs of War on
    Land and its Annex: Regulations concerning the Laws and Customs
    of War on Land 135
1919 Covenant of the League of Nations 9–10
1919 Peace Treaty of Versailles 9–10
1925 Protocol for the Prohibition of the Use of Asphyxiating, Poisonous
    or Other Gases, and of Bacteriological Methods of Warfare 36, 43–44, 58
1945 Charter of the United Nations 7–8, 10, 34
1949 Geneva Conventions 37–38, 134, 135
1959 Antarctic Treaty 11, 86, 159
1963 Treaty Banning Nuclear Weapon Tests in the Atmosphere, in
    Outer Space and Under Water 11, 27–28, 76–77, 158–59
1967 Treaty on Principles Governing the Activities of States in
    the Exploration and Use of Outer Space, including the Moon
    and Other Celestial Bodies 11, 92–93
1967 Treaty for the Prohibition of Nuclear Weapons in Latin America and
    the Caribbean (Treaty of Tlatelolco) 86–87
1968 Treaty on the Non-Proliferation of Nuclear Weapons 5–6, 11, 19–20,
    27, 31, 69–71, 74, 96
1969 Vienna Convention on the Law of Treaties 39, 54
1971 Treaty on the Prohibition of the Emplacement of Nuclear Weapons
    and Other Weapons of Mass Destruction on the Sea-Bed and the
    Ocean Floor and in the Subsoil Thereof 19–20
1971 Convention on the Prohibition of the Development, Production and
    Stockpiling of Bacteriological (Biological) and Toxin Weapons and
    on Their Destruction 11, 23, 25–27, 29–31, 32,
    36, 43–48, 54–62

1972 Treaty Between the United States of America and the Union of
Soviet Socialist Republics on the Limitation of Anti-Ballistic
Missile Systems (ABM Treaty) 78–79, 84
1972 Interim Agreement Between the United States of America and the Union
of Soviet Socialist Republics on Certain Measures with respect to the
Limitation of Strategic Offensive Arms (SALT I) 11–12, 79
1976 Convention on Environmental Modification 19–20
1977 Protocol Additional to the Geneva Conventions of 12 August 1949,
and Relating to the Protection of Victims of International Armed
Conflicts (Protocol I), of 8 June 1977 (1977 Additional Protocol I to
the Geneva Conventions) 36–37, 135
1977 Protocol Additional to the Geneva Conventions of 12 August 1949,
and Relating to the Protection of Victims of Non-International Armed
Conflicts (Protocol II), of 8 June 1977 (1977 Additional Protocol II to
the Geneva Conventions) 36–38, 119, 122
1979 Agreement Governing the Activities of States on the Moon and Other
Celestial Bodies (Moon Treaty) 158–59
1980 Convention on Prohibitions or Restrictions on the Use of Certain
Conventional Weapons Which May Be Deemed to Be Excessively
Injurious or to Have Indiscriminate Effects (Convention on Certain
Conventional Weapons) 2, 36–37, 105, 122–24
  Protocol I on Non-Detectable Fragments (1980). 36–37, 123
  Protocol II on Mines (1980) 2, 105
  Protocol III on Incendiary Weapons (1980). 36–37, 123
  Protocol IV on Blinding Laser Weapons (1995) 31, 36–37, 123–24
  Amended Protocol II on Mines (1996). 29, 30, 31, 36–37, 105
  Protocol V on Explosive Remnants of War (2003) 124
1985 South Pacific Nuclear Free Zone Treaty (Treaty of Rarotonga) 87–88
1987 Treaty Between the United States of America and the Union of
Soviet Socialist Republics on the Elimination of Their
Intermediate-Range and Shorter-Range Missiles. 12–13, 80–81, 164–66
1990 Treaty on Conventional Armed Forces in Europe
(CFE Treaty) 103, 124–25
1991 START I 13, 82–84, 161–62
1992 Convention on the Prohibition of the Development, Production,
Stockpiling and Use of Chemical Weapons and on their
Destruction. 22, 25–27, 29–31, 35, 36,
39–40, 48–62
1992 Treaty on Open Skies 20–21, 103, 125–26, 167–69
1995 Treaty on the Southeast Asia Nuclear-Weapon-Free Zone
(Treaty of Bangkok) 89
1995 Protocol IV on Blinding Laser Weapons to the CCW. 31, 36–37, 105–6
1996 Protocol on Prohibitions or Restrictions on the Use of Mines,
Booby-Traps and Other Devices as amended on 3 May 1996
(Amended Protocol II) to the CCW. 30, 31, 36–37, 105
1996 African Nuclear-Weapon-Free Zone Treaty (Treaty
of Pelindaba). 90–91
1996 Comprehensive Nuclear-Test-Ban Treaty 17, 19–20, 27–28,
63–64, 77, 159–61

1997 Convention on the Prohibition of the Use, Stockpiling, Production and
     Transfer of Anti-Personnel Mines and on Their Destruction. . . . 23, 25–27, 28,
                                                          29–32, 33, 37, 104–18
1998 Rome Statute of the International Criminal Court 37–39, 44, 51–52, 135
2002 Strategic Offensive Reductions Treaty (Treaty of Moscow) 162
2003 Protocol on Explosive Remnants of War (Protocol V) to the CCW 124
2006 ECOWAS Convention on Small Arms and Light Weapons, Their
     Ammunition and Other Related Materials. 128, 141
2008 Convention on Cluster Munitions 23, 25–27, 28,
                                                          29–31, 37, 119–22
2009 Treaty on a Nuclear-Weapon-Free Zone in Central Asia (Treaty of
     Semipalatinsk) 91–92
2010 Central African Convention for the Control of Small Arms and Light
     Weapons, their Ammunition and all Parts and Components that can be
     used for their Manufacture, Repair and Assembly. 128, 141–42
2010 Treaty between The United States of America and the Russian Federation
     on Measures for the Further Reduction and Limitation of Strategic
     Offensive Arms (New START) 29, 63–64, 162–64
2013 Arms Trade Treaty. 13, 14, 17, 24, 30, 128
2017 Treaty on the Prohibition of Nuclear Weapons 17, 25–27, 30–31, 37,
                                                          63–64, 94–96

DIRECTIVES

European Union Common Position 2008/944/CFSP of 8 December 2008. 128

SOFT LAW INSTRUMENTS AND GUIDELINES

2005 International Instrument to Enable States to Identify and Trace, in
     a Timely and Reliable Manner, Illicit Small Arms and Light Weapons 132
2011 OSCE Vienna Document on Confidence- and Security-building
     Measures 103, 127
2015 Joint Comprehensive Plan of Action 15–16, 20–21, 72, 97–98
Australia Group Guidelines for Transfers of Sensitive Chemical or
     Biological Items 60–62
Wassenaar Arrangement Initial Elements. 143
Missile Technology Control Regime (MTCR) Guidelines for Sensitive
     Missile-Relevant Transfers 144–46
Nuclear Suppliers Group Guidelines 73

CASES

International Court of Justice

Case Concerning Military and Paramilitary Activities In and Against Nicaragua
     (*Nicaragua* v. *United States*), Judgment (Merits), 27 June 1986. 129–30
Legality of the Threat or Use of Nuclear Weapons, Advisory Opinion,
     8 July 1996 34–35

European Court of Human Rights

Finogenov and others v. *Russia*, Final Judgment, 4 June 2012 4

UNITED NATIONS RESOLUTIONS

General Assembly

Resolution 1(I) 10–11
Resolution 1652 (XVI). 90
Resolution 1962 (XVIII) 92
Resolution 2222 (XXI). 92
Resolution 3472B (XXX). 85
Resolution 3477 (XXX) 87
Resolution 45/56A 90
Resolution 45/57. 58
Resolution 61/89. 130
Resolution 71/258. 94
Resolution 74/56. 18
Resolution S-10/2 18–19

Security Council

Resolution 620 58
Resolution 1540 . . . . .3, 25, 41–42
Resolution 1977 41–42
Resolution 2083 40
Resolution 2209 53–54
Resolution 2231 . . . . .15–16, 97
Resolution 2235 22
Resolution 2319 22
Resolution 2356 98–99
Resolution 2375 . . . . .16, 156–57

Glossary of Abbreviations and Acronyms

ABM	Anti-ballistic missile
ASEAN	Association of Southeast Asian Nations
ATT	Arms Trade Treaty (2013)
CCW	Convention on Conventional Weapons (1980)
CD	Conference on Disarmament
CoCom	Coordinating Committee for Multilateral Export Controls
CSA	Comprehensive Safeguards Agreement
CST	Collective Security Treaty
CTBT	Comprehensive Nuclear-Test-Ban Treaty (1996)
CTBTO	Comprehensive Nuclear-Test-Ban Treaty Organization
DDR	Disarmament, demobilization, and reintegration
DPRK	Democratic People's Republic of Korea
ECOWAS	Economic Community of West African States
EEZ	Exclusive economic zone
EMP	Electromagnetic pulses
FFM	Fact-Finding Mission
G-7	Group of Seven (industrialized nations)
IAEA	International Atomic Energy Agency
ICBM	Intercontinental ballistic missile
ICC	International Criminal Court
ICJ	International Court of Justice
ICRC	International Committee of the Red Cross
IHL	International humanitarian law
IIT	Investigation and Identification Team (OPCW)
IMS	International Monitoring System
INF	Intermediate Nuclear Forces (Treaty)
JCPOA	Joint Comprehensive Plan of Action (2015)
MIRV	Multiple independently targeted re-entry vehicles
MTCR	Missile Technology Control Regime
NATO	North Atlantic Treaty Organization
New START	New Strategic Arms Reduction Treaty (2010)
NPT	Treaty on the Non-Proliferation of Nuclear Weapons
NSG	Nuclear Suppliers Group
NTI	Nuclear Threat Initiative

OAS	Organization of American States
OPCW	Organization for the Prohibition of Chemical Weapons
OSCC	Open Skies Consultative Commission
OSCE	Organization for Security and Co-operation in Europe
OSI	On-site inspection
RCA	Riot control agent
SALT	Strategic Arms Limitation Talks
SALW	Small arms and light weapons
SLBM	Submarine-launched ballistic missile
START	Strategic Arms Reduction Treaty (1991)
TPNW	Treaty on the Prohibition of Nuclear Weapons (2017)
UN	United Nations
UNODA	United Nations Office for Disarmament Affairs
UNROCA	United Nations Register of Conventional Arms
US	United States
WMD	Weapon of mass destruction

Introduction

Arms control and disarmament are key contributors to international peace and security. That said, the precise ambit of each term is not settled in either international law or doctrine, while the measures that are necessary to implement and monitor relevant multilateral and bilateral treaties can sometimes be technically complex. The aim of this book is therefore to provide a concise and objective appraisal of arms control and disarmament, with a primary focus on international law, but also with reference to key mechanisms and institutions. Evolving trends, in particular as a result of new technologies, are a cross-cutting theme.

This introduction serves as background and context to the study of arms control and disarmament. It first offers definitions of certain fundamental terms: arms and weapons, weapons of mass destruction, conventional weapons, disarmament, arms control, and non-proliferation. It then summarizes the evolution of arms control and disarmament over the past 150 years into the modern era. Finally, the role of multilateral institutions in disarmament and arms control is outlined.

Definition of key terms

The following definitions are intended to aid understanding, even though they are not necessarily reflective of treaty or general international law. This is because the terms described are widely employed in treaty and literature without either being subject to a negotiated definition or enjoying consensus in State practice or among publicists. Where there is disagreement on definitions, this is noted and discussed.

Arms and weapons

First and foremost, no agreed definition exists of either 'arms' (or the synonymous 'armaments') or 'weapons'. That said, the notion of a weapon is generally understood to be broader in ambit than is the case with respect to arms or armaments. Arms and armaments denote those weapons that are mass-produced in a factory—especially when they are intended for the military—including assault rifles, tanks, and combat aircraft. They are therefore a subset of the broader category of weapons.

Weapons comprise, in addition to arms, those tools and devices that are used, constructed, or adapted with a view to killing, harming, disorientating, or incapacitating a person, or for damaging or even destroying buildings or *matériel*. A good example of the distinction between arms and weapons is seen in the case of landmines, that is to say, explosive munitions that are designed to be victim-activated. Factory-produced landmines, a form of munition, are arms. But a landmine may also be improvised in the field—for example, by attaching a tripwire to a hand grenade—in which case it is a weapon. This notion of improvisation is duly reflected in the title of the 1980 Convention on Certain Conventional Weapons.[1] The Protocol II annexed to the Convention, which was adopted in 1980, covers not only factory-produced mines but also booby-traps, which are defined as 'any device or material which is designed, constructed *or adapted* to kill or injure and which functions unexpectedly when a person disturbs or approaches an apparently harmless object or performs an apparently safe act'.[2]

Weapons and weapon systems (and their parts and components) are distinguished from so-called dual-use items by their deliberate design for a violent purpose. Dual-use items are those that can be used for both hostile and peaceful, civilian purposes.[3] Examples include navigation systems, which can be used to help pilot a civilian airliner to a safe landing or to direct a ballistic missile to its target.

---

[1] Convention on Prohibitions or Restrictions on the Use of Certain Conventional Weapons which May Be Deemed to Be Excessively Injurious or to Have Indiscriminate Effects; adopted at Geneva, 10 October 1980; entered into force, 2 December 1983, *UNTS* Vol. 1342, Reg. No. 22495.

[2] Art. 2(2), Protocol on Prohibitions or Restrictions on the Use of Mines, Booby-Traps and Other Devices (Protocol II); adopted at Geneva, 10 October 1980; entered into force, 2 December 1983, *UNTS* Vol. 2048, Reg. No. 22495 [added emphasis].

[3] See, e.g., United Kingdom Government, 'Export Controls: Dual-Use Items, Software and Technology, Goods for Torture and Radioactive Sources', Last updated 3 March 2021, at: https://www.gov.uk/guidance/export-controls-dual-use-items-software-and-technology-goods-for-torture-and-radioactive-sources.

Weapons of mass destruction

The term 'weapon of mass destruction' (WMD) is generally taken to denote a small group of weapons with a very high lethality rate over a wide area: biological weapons, chemical weapons, and nuclear weapons. It was used in this sense in United Nations (UN) Security Council Resolution 1540, adopted in 2004.[4] The first preambular paragraph affirms that the proliferation of nuclear, chemical, and biological weapons constitutes a threat to international peace and security while the second refers to the need for all UN member States to prevent proliferation of all weapons of mass destruction in all its aspects.

Also potentially covered by the term are radiological weapons; these are weapons, sometimes called 'dirty bombs', that use conventional explosives to disperse radiation and that may kill significant numbers of people, but which do not involve a nuclear explosion. In its valuable *Dictionary of Military and Associated Terms*, the United States (US) Department of Defense defines WMD as: 'Chemical, biological, radiological, or nuclear weapons capable of a high order of destruction or causing mass casualties, excluding the means of transporting or propelling the weapon where such means is a separable and divisible part from the weapon.'[5] This definition excludes toxic chemicals used as 'less lethal' weapons, particularly tear gas. Exceptionally, however, under US domestic criminal law, the term WMD is defined far more broadly to encompass also conventional explosive and incendiary devices.[6] This definition does not apply to international law.

Conventional weapons

According to the approach taken by the UN Commission for Conventional Armaments in 1948, conventional weapons comprise all weapons other than WMD.[7] The definition used by the Commission explicitly included as

---

[4] UN Security Council Resolution 1540, adopted unanimously on 28 April 2004.

[5] US Department of Defense (DOD), *DOD Dictionary of Military and Associated Terms*, Washington DC, January 2021, at: https://www.jcs.mil/Portals/36/Documents/Doctrine/pubs/dictionary.pdf, p. 230.

[6] 18 US Code §2332a ('Use of weapons of mass destruction'), at: https://www.govinfo.gov/content/pkg/USCODE-2011-title18/pdf/USCODE-2011-title18-partI.pdf; and 18 US Code §921 ('Definitions'), at: https://www.law.cornell.edu/uscode/text/18/921#, para. 4.

[7] Report of the Conventional Armaments Commission, UN doc. S/C.3/32/Rev.1, 18 August 1948, at: https://undocs.org/en/S/C.3/32/Rev.1.

weapons of mass destruction 'radio-active material weapons, lethal chemical and biological weapons'.[8] This reflects the term's general understanding in international law today. That said, the precise scope of the term may be uncertain. It is, for instance, not settled whether riot control agents, such as tear gas, fall within the category of conventional weapons.[9]

There is greater clarity as to the classification of chemical incapacitants. The definition of a toxic chemical under the 1992 Chemical Weapons Convention is: 'Any chemical which through its chemical action on life processes can cause death, temporary incapacitation or permanent harm to humans or animals.'[10] In turn, toxic chemicals are defined to be chemical weapons.[11] This is so unless they are used for law enforcement purposes.[12] The *Finogenov* case before the European Court of Human Rights concerned use of what appears to have been a derivative of fentanyl—a powerful narcotic gas—by Russian Special Forces to bring an end to a hostage crisis. In its judgment on applications by survivors or relatives of some of the deceased hostages, the Court stated that since the exact formula of the gas was not revealed by the authorities, it was 'impossible' for it to determine whether or not it was a 'conventional weapon'.[13] The Court was therefore undecided whether Russia had used a prohibited weapon, and did not discuss whether that use occurred during and in connection with a situation of armed conflict (making it a chemical weapon and also a WMD).

It may be doubted whether cyber attacks are to be considered as conventional weapons, or whether instead they represent a distinct third category of weapons.[14] Cyberspace is defined by the US Department of Defense as a

---

[8] Ibid., p. 2, Resolution adopted by the Commission for Conventional Armaments at its Thirteenth Meeting, 12 August 1948.

[9] Under the 1992 Chemical Weapons Convention, riot control agent is defined as 'Any chemical not listed in a Schedule [to the Convention], which can produce rapidly in humans sensory irritation or disabling physical effects which disappear within a short time following termination of exposure.' Art. II(7), Convention on the Prohibition of the Development, Production, Stockpiling and Use of Chemical Weapons and on Their Destruction; adopted at Geneva, 3 September 1992; entered into force, 29 April 1997.

[10] Art. II(2), 1992 Chemical Weapons Convention.

[11] Art. II(1)(a), 1992 Chemical Weapons Convention.

[12] Art. II(9), 1992 Chemical Weapons Convention. But see also on this issue International Committee of the Red Cross (ICRC), *Expert Meeting: 'Incapacitating Chemical Agents', Law Enforcement, Human Rights Law And Policy Perspectives, Montreux, Switzerland, 24–26 April 2012*, Report, Geneva, 2013, at: https://www.icrc.org/en/doc/assets/files/publications/icrc-002-4121.pdf.

[13] European Court of Human Rights, *Finogenov and others* v. *Russia*, Final Judgment, 4 June 2012, at: https://hudoc.echr.coe.int/eng#{%22itemid%22:[%22001-108231%22]}, para. 229.

[14] See, e.g., S. Kreps and J. Schneider, 'Escalation Firebreaks in the Cyber, Conventional, and Nuclear Domains: Moving beyond Effects-Based Logics', *Journal of Cybersecurity*, Vol. 5, No. 1 (2019), at: https://academic.oup.com/cybersecurity/article/5/1/tyz007/5575971.

'global domain within the information environment consisting of the inter-dependent networks of information technology infrastructures and resident data, including the Internet, telecommunications networks, computer systems, and embedded processors and controllers'. In turn, a cyberspace attack encompasses actions taken in cyberspace 'that create noticeable denial effects (i.e., degradation, disruption, or destruction) in cyberspace or manipulation that leads to denial that appears in a physical domain'.[15] Such an attack is considered a form of 'fires' by the United States, which involves the 'use of weapon systems or other actions to create specific lethal or non-lethal effects on a target'.[16]

Disarmament

The term 'disarmament' has often been used as a generic term for all forms of control on weapons under international law,[17] but disarmament as a discipline is better understood, as it is in this book, as more narrowly pertaining to the elimination of weapons, particularly through the destruction of stockpiles. For instance, the North Atlantic Treaty Organization (NATO) defines disarmament as 'the act of eliminating or abolishing weapons (particularly offensive arms) either unilaterally (in the hope that one's example will be followed) or reciprocally. It may refer either to reducing the number of arms, or to eliminating entire categories of weapons.'[18]

The term 'general and complete disarmament' has often been employed, in particular within the United Nations (UN), to denote the elimination of all weapons of mass destruction, but may also include all offensive conventional weapons. In 1961, at its first Summit, the Non-Aligned Movement (NAM) referred to the notion of general and complete disarmament as including a 'total prohibition of the production, possession and utilization of nuclear and thermo-nuclear arms, bacteriological and chemical weapons as well as the elimination of equipment and installations for the delivery

---

[15] US Department of Defense (DOD), *DOD Dictionary of Military and Associated Terms*, January 2021, p. 55.

[16] Ibid., p. 82. See also S. Halpern, 'Annals of Technology: How Cyber Weapons Are Changing the Landscape of Modern Warfare', *The New Yorker*, 18 July 2019, at: https://www.newyorker.com/tech/annals-of-technology/how-cyber-weapons-are-changing-the-landscape-of-modern-warfare.

[17] J. Kierulf, *Disarmament under International Law*, Djof Publishing, Denmark, 2017, p. 5.

[18] NATO, 'Arms Control, Disarmament and Non-Proliferation in NATO', Last updated 16 February 2021, at: https://www.nato.int/cps/ua/natohq/topics_48895.htm.

and placement and operational use of weapons of mass destruction on national territories'.[19] Article VI of the 1968 Treaty on the Non-Proliferation
of Nuclear Weapons (NPT) stipulated in part that: 'Each of the Parties to
the Treaty undertakes to pursue negotiations in good faith … on a treaty on
general and complete disarmament under strict and effective international
control'.[20]

In the Final Document of the First Special Session of the UN General
Assembly on Disarmament, convened in 1978, it was stated that

> general and complete disarmament under strict and effective inter-
> national control shall permit States to have at their disposal only those
> non-nuclear forces, armaments, facilities and establishments as are
> agreed to be necessary to maintain internal order and protect the per-
> sonal security of citizens and in order that States shall support and pro-
> vide agreed manpower for a United Nations peace force.[21]

This would comprise the elimination of all offensive conventional weapons
in addition to the elimination of all weapons of mass destruction.

Arms control

The term 'arms control' was first coined in the 1950s in the context of the
arms race between the United States of America and the Soviet Union.[22] It
is a broad term—considerably broader than disarmament—which is used
to describe a range of restraints short of total elimination that are imposed
under international law upon the development, production, stockpiling,
deployment, transfer, and use of both conventional weapons and WMD.[23]

---

[19] NAM, Summary of the 1st Heads of State Summit, Belgrade, 1961, 'Final Document',
para. 16.

[20] Art. VI, Treaty on the Non-Proliferation of Nuclear Weapons; opened for signature at
London, Moscow, and Washington, DC, 1 July 1968; entered into force, 5 March 1970, *UNTS*
Vol. 729, Reg. No. 10485. As of 1 March 2021, 190 States were party to the NPT.

[21] First Special Session of the UN General Assembly on Disarmament, Final Document,
New York, 1978, para. 111. Epstein, however, suggests that serious negotiations on general
and complete disarmament had been effectively abandoned back in 1963. W. Epstein, *The Last
Chance: Nuclear Proliferation and Arms Control*, The Free Press, New York, 1976, p. 48.

[22] J. Borrie and T. Caughley, 'Viewing Weapons through a Humanitarian Lens: From
Cluster Munitions to Nukes?' *Irish Studies in International Affairs*, Vol. 25 (2014), pp. 23–43.

[23] See, e.g., NATO, 'Arms Control, Disarmament and Non-Proliferation in NATO'.

This is how Jozef Goldblat understood the term in his seminal work on arms control, last reprinted in 2002.[24]

Although it may be awkward to refer to restrictions on the use of weapons under the law of armed conflict/international humanitarian law as 'arms control', this broad-brush approach to the notion is becoming more widely accepted.

Non-proliferation

Non-proliferation is closely related to both arms control and disarmament. It is sometimes considered as a subset of either concept, and sometimes deemed a distinct discipline standing on its own. Horizontal non-proliferation concerns efforts to prevent the spread of weapons (and related technologies) to those that do not yet have them, whether they be States or non-State actors. Vertical proliferation refers to increases in the number, quality, or destructive capacity of existing arsenals of specific weapons by those possessor States.

While non-proliferation also applies to conventional weapons, especially with respect to missiles and missile technology, the discipline is primarily concerned with WMD.[25] For example, the NPT, which entered into force on 5 March 1970, seeks to prevent all States other than the five 'nuclear-weapon States' effectively designated as such under the NPT (China, France, Russia, the United Kingdom, and the United States), as well as any non-State actors, from obtaining nuclear weapons or other nuclear explosive devices.[26] The NPT is discussed in further detail in Chapter 3.

A brief history of arms control and disarmament

Prior to the adoption of the Charter of the United Nations[27] (UN Charter), which entered into force on 24 October 1945, most of the prohibitions

---

[24] J. Goldblat, *Arms Control: The New Guide to Negotiations and Agreements*, Sage, Thousand Oaks, CA, 2002.

[25] See UN Security Council Resolution 1540, adopted on 28 April 2004 by unanimous vote in favour.

[26] This concept concerns nuclear devices that have not been weaponized, which occurs, in particular, by their miniaturization in a warhead and incorporation in a bomb or missile.

[27] Charter of the United Nations; signed at San Francisco, 26 June 1945; entered into force, 24 October 1945, *UNTS* Vol. I. As of 1 March 2021, 193 States were members of the United Nations.

imposed on weapons were adopted in the context of the law of armed conflict/law of war rather than disarmament or arms control. An early example of this was the 1868 St Petersburg Declaration, which outlawed the use of exploding bullets against personnel in warfare.[28] Subsequent peace conferences held in The Hague, first in 1899 and then in 1907, adopted further agreements on the law of war/law of armed conflict[29] (nowadays more popularly known as international humanitarian law),[30] the law of neutrality,[31] and *jus ad bellum*[32] (the law on inter-State use of force), but they failed to agree on measures of disarmament.

Of particular importance to early arms control efforts during warfare were the Regulations annexed to the 1899 Convention on Land Warfare[33] and its 1907 revision.[34] These Regulations, which would be the basis for the prosecution of war crimes at the Nuremburg Tribunal after the end of the Second World War, prohibited the use of poison or poisoned arms and arms of a nature to cause superfluous injury or unnecessary suffering.[35] Other important treaties were the 1899 Declaration on asphyxiating or

[28] Declaration Renouncing the Use, in Time of War, of Explosive Projectiles under 400 Grammes Weight; adopted at St Petersburg, 11 December 1868; entered into force, 4 September 1900.

[29] These include specific prohibitions on the use of 'asphyxiating or deleterious gases' and expanding 'dum-dum' bullets, both adopted in 1899, as well as binding rules ('regulations') for warfare on land, adopted in 1899 and revised minimally in 1907. See, e.g., S. Casey-Maslen with S. Haines, *Hague Law Interpreted: The Conduct of Hostilities under the Law of Armed Conflict*, Hart, Oxford, 2018, pp. 6–7.

[30] There are various descriptors for the branch of international law that regulates the acts of parties during and in connection with an armed conflict. The International Committee of the Red Cross prefers the term international humanitarian law; this was also the term employed by the erstwhile International Criminal Tribunal for the former Yugoslavia (ICTY). The United States typically employs the older term of law of war. The present author prefers the term law of armed conflict, as being more neutral. Gary Solis notes 'the irony of how a body of law defining how non-combatants may lawfully be killed … is "humanitarian"': G. D. Solis, *The Law of Armed Conflict: International Humanitarian Law in War*, 2nd edn, Cambridge University Press, New York, 2016, p. 23. See also S. Haines, "War at Sea: Nineteenth-century Laws for Twenty-first Century Wars?', *International Review of the Red Cross*, Vol. 98, No. 2 (2016) pp. 419–47, at 420, fn 3.

[31] Convention (V) respecting the Rights and Duties of Neutral Powers and Persons in Case of War on Land; adopted at The Hague, 18 October 1907; entered into force, 26 January 1910.

[32] Convention (III) relative to the Opening of Hostilities; adopted at The Hague, 18 October 1907; entered into force, 26 January 1910.

[33] Convention (II) with Respect to the Laws and Customs of War on Land and its Annex: Regulations Concerning the Laws and Customs of War on Land; adopted at The Hague, 29 July 1899; entered into force, 4 September 1900.

[34] Convention (IV) respecting the Laws and Customs of War on Land and its Annex: Regulations Concerning the Laws and Customs of War on Land; adopted at The Hague, 18 October 1907; entered into force, 26 January 1910.

[35] Art. 23(a) and (e), 1899 Hague Regulations; and Art. 23(a) and (e), 1907 Hague Regulations.

deleterious gases,[36] which was the first treaty prohibition on the use of chemical weapons, and the 1899 Declaration on expanding bullets.[37]

The failure of the 1899 Hague Peace Conference to achieve concrete measures of disarmament was duly reflected in its final declaration: 'The Conference is of [the] opinion that the restriction of military charges, which are at present a heavy burden on the world, is extremely desirable for the increase of the material and moral welfare of mankind.' Eight years later, in his closing address to the final plenary, the British representative proposed to the 1907 Hague Peace Conference the following wording for its final declaration:

> The Conference confirms the resolution adopted by the Conference of 1899 in regard to the limitation of military expenditure; and inasmuch as military expenditure has considerably increased in almost every country since that time, the Conference declares that it is eminently desirable that the Governments should resume the serious examination of this question.

The British proposal was unanimously adopted.[38]

An exception to the general trend was the 1890 Brussels General Act, the first international instrument serving to regulate the arms trade in the modern era.[39] In fact, however, the Act was a treaty primarily dedicated to ending the slave trade in Africa. But the contracting colonial powers declared that the 'most effective means' of tackling the slave trade in Africa included restrictions on the 'importation' of firearms.[40] The colonial powers of the day were seeking generally to prohibit the import by others of firearms, 'and especially of rifles and improved weapons, as well as of powder, ball and cartridges', into the African countries they controlled.[41]

As a result of the outbreak of the First World War, a third international peace conference, scheduled for 1915 again in The Hague, did not take

---

[36] Declaration (IV, 2) concerning asphyxiating or deleterious gases; adopted at The Hague, 29 July 1899; entered into force, 4 September 1900.

[37] Declaration (IV, 3) concerning expanding bullets; adopted at The Hague, 29 July 1899; entered into force, 4 September 1900.

[38] '1907 Second Hague Peace Conference', *Global Security*, undated but accessed 18 March 2020, at: https://www.globalsecurity.org/military/world/naval-arms-control-1907.htm.

[39] General Act on the Slave Trade and Importation into Africa of Firearms, Ammunition, and Spirituous Liquors; signed at Brussels, 2 July 1890.

[40] Art. I(7), 1890 Brussels General Act.

[41] Art. VII, 1890 Brussels General Act.

place. The remit for the conference would have again concerned disarmament. Instead, the 1919 Treaty of Versailles that formally brought the war to an end imposed stringent disarmament obligations upon Germany. This was done with a view to making possible 'the initiation of a general limitation of the armaments of all nations'.[42] In addition, the Covenant of the League of Nations, also concluded in 1919, contained a number of provisions pertaining to disarmament. Under the Covenant, it was recognized 'that the maintenance of peace requires the reduction of national armaments to the lowest point consistent with national safety and the enforcement by common action of international obligations'.[43] By virtue of Article 23(d) of the Covenant, the League was entrusted with 'the general supervision of the trade in arms and ammunition with the countries in which the control of this traffic is necessary in the common interest'. This supervision formally ended with the death of the League in 1946, but in truth it had ceased to play this role more than a decade earlier.

The UN Charter, which was negotiated towards the end of the Second World War, was intended to put an end to the scourge of warfare. The Charter refers, in its Article 26, to the value of promoting 'the establishment and maintenance of international peace and security with the least diversion for armaments of the world's human and economic resources'. The Charter also gives the UN General Assembly the authority to consider 'the general principles of cooperation in the maintenance of international peace and security, including the principles governing disarmament and regulation of armaments'.[44] Nonetheless, the infrequency of mention of either disarmament or the regulation of armaments in an instrument adopted in the context of a war that had seen unprecedented expenditure on arms and the highest number of deaths in warfare in human history is noteworthy.[45]

That said, the first resolution of the first session of the UN General Assembly in January 1946 was dedicated to disarmament, calling for the establishment of a Commission to make recommendations 'for the elimination from national armaments of atomic weapons and of all other major weapons adaptable to mass destruction'.[46] This followed the dropping of the

---

[42]   Arts 159–213, Peace Treaty of Versailles, 1999, text available at: https://net.lib.byu.edu/~rdh7/wwi/versa/versa4.html.

[43]   Art. 8, Covenant of the League of Nations; signed at Paris, 28 June 1919; entered into force, 10 January 1920.

[44]   Art. 11, UN Charter.

[45]   Epstein, *The Last Chance: Nuclear Proliferation and Arms Control*, p. 3.

[46]   UN General Assembly Resolution 1(I), adopted on 24 January 1946 by 47 votes to 0 without abstention, para. 5(c).

atomic bombs at Hiroshima and Nagasaki by the United States at the end of the Second World War.

In the Cold War decades after 1945, nuclear disarmament was expected to prefigure general and complete disarmament.[47] This would be reflected in Article VI of the NPT, which stipulated: 'Each of the Parties to the Treaty undertakes to pursue negotiations in good faith on effective measures relating to cessation of the nuclear arms race at an early date and to nuclear disarmament, and on a treaty on general and complete disarmament under strict and effective international control.' Before the conclusion of the NPT, States, led by the two superpowers, negotiated and adopted the 1959 Antarctic Treaty[48] and the 1967 Outer Space Treaty[49] as well as the 1963 Partial Nuclear-Test Ban Treaty,[50] limiting the ability to test nuclear weapons in certain places or to deploy them to certain regions. After the NPT, the most significant global disarmament agreement was the 1971 Biological Weapons Convention.[51]

Much of the arms control negotiations during the Cold War took place bilaterally between the two superpowers. On 1 July 1968, at the signing of the NPT, US President Lyndon Johnson announced that agreement had been reached with the Soviets to begin discussions on limiting and reducing both strategic nuclear weapons delivery systems and defence against ballistic missiles.[52] The Strategic Arms Limitation Talks (SALT) had been due to start later that very year, but were delayed following the Soviet invasion

---

[47] See the definition of disarmament above. See also, e.g., 'General and Complete Disarmament: Principles and Objectives (Basic Documents)', *Bulletin of Peace Proposals*, Vol. 9, No. 1 (1 January 1978), pp. 90–93.

[48] The Antarctic Treaty; adopted at Washington, DC, 1 December 1959; entered into force, 23 June 1961, *UNTS* Vol. 402, Reg. No. 5778. As of 1 March 2021, fifty-four States were party to it.

[49] Treaty on Principles Governing the Activities of States in the Exploration and Use of Outer Space, including the Moon and Other Celestial Bodies, adopted on 19 December 1966; entry into force, 10 October 1967, UNTS Vol. 610, Reg. No. 23002. As of 1 March 2021, 110 States were party to the Treaty.

[50] Treaty Banning Nuclear Weapon Tests in the Atmosphere, in Outer Space and Under Water; opened for signature at London, Moscow, and Washington, DC, 8 August 1963; entered into force, 10 October 1963, *UNTS* Vol. 480, Reg. No. 6964. As of 1 March 2021, 125 States were party to the Treaty.

[51] Convention on the Prohibition of the Development, Production and Stockpiling of Bacteriological (Biological) and Toxin Weapons and on Their Destruction; opened for signature at London, Moscow, and Washington, DC, 10 April 1972; entered into force, 26 March 1975, *UNTS* Vol. 1015, Reg. No. 14860. As of 1 March 2021, 183 States were party to the Convention.

[52] Federation of American Scientists, 'Strategic Arms Limitation Talks (SALT I)', at: http://bit.ly/3tTLFsd.

of Czechoslovakia.[53] The first series of the Talks began in November 1969 under the Johnson administration, first in Helsinki and later in Vienna, continuing through to May 1972 under President Nixon. The first round of SALT ended with the conclusion of two treaties, the first addressing defensive systems against the threat from ballistic missiles[54] and the second imposing a (very limited) capping of the two nations' strategic nuclear arsenals.[55]

Subsequent SALT talks would take place in Geneva. SALT II set specific aggregate limits on strategic nuclear-weapon delivery systems and the number of multiple independently targetable vehicles (MIRVs) that could be incorporated into each ballistic missile.[56] MIRVs are multiple warheads incorporated into a single missile which, if used, would overwhelm missile defence systems. Some MIRVed missiles can hit targets as far as 1,500 kilometres apart.[57] But SALT II, which was signed by both the Soviet Union and the United States in June 1979, would never enter into force, a victim of the Soviet invasion of Afghanistan.

When Ronald Reagan came to power in 1980, he was initially reluctant to support arms control with the Soviet Union. But later he would engage wholeheartedly in arms control efforts. Indeed, in resuming strategic arms negotiations with the Soviet Union in 1982, the Reagan administration proposed radical reductions, rather than merely limitations, in each superpower's existing stocks of missiles and warheads. Reagan's successes include agreement on the first Cold War treaty that eliminated nuclear weapons from the arsenals of the two nuclear superpowers. The 1987 Treaty between the United States and the Soviet Union on the elimination of their

---

[53] Epstein, *The Last Chance: Nuclear Proliferation and Arms Control*, p. 27. For detail on the SALT talks, see generally M. J. Ambrose, *The Control Agenda: A History of the Strategic Arms Limitation Talks*, Cornell University Press, Ithaca, NY, 2018.

[54] Treaty Between the United States of America and the Union of Soviet Socialist Republics on the Limitation of Anti-Ballistic Missile Systems (ABM Treaty); adopted at Moscow, 26 May 1972; entered into force, 3 October 1972; expired 13 June 2002, *UNTS* Vol. 944, Reg. No. 13446.

[55] Interim Agreement Between the United States of America and the Union of Soviet Socialist Republics on Certain Measures with respect to the Limitation of Strategic Offensive Arms (SALT I); adopted at Moscow, 26 May 1972; entered into force, 3 October 1972; expired 3 October 1977, *UNTS* Vol. 944, Reg. No. 13445.

[56] P. H. Nitze, 'The Vladivostok Accord and SALT II', *The Review of Politics*, Vol. 37, No. 2 (April 1975), 147–60.

[57] Center for Arms Control and Non-Proliferation, 'Multiple Independently-targetable Reentry Vehicle (MIRV)', 28 August 2017, at: https://armscontrolcenter.org/wp-content/uploads/2017/08/Multiple-Independently_New.pdf. For a useful history of the development of MIRVed missiles in the 1960s and 1970s, see M. Leitenberg, Studies of Military R&D and Weapons Development, 'Case Study 3: The Origin of MIRV', Federation of American Scientists, 9 June 2010, at: https://fas.org/man/eprint/leitenberg/mirv.pdf.

intermediate-range and shorter-range missiles,[58] better known as the INF Treaty, eliminated from Europe an entire category of non-strategic missiles (those with a range of between 500 and 5,000 kilometres). Both nuclear and conventional missiles fell within the disarmament agreement. The Treaty became defunct in August 2019 following the withdrawal of first the United States and then the Russian Federation.[59]

The success of the INF Treaty, including and especially its intrusive on-site verification system, would be reflected in the Strategic Arms Reduction Treaty (START I), which was adopted by President Reagan's successor George H. W. Bush and opened for signature in 1991. The Treaty's entry into force was complicated by the collapse of the Soviet Union but as a result of START I, by the late 1990s Russian and US arsenals were down to around 10,000 warheads each,[60] a reduction of two-thirds from the height of the Cold War in the mid-1980s.[61]

Thus, during the Cold War that began in the aftermath of the Second World War, disarmament focused on efforts to eliminate certain WMD and limit first horizontal and then vertical proliferation of nuclear weapons. In contrast, evolving arms control addressed both WMD and conventional weapons. Since the end of the Cold War in 1991, the scope of disarmament has broadened to encompass also the elimination of certain conventional weapons (munitions) from stockpiles, in particular anti-personnel mines and cluster munitions. Within arms control, rules and regulations have also been adopted to limit or prohibit the use of certain conventional weapons (incendiary weapons and blinding laser weapons in particular). Arms control has also restricted the supply of armaments to regimes and armed forces that might misuse them in violation of international humanitarian law and human rights. The best example of this at the global level, with re-spect to conventional weapons, is the UN Arms Trade Treaty,[62] which is discussed in detail in Chapter 5.

---

[58] Treaty Between the United States of America and the Union of Soviet Socialist Republics on the Elimination of Their Intermediate-Range and Shorter-Range Missiles (INF Treaty); signed at Washington DC, 8 December 1987; entered into force, 1 June 1988; expired (de facto), 2 August 2019, *UNTS* Vol. 1657, Reg. No. 28521.

[59] Russia was the primary successor State to the Soviet Union for the purpose of the INF Treaty.

[60] 'Introduction', in S. I. Schwartz (ed.), *Atomic Audit: The Costs and Consequences of U.S. Nuclear Weapons since 1940*, The Brookings Institution, Washington DC, 1998, p. 2.

[61] H. M. Kristensen and M. Korda, 'Nuclear Notebook', Federation of American Scientists, accessed 1 February 2021, at: http://bit.ly/2miTj16.

[62] Arms Trade Treaty; adopted at New York, 2 April 2013; entered into force, 24 December 2014, *UNTS* Vol. 3013, Reg. No. 52373.

The role of multilateral institutions in arms control and disarmament

While the UN has been central to many arms control and disarmament initiatives, much has also been achieved either bilaterally or multilaterally outside its auspices. Sometimes this has been for perceived reasons of negotiating efficiency, while at other times the practice of concluding agreements by consensus has impeded effectiveness. Equally, a failure to achieve an agreement either outside UN fora or within a UN-convened diplomatic conference has, on occasion, been overcome by the adoption of a resolution within the UN General Assembly. There a two-thirds majority—or even arguably a simple majority—is required for the adoption of a treaty.[63] In recent times, this was the case with the Arms Trade Treaty, whose adoption in 2013 at a specially convened UN diplomatic conference had been blocked by three States: Iran, North Korea, and Syria. A few days later, the General Assembly adopted the Treaty by overwhelming majority.

The role of the United Nations

Action in the Security Council

Under the Charter, the UN Security Council is granted primary responsibility by UN member States for the maintenance of international peace and security.[64] This broad duty inevitably encapsulates measures of disarmament, arms control, and non-proliferation. At one end of the weapons spectrum, this concerns the non-proliferation of nuclear weapons, the most destructive weapons ever invented, while at the other, so-called micro-disarmament of small arms and light weapons (SALW) is exhorted in conflict-affected States within the context of disarmament, demobilisation, and reintegration (DDR) initiatives. Thus, for instance, the Council has encouraged governments in the Lake Chad Basin region to develop and implement a strategy that 'encompasses transparent, inclusive, human rights-compliant disarmament, demobilisation, de-radicalisation,

---

[63] According to Rule 83 of the Assembly's Rules of Procedure, decisions on 'important questions' shall be made by a two-thirds majority of the members present and voting. The adoption of a treaty is not explicitly listed as an important question. Rules of Procedure of the General Assembly, UN doc. A/520/Rev.19, New York, 2021, at: https://undocs.org/pdf?symbol=A/520/Rev.19#page=47, Rule 83.

[64] Art. 24(1), UN Charter.

rehabilitation and reintegration initiatives' for persons associated with Boko Haram and Islamic State.[65]

In 2015, then UN Secretary-General Ban Ki-moon told the Security Council that the widespread availability of weapons was a major factor in the more than 250 conflicts of the preceding decade, leading to more than 50,000 deaths each year and record-high levels of displacement.[66] 'Deny access to illegal weapons and ammunition, and you deny criminals, armed groups and extremists a central means to perpetrate violence intimidation and harm', he said. In his report to the Security Council, the UN Secretary-General stated that it was 'vital that traditional arms control measures be linked and integrated with disarmament, demobilization, and reintegration and security sector reform'.[67] In December 2020, the Security Council explicitly recognized the interlinkage between security sector reform on the one hand and disarmament, demobilization, and reintegration of former combatants, as well as national small arms and light weapons management, on the other.[68]

With the intention of preventing the proliferation of nuclear weapons, the Security Council has been especially active since the 1990s. On 6 June 1998, in response to nuclear test detonations by India and then Pakistan the month before, the UN Security Council unanimously adopted Resolution 1172, condemning both nations' nuclear tests.[69] In 2006, the Council adopted Resolution 1696 in which it called upon Iran 'without further delay' to take the steps necessary 'to build confidence in the exclusively peaceful purpose of its nuclear programme and to resolve outstanding questions'. The Council further demanded that Iran 'suspend all enrichment-related and reprocessing activities, including research and development'.[70] In July 2015, the Council unanimously adopted Resolution 2231, which endorsed the Joint Comprehensive Plan of Action (JCPOA), a political agreement

---

[65] UN Security Council Resolution 2349, adopted unanimously on 31 March 2017, operative para. 29.

[66] UN, 'Human Cost of Illicit Flow of Small Arms, Light Weapons Stressed in Security Council Debate', UN doc. SC/11889, 13 May 2015, at: https://www.un.org/press/en/2015/sc11889.doc.htm.

[67] 'Small Arms and Light Weapons, Report of the Secretary-General', UN doc. S/2015/289, 27 April 2015, at: https://undocs.org/S/2015/289, para. 87.

[68] UN Security Council Resolution 2553, adopted unanimously on 3 December 2020, twenty-fourth preambular para.

[69] UN Security Council Resolution 1172, adopted unanimously on 6 June 1998, operative para. 1.

[70] UN Security Council Resolution 1696, adopted by 14 votes to 1 (Qatar) on 31 July 2006, operative paras 1 and 2.

with Iran that sought to build confidence that Iran would not engage in a nuclear weapons programme in the future.[71] The Council affirmed that the conclusion of the JCPOA marked a fundamental shift in its consideration of the Iranian nuclear issue and expressed its desire to build a new relationship with Iran.[72] At the time of writing, the future of the JCPOA hung in the balance.[73]

Lately concern has focused on North Korea, which has continued to test-detonate nuclear weapons, most recently in early September 2017 when it exploded a thermonuclear device underground. In its Resolution 2375 of 2017, the Council reaffirmed that the proliferation of nuclear, chemical, and biological weapons, as well as their means of delivery, constitutes a threat to international peace and security, and reaffirmed its earlier decision that the Democratic People's Republic of Korea 'shall immediately abandon all nuclear weapons and existing nuclear programs in a complete, verifiable and irreversible manner'.[74]

Action in the General Assembly

In fulfilling its mandate under the UN Charter to consider 'principles governing disarmament and the regulation of armaments', the General Assembly is further empowered to make recommendations on these issues to UN member States as well as to the Security Council.[75] In 1978, the first Special Session of the General Assembly devoted to disarmament (see below) established a Disarmament Commission as a subsidiary organ of the Assembly, composed of all UN member States. Created as a deliberative but not a decision-making body, with the function of considering and making recommendations on various issues in the field of disarmament, it reports annually to the General Assembly. The Commission, which meets for three weeks in the spring, is chaired by the five geographical groupings in turn.[76] Most recently, in 2017 it published recommendations on practical confidence-building measures in the field of conventional weapons.

---

[71] UN Security Council Resolution 2231, adopted unanimously on 20 July 2015, operative para. 1.

[72] UN Security Council Resolution 2231, seventh preambular para.

[73] See, e.g., K. Robinson, 'What Is the Iran Nuclear Deal?', Backgrounder, Council on Foreign Relations, Last updated 25 February 2021, at: https://www.cfr.org/backgrounder/what-iran-nuclear-deal.

[74] UN Security Council Resolution 2375, adopted unanimously on 11 September 2017, second preambular para. and operative para. 2.

[75] Art. 11(1), UN Charter.

[76] African Group; Asia-Pacific Group; Eastern European Group; Latin American and Caribbean Group (GRULAC); and Western European and Others Group (WEOG).

Among the recommendations were the call to member States to implement fully the 2001 Programme of Action on Small Arms and Light Weapons[77] and encouragement to continue 'preventing, combating and eradicating the diversion of conventional weapons into the illicit market or to criminals, illegal armed groups, terrorists or other unauthorized recipients'.[78]

In addition, in the past few decades the Assembly has either adopted or caused to be adopted a number of significant global disarmament and arms control treaties. This includes (albeit in controversial circumstances) the Comprehensive Nuclear-Test-Ban Treaty (CTBT) in 1996[79] and, more recently, the UN Arms Trade Treaty in 2013,[80] both of which were adopted directly by the General Assembly after diplomatic conferences failed to achieve the requisite consensus.[81] In contrast, the 2017 Treaty on the Prohibition of Nuclear Weapons, which entered into force in January 2021, was adopted on 7 July 2017 by vote at a diplomatic conference specifically mandated for the task by the Assembly.[82]

Special Sessions of the General Assembly on Disarmament

The Assembly has also convened three Special Sessions dedicated to broad-based discussions on disarmament (in 1978, 1982, and 1988). Only the first of these, however, culminated in agreement upon a final document with decisions and recommendations.[83] The second Special Session, convened in 1982 at a high point of tension in the Cold War, noted the disappointing results achieved since 1978. States concluded that 'The arms race ... in

[77] Programme of Action to Prevent, Combat and Eradicate the Illicit Trade in Small Arms and Light Weapons in All Its Aspects and the International Instrument to Enable States to Identify and Trace, in a Timely and Reliable Manner, Illicit Small Arms and Light Weapons, in 'Report of the United Nations Conference on the Illicit Trade in Small Arms and Light Weapons in All Its Aspects', New York, 9–20 July 2001, at: https://undocs.org/en/A/CONF.192/15(SUPP).

[78] *Report of the Disarmament Commission for 2017*, UN doc. A/72/42, 'Recommended Practical Confidence-building Measures in the Field of Conventional Weapons', at: https://undocs.org/en/A/72/42, paras 4.4 and 4.5.

[79] Comprehensive Nuclear-Test-Ban Treaty; adopted at New York, 10 September 1996; not yet in force. As of 1 March 2021, 170 States had signed and ratified the CTBT, but eight named States were required to ratify it to trigger its entry into force.

[80] Arms Trade Treaty; adopted at New York, 2 April 2013; entered into force, 24 December 2014, UNTS Vol. 3013, Reg. 52373. As of 1 March 2021, 110 States were party to the Treaty.

[81] India blocked the adoption of the CTBT in 1996, while Iran, North Korea, and Syria blocked the adoption of the Arms Trade Treaty.

[82] Treaty on the Prohibition of Nuclear Weapons; adopted at New York, 7 July 2017; entered into force, 22 January 2021. As of 1 March 2021, fifty-four States were party to the Treaty.

[83] 'Resolutions and Decisions adopted by the UN General Assembly during its Tenth Special Session, 23 May–30 June 1978', UN doc. A/S-10/4, New York, 1978, at: https://www.un.org/disarmament/wp-content/uploads/2017/05/A-S10-4.pdf.

particular the nuclear-arms race, has assumed more dangerous proportions and global military expenditures have increased sharply'.[84] In 1988, States were able to agree upon little more in the concluding document than to list the papers and proposals that had been made.[85]

Calls have been made for a fourth Special Session on disarmament to be held, most recently in General Assembly Resolution 74/56, adopted by UN member States on 12 December 2019 by 179 votes to 0 (with 4 abstentions). An Open-ended Working Group in 2016–17 had recommended that a Fourth Session comprehensively assess the situation in disarmament and review the international disarmament machinery with a view to maintaining its relevance and increasing its effectiveness.[86] As of the time of writing, no formal agreement had been reached to hold the Session, much less to set a date for it to be convened.

The role of the Conference on Disarmament

In earlier decades, a key and active component in the international disarmament machinery was the Conference on Disarmament (CD). Indeed, in 1978 its predecessor, the Committee on Disarmament, was designated as the principal multilateral disarmament negotiating forum by the UN General Assembly in its Resolution S-10/2 of 30 June 1978. The CD, whose membership originally comprised 40 States, was expanded several times; it had 65 member States as of March 2021.[87] While the CD is not

[84] Review of the Implementation of the Recommendations and Decisions Adopted by the General Assembly at its Tenth Special Session, UN doc. A/S-12/32, 9 July 1982, at: https://www.undocs.org/A/S-12/32, pp. 22–23.

[85] Assessment of the Implementation of the Decisions and Recommendations Adopted by the General Assembly at its Tenth and Twelfth Special Sessions, UN doc. A/S-15/50, June 1988, at: https://www.undocs.org/A/S-15/50.

[86] Report of the Open-ended Working Group on the fourth special session of the General Assembly devoted to disarmament, UN doc. A/AC.268/2017/2, 16 June 2017, at: https://www.un.org/disarmament/wp-content/uploads/2017/07/A-268-2017-2_Report-OEWG-SSODIV.pdf.

[87] UN, 'Conference on Disarmament', undated but accessed 1 March 2021 at: https://www.un.org/disarmament/conference-on-disarmament/. The sixty-five States are: Algeria, Argentina, Australia, Austria, Bangladesh, Belarus, Belgium, Brazil, Bulgaria, Cameroon, Canada, Chile, China, Colombia, Cuba, Democratic Republic of the Congo, Ecuador, Egypt, Ethiopia, Finland, France, Germany, Hungary, India, Indonesia, Iran, Iraq, Ireland, Israel, Italy, Japan, Kazakhstan, Kenya, Democratic People's Republic of Korea, Republic of Korea, Malaysia, Mexico, Mongolia, Morocco, Myanmar, the Netherlands, New Zealand, Nigeria, Norway, Pakistan, Peru, Poland, Romania, Russian Federation, Senegal, Slovakia, South Africa, Spain, Sri Lanka, Sweden, Switzerland, Syrian Arab Republic, Tunisia, Turkey, Ukraine, the United Kingdom, the United States, Venezuela, Viet Nam, and Zimbabwe.

formally a UN body—it adopts its own rules of procedure and agenda—it has a very close relationship with the United Nations, reporting annually to the General Assembly and taking into account recommendations by the Assembly.[88]

The CD's permanent agenda, which is known as the Decalogue,[89] now comprises only nine issues, following the successful adoption of the Chemical Weapons Convention in 1992:[90]

- Nuclear weapons in all aspects
- Other weapons of mass destruction
- Conventional weapons
- Reduction of military budgets
- Reduction of armed forces
- Disarmament and development
- Disarmament and international security
- Collateral measures; confidence-building measures; effective verification methods in relation to appropriate disarmament measures, acceptable to all parties
- Comprehensive programme of disarmament leading to general and complete disarmament under effective international control.

The CD and its forerunners successfully negotiated the NPT, the 1971 Sea-bed Treaty,[91] the 1971 Biological Weapons Convention,[92] the 1976

Since 1982, requests for membership have been received from the following twenty-seven non-members, in chronological order: Greece, Croatia, Kuwait, Portugal, Slovenia, Czechia, Costa Rica, Denmark, North Macedonia, Cyprus, Lithuania, Ghana, Luxembourg, Uruguay, Philippines, Azerbaijan, Libya, Armenia, Thailand, Georgia, Jordan, Estonia, Latvia, Malta, Serbia, Moldova, and Qatar.

[88] The annual reports are available at: https://meetings.unoda.org/section/cd-reports/.

[89] See, e.g., Nuclear Threat Initiative (NTI), 'CONFERENCE ON DISARMAMENT (CD)', Last updated 16 December 2020, at: https://www.nti.org/learn/treaties-and-regimes/conference-on-disarmament/.

[90] Convention on the Prohibition of the Development, Production and Stockpiling of Development, Production, Stockpiling and Use of Chemical Weapons and on their Destruction; adopted at Geneva, 3 September 1992; entered into force, 29 April 1997, UNTS Vol. 1975, Reg. No. 33757. As of 1 March 2021, 193 States were party to the Convention.

[91] Treaty on the Prohibition of the Emplacement of Nuclear Weapons and Other Weapons of Mass Destruction on the Sea-Bed and the Ocean Floor and in the Subsoil Thereof; opened for signature at London, Moscow, and Washington, DC, 11 February 1971; entered into force, 18 May 1972, *UNTS* Vol. 955, Reg. No. 13678. As of 1 March 2021, ninety-four States were party to the Treaty.

[92] Convention on the Prohibition of the Development, Production and Stockpiling of Bacteriological (Biological) and Toxin Weapons and on Their Destruction; opened for

Convention on Environmental Modification,[93] and the 1992 Chemical Weapons Convention. Since its failure to adopt the CTBT in 1996, however, the CD has been effectively deadlocked, unable to make progress on any disarmament or arms control instruments.[94] The sole exception was a few weeks in 1998 during which the Conference convened negotiations on a fissile material cut-off treaty (FMCT), which would prohibit the production of plutonium and highly enriched uranium for weapons. But no agreement resulted from the talks and no progress has been achieved since.[95]

The opening of business in the CD in 2021 did not suggest the twenty-five-year impasse was about to be overcome. In January, talks seeking to surmount the deadlock began with acrimony, with Iran blocking Saudi Arabia and the United Arab Emirates from joining as observers, while Turkey blocked the involvement of Cyprus. Marc Finaud, a security expert at the Geneva Centre for Security Policy (GCSP), told the Reuters press agency: 'It is a sign that the Conference on Disarmament is at a crossroads and if it wants to remain relevant and useful it has to do some soul-searching.'[96]

In February, at the High-Level Segment of the 2021 Session of the Conference, the Russian Minister of Foreign Affairs, Sergey Lavrov, observed that 2020 had been 'a difficult year in all respects'. It had seen, he said, 'a growing destructive trend toward the collapse of the existing international arms control, disarmament and non-proliferation regimes, an increasing tension and lack of trust between UN Member States'.[97] Unfortunately, the Minister declared, 'the United States continued taking

---

signature, 10 April 1972; entered into force, 25 March 1975, *UNTS* Vol. 1015, Reg. No. 14860. As of 1 March 2021, 183 States were party to the Convention.

[93] Convention on the Prohibition of Military or Any Other Hostile Use of Environmental Modification Techniques (ENMOD); adopted at New York, 10 December 1976; entered into force, 5 October 1978, *UNTS* Vol. 1108, Reg. No. 17119. As of 1 March 2021, seventy-eight States were party to the Convention.

[94] The CTBT was drafted in the Conference on Disarmament but could not be adopted as a result of opposition by India. The text of the treaty was forwarded by Australia to the UN General Assembly where it was adopted by 158 votes to 3 (Bhutan, India, and Libya). UN General Assembly Resolution 50/245, adopted on 10 September 1996 by 158 votes to 3, with 5 abstentions.

[95] W. Boese, 'Conference on Disarmament Stalemate Persists', *Arms Control Today*, June 2007, at: https://www.armscontrol.org/act/2007_06/CDStalemate.

[96] E. Farge, 'CORRECTED—Iran, Turkey block rivals from joining U.N. disarmament talks', *Reuters*, 19 January 2021, at: https://www.reuters.com/article/un-arms-idUSL8N2JU28V.

[97] Ministry of Foreign Affairs of the Russian Federation, 'Address by Sergey Lavrov, Minister of Foreign Affairs of the Russian Federation, to the High Level Segment of the Conference on Disarmament', Moscow, 24 February 2021, at: https://www.mid.ru/en/foreign_policy/news/-/asset_publisher/cKNonkJE02Bw/content/id/4594359.

steps to substitute some global "rules-based order" imposed by Washington for international law and the central role of the United Nations. After withdrawing from the JCPOA in 2018 and dismantling the INF Treaty in 2019, the United States decided, in 2020, to withdraw from the Treaty on Open Skies, thereby undermining international security.'[98]

US Secretary of State Antony Blinken observed that after Joe Biden took office as President, 'the United States and the Russian Federation extended New START for five years. That decision made our countries and the world safer, and it was only the beginning of our efforts to address nuclear threats.'[99] The United States was, he said, 'ready to engage Russia in strategic stability discussions on arms control and emerging security issues. We will be clear-eyed about the broader challenges posed by Russia and how our respective nuclear arsenals represent existential threats to each other.'[100]

Sohail Mahmood, Pakistan's Foreign Secretary, said that while the Conference on Disarmament was an 'indispensable part' of the UN disarmament machinery, militarily significant States were only willing to advance proposals which were cost-free for them. The Conference needed to take up negotiations on a legally binding treaty for the prevention of an arms race in outer space, he said.[101] Earlier in the month, China had stated its readiness 'to conduct bilateral dialogues, on the basis of equality and mutual respect, on issues related to strategic security with other nuclear-weapon States, including the US and Russia, so as to enhance strategic trust'.[102] It was also ready to participate in dialogues and cooperation in multilateral fora, such as the P5 mechanism, the NPT review process, and the CD, 'with a view to maintaining the strategic stability, enhancing international peace and security, and promoting international arms control, disarmament and non-proliferation process'.[103]

---

[98] Ibid.

[99] US Mission to the United Nations in Geneva, 'Secretary of State Antony J. Blinken, Remarks at the High-level Segment of the Conference on Disarmament', 22 February 2021, at: https://geneva.usmission.gov/2021/02/22/secretary-blinken-cd/.

[100] Ibid.

[101] UN, 'Conference on Disarmament Concludes High-level Segment', Meeting Summary, 24 February 2021, at: https://www.ungeneva.org/en/news-media/meeting-summary/2021/02/conference-disarmament-concludes-high-level-segment.

[102] Remarks by H. E. Amb. Li Song of China at the Plenary Meeting on 4 February 2021 of the Conference on Disarmament, 4 February 2021, at: http://www.china-un.ch/eng/dbdt/t1851357.htm.

[103] Ibid.

The role of treaty-based mechanisms

Several global disarmament treaties have established monitoring or implementation mechanisms to support the relevant treaties' application. By far the most significant, in terms of mandate, resources, and impact, is the Organization for the Prohibition of Chemical Weapons (OPCW), established by the 1992 Chemical Weapons Convention. The States Parties to the Convention established the OPCW to 'achieve the object and purpose of th[e] Convention, to ensure the implementation of its provisions, including those for international verification of compliance with it, and to provide a forum for consultation and cooperation among States Parties'.[104]

Alone among such treaty-based institutions, the OPCW is empowered to investigate alleged use of the weapons prohibited by the treaty. To date, this has concentrated on alleged use in Syria. Thus, for example, in May 2018, the OPCW Fact-Finding Mission for Syria reported that chlorine had been used as a chemical weapon on 4 February of the same year in Saraqib in Idlib governorate.[105] Until a decision by the Conference of States Parties to the Convention in June 2018, however, a Fact-Finding Mission had not been authorized to seek to attribute *responsibility* for use of chemical weapons by or on the territory of a State Party.[106]

Previously, for a period of two years, a joint UN–OPCW mechanism had been investigating alleged use in Syria. UN Security Council Resolution 2235 (2015), unanimously adopted on 7 August 2015, had established the OPCW–UN Joint Investigative Mechanism (JIM) 'to identify to the greatest extent feasible individuals, entities, groups, or governments who were perpetrators, organisers, sponsors or otherwise involved in the use of chemicals as weapons'.[107] The Council renewed the JIM's mandate for a further period of one year in its Resolution 2319, unanimously adopted on 17 November 2016, but on 16 November 2017 the Security Council did not renew the mandate of the JIM again, following Russia's wielding of its veto.

---

[104] Art. VIII(1), Chemical Weapons Convention.

[105] OPCW, 'OPCW Fact-finding Mission Confirms Likely Use of Chlorine in Saraqib, Syria', Press release, 16 May 2018, at: https://www.opcw.org/media-centre/news/2018/05/opcw-fact-finding-mission-confirms-likely-use-chlorine-saraqib-syria.

[106] OPCW, 'CWC Conference of the States Parties Adopts Decision Addressing the Threat from Chemical Weapons Use', News release, The Hague, 27 June 2018, at: https://www.opcw.org/media-centre/news/2018/06/cwc-conference-states-parties-adopts-decision-addressing-threat-chemical. The decision was adopted by 82 votes to 24.

[107] UN Security Council Resolution 2235, unanimously adopted on 7 August 2015, operative paragraph 1.

On 5 November 2019 the Director-General of the OPCW, Fernando Arias, briefed the UN Security Council and senior UN officials on issues related to chemical weapons and Syria. He noted that the two bodies 'work in a complementary manner, as has been manifested in OPCW decisions and resolutions of the UN Security Council and the General Assembly'.[108] Subsequently, the Council issued a Presidential Statement in which the Council welcomed continuing cooperation between the UN and the OPCW, and expressed its strong support for 'the efforts of the OPCW to achieve the object and purpose of the Convention and to ensure the full implementation of its provisions'.[109]

States Parties to other disarmament treaties, notably the 1971 Biological Weapons Convention, the 1997 Anti-Personnel Mine Ban Convention, and the 2008 Convention on Cluster Munitions, have established small Implementation Support Units (ISUs) to support the implementation of the respective treaty. These mechanisms are discussed further in Chapter 2 and Chapter 4.

---

[108] OPCW, 'OPCW Director-General Briefs United Nations Security Council on Syria', News, 7 November 2019, at: https://www.opcw.org/media-centre/news/2019/11/opcw-director-general-briefs-united-nations-security-council-syria.

[109] Statement by the President of the Security Council, UN doc. S/PRST/2019/14, 22 November 2019, at: https://www.securitycouncilreport.org/atf/cf/%7B65BFCF9B-6D27-4E9C-8CD3-CF6E4FF96FF9%7D/s_prst_2019_14.pdf.

1

Key Components of Arms Control and Disarmament

This chapter defines and describes the different components within arms control and disarmament law treaties, specifically development and testing, production, stockpiling, transfer, and use. Verification and other confidence-building measures, discussed elsewhere in this work, seek to monitor and promote implementation of agreed commitments while assuring other States that those commitments are being respected.

Weapons development includes testing of prototypes. With respect specifically to test-detonation of nuclear weapons and other nuclear explosive devices this issue is also addressed in dedicated provisions and treaties. Production is one form of acquisition of armaments but it is not the only means by which a State may come to possess or control a weapon. Stockpile destruction may be total, but certain treaties may allow a small number of prohibited weapons to be retained, for instance for use in training and testing of environmental remediation processes.

Transfer certainly encompasses export, but whether it includes transit of weapons over national territory and also gifts, loans, and leases is sometimes disputed in the context of specific treaty regimes. Furthermore, in a number of treaties, it is made explicit that the meaning of transfer is not limited to export. In the United Nations (UN) Arms Trade Treaty, for instance, transfer is stipulated to also apply to import, trans-shipment, and brokering.[1] The nature of the prohibition on assisting or encouraging prohibited activities incorporated in many global disarmament law treaties is also briefly addressed in this chapter.

This chapter further summarizes the inter-relationship between arms control and disarmament law and other branches of international law, particularly *jus ad bellum*, international humanitarian law (IHL), and

---

[1] Art. 2(2), Arms Trade Treaty; adopted at New York, 2 April 2013; entered into force, 24 December 2014, UNTS Vol. 3013, Reg. No. 52373. As of 1 June 2021, 110 States were party to the Treaty.

international criminal law. It is often said that *jus ad bellum* is weapons-neutral, but the reality is more nuanced, particularly with respect to nuclear weapons. Use of all weapons during armed conflict was traditionally the preserve of IHL, but a disarmament treaty may prohibit use in all circumstances, including peacetime as well as armed conflict.

The chapter also touches on national implementation of arms control and disarmament rules, both through multilateral treaty regimes and also through binding provisions in resolutions adopted by the UN Security Council, such as those contained in its landmark Resolution 1540 regarding the non-proliferation of weapons of mass destruction.[2] Verification and compliance, which are especially difficult issues in an arms control or disarmament treaty because of their implications at domestic level, are discussed in subsequent chapters. States are the primary addressees of arms control and disarmament obligations but non-State actors within their jurisdiction, such as companies operating or headquartered on their territory, are also encompassed by the obligations imposed on the territorial States.

The general scope of prohibitions

The core prohibitions in a disarmament treaty are generally formulated in positive terms as an undertaking 'never under any circumstances' to engage in certain conduct. This is the case in the 1971 Biological Weapons Convention,[3] the 1992 Chemical Weapons Convention,[4] the 1997 Anti-Personnel Mine Ban Convention,[5] the 2008 Convention on Cluster Munitions,[6] and the 2017 Treaty on the Prohibition of Nuclear Weapons

---

[2] UN Security Council Resolution 1540, adopted unanimously on 28 April 2004.

[3] Art. I, Convention on the Prohibition of the Development, Production and Stockpiling of Bacteriological (Biological) and Toxin Weapons and on Their Destruction; adopted at New York, 16 December 1971; entered into force, 25 March 1975, *UNTS* Vol. 1015, Reg. No. 14860. As of 1 June 2021, 183 States were party to the Convention.

[4] Art. I(1), Convention on the Prohibition of the Development, Production and Stockpiling of Development, Production, Stockpiling and Use of Chemical Weapons and on Their Destruction; adopted at Geneva, 3 September 1992; entered into force, 29 April 1997, *UNTS* Vol. 1975, Reg. No. 33757. As of 1 June 2021, 193 States were party to the Convention.

[5] Art. 1(1), Convention on the Prohibition of the Use, Stockpiling, Production and Transfer of Anti-Personnel Mines and on Their Destruction; adopted at Oslo, 18 September 1997; entered into force, 1 March 1999, *UNTS* Vol. 2056, Reg. No. 35597. As of 1 June 2021, 164 States were party to the Convention.

[6] Art. 1(1), Convention on Cluster Munitions; adopted at Dublin, 30 May 2008; entered into force, 1 August 2010, *UNTS* Vol. 2699, Reg. No. 47713. As of 1 June 2021, 110 States were party to the Convention.

(TPNW).[7] In the Chemical Weapons Convention, the Anti-Personnel Mine Ban Convention, and the 2008 Convention on Cluster Munitions, the article is entitled 'General Obligations'. In the TPNW, the article is entitled 'Prohibitions'.

In any event, the undertaking is binding on the State Party itself, meaning that the authorities cannot engage in the prohibited conduct either directly or through their agents. It is further understood that this form of undertaking also demands that each State effectively prohibit corporations, other forms of enterprise or group, and individuals within its jurisdiction from engaging in prohibited conduct. Non-State actors, including armed groups, are not directly bound by these treaty obligations. This distinguishes arms control and disarmament from IHL, which is generally agreed to bind non-State armed groups as a matter of international law.[8]

Prohibitions and controls on development and testing

Arms control and disarmament treaties often—but not always—prohibit or control weapons development and testing. It is specifically prohibited to develop the weapons outlawed in the 1971 Biological Weapons Convention,[9] the 1992 Chemical Weapons Convention, the 1997 Anti-Personnel Mine Ban Convention,[10] the 2008 Convention on Cluster Munitions,[11] and the TPNW.[12] The terms 'develop' or 'development' are not defined in any of these treaties, but they are ordinarily taken to encompass all dedicated research and related activities that typically take place before a weapon enters production. In the context of the Chemical Weapons Convention, to '"develop" is said to be, by virtue of its purpose, the preparation of the production of chemical weapons as distinct from permitted research'.[13] This

---

[7] Treaty on the Prohibition of Nuclear Weapons; adopted at New York, 7 July 2017; entered into force, 22 January 2021. As of 1 June 2021, fifty-four States were party to the Convention.

[8] See, e.g., International Committee of the Red Cross, Commentary on Article 3 of the 1949 Geneva Convention III on Prisoners of War, 2020, at: https://ihl-databases.icrc.org/applic/ihl/ihl.nsf/Comment.xsp?action=openDocument&documentId=31FCB9705FF00261 C1258585002FB096, paras 539–42.

[9] Art. I, Biological Weapons Convention.

[10] Art. 1(1)(b), Anti-Personnel Mine Ban Convention.

[11] Art. 1(1)(b), Convention on Cluster Munitions.

[12] Art. 1(1)(a), TPNW.

[13] W. Krutzsch and R. Trapp, *A Commentary on the Chemical Weapons Convention*, Martinus Nijhoff, The Netherlands, 1994, p. 13.

conceptualization of development is generally understood to encompass testing of prototypes and even, in certain circumstances, computer modelling or simulations.[14]

The absence of a reference to development as a prohibited activity in a treaty implies that research and development that do not culminate in production or acquisition of a prohibited weapon are not unlawful. This issue has provoked considerable discussion in the context of the 1968 Treaty on the Non-Proliferation of Nuclear Weapons, which prohibits the acquisition of any nuclear explosive device by non-nuclear-weapon States Parties but not its development.[15] Given this fact, a number of leading commentators have argued that preliminary activities of research and development that fall short of the completion of a nuclear explosive device are lawful.[16] Thus, the international arms control expert Daniel Joyner has observed:

> Some current and former government officials and other observers, particularly in the United States, hold that the prohibition on manufacturing a nuclear explosive device entails a scope which reaches far back along the knowledge acquisition and development line of a nuclear weapons program to the concept, capacity building, design, research and experimentation stages. Under this interpretation, the information presented in this new IAEA [International Atomic Energy Agency] report might be considered evidence of a breach. However, this interpretation is incorrect by reference to the plain meaning of the terms of Article II, as confirmed by the negotiating history of the NPT.[17]

Testing of a weapon means its use in controlled conditions on sovereign territory or extraterritorially with the valid consent of the territorial State. This is distinguished from the notion of 'use' under international law, which means hostile use against an adverse party, particularly in an armed

---

[14] S. Casey-Maslen and T. Vestner, *A Guide to International Disarmament Law*, Routledge, Abingdon/New York, 2019, para. 2.11.

[15] Art. II, Treaty on the Non-Proliferation of Nuclear Weapons; opened for signature at London, Moscow, and Washington, DC, 1 July 1968; entered into force, 5 March 1970, *UNTS* Vol. 729, Reg. No. 10485. As of 1 June 2021, 190 States were party to the NPT of which 185 were non-nuclear-weapons States Parties.

[16] W. Epstein, *The Last Chance: Nuclear Proliferation and Arms Control*, The Free Press, New York, 1976, p. 90; D. Joyner, 'Iran's Nuclear Program and the Legal Mandate of the IAEA', Blog entry, *Jurist*, 9 November 2011, at: http://bit.ly/3er3UNz.

[17] Ibid. See also J. Woodliffe, 'Nuclear Weapons and Non-Proliferation: The Legal Aspects', Chap. 5 in I. Pogany (ed.), *Nuclear Weapons and International Law*, Avebury, Aldershot, 1987, p. 91.

conflict.[18] While the testing of a weapon generally falls within the notion of development, in a number of disarmament or arms control agreements it is treated as a distinct element. In the specific cases of the 1963 Partial Nuclear-test-ban Treaty[19] and the 1996 Comprehensive Nuclear-Test-Ban Treaty (not yet in force),[20] the prohibition of certain forms of testing and in specified locations is the object and purpose of the treaty. Of course, with respect to nuclear weapons, explosive testing of any kind has highly significant safety and environmental implications. Article 1(1)(a) of the TPNW prohibits the explosive testing of any nuclear weapons or nuclear explosive devices. Other forms of testing, such as computer modelling and sub-critical testing, are prohibited under the TPNW as illegal development.[21]

In the case of specific conventional weapons that are outlawed by disarmament treaty, continued testing may be permitted under certain circumstances. This is notably the case with respect to the development of techniques in the clearance and destruction of anti-personnel mines or unexploded submunitions, under the 1997 Anti-Personnel Mine Ban Convention[22] and the 2008 Convention on Cluster Munitions,[23] respectively.

Prohibitions and controls on production

A comprehensive prohibition on the production and/or manufacture of the weapon is typically included in a disarmament treaty. This is the case in the Biological Weapons Convention, the Chemical Weapons Convention, the Anti-Personnel Mine Ban Convention, the Convention on Cluster Munitions, and the TPNW. (The Chemical Weapons Convention also obligates the destruction of production facilities.) Neither production nor manufacture is defined in any of those treaties. The terms production or produce are, though, broader than the notion of manufacture—which in

---

[18] Casey-Maslen and T. Vestner, *A Guide to International Disarmament Law*, para. 2.12.

[19] Treaty Banning Nuclear Weapon Tests in the Atmosphere, in Outer Space and Under Water; concluded at Moscow, 5 August 1963; entered into force, 10 October 1963, *UNTS* Vol. 480, Reg. No. 6964.

[20] Comprehensive Nuclear-Test-Ban Treaty; adopted at the UN General Assembly in New York, 10 September 1996; not yet in force.

[21] See further S. Casey-Maslen, *Treaty on the Prohibition of Nuclear Weapons: A Commentary*, Oxford University Press, Oxford, 2019, paras 1.36–1.39.

[22] Art. 3(1), 1997 Anti-Personnel Mine Ban Convention.

[23] Art. 3(6), 2008 Convention on Cluster Munitions.

ordinary parlance denotes production in a factory—given that production applies to the local artisanal fabrication or improvisation of weapons as well as to the adaptation of existing weapons.

Under Article II of the NPT, a non-nuclear-weapon State Party undertakes not to 'manufacture or otherwise acquire' nuclear weapons or other nuclear explosive devices. A limited prohibition on production—in particular, of non-detectable anti-personnel mines—is also included in the 1996 Amended Protocol II to the Convention on Certain Conventional Weapons,[24] which is primarily an IHL treaty.

Prohibitions and controls on stockpiling

Central to a disarmament treaty are a prohibition on stockpiling and a corresponding obligation to destroy stockpiles of the weapon being outlawed. A stockpile is not formally defined in international law but may be taken to mean an accumulation of one or more stored weapons prior to their deployment or use. In some treaties, stockpiling does not encompass deployed weapons. This is the case in certain bilateral nuclear arms treaties, such as the 2010 New START Treaty,[25] as well as the 1992 Chemical Weapons Convention. This explains the broad formulation in the Convention of the duty on each State Party to 'destroy chemical weapons it owns or possesses, or that are located in any place under its jurisdiction or control'.[26]

The obligation to destroy some or all of the weapons held in a stockpile (or operationally deployed but not used) is normally contained in a time-bound deadline. The deadline may depend either on the date of entry into force of the treaty (as is the case in the Biological Weapons Convention and the Chemical Weapons Convention) or on the date on which a State becomes party to the treaty (as in the Anti-Personnel Mine Ban Convention or the Convention on Cluster Munitions). Sometimes the deadlines for

---

[24] Technical Annex, para. 1(d), Protocol on Prohibitions or Restrictions on the Use of Mines, Booby-Traps and Other Devices as amended on 3 May 1996 (Amended Protocol II), annexed to the Convention on Prohibitions or Restrictions on the Use of Certain Conventional Weapons Which May Be Deemed to Be Excessively Injurious or to Have Indiscriminate Effects; adopted at Geneva, 3 May 1996; entered into force, 3 December 1998, *UNTS* Vol. 2048, Reg. No. 22495. As of 1 June 2021, 106 States were party to the 1996 Amended Protocol II.

[25] Treaty between the United States of America and the Russian Federation on Measures for the Further Reduction and Limitation of Strategic Offensive Arms (New START); signed at Prague, 8 April 2010; entered into force, 5 February 2011; duration extended to 5 February 2026.

[26] Art. I(2), 1992 Chemical Weapons Convention.

stockpile destruction are fixed and may not be extended (this is so under the Biological Weapons Convention). In other instances, the deadline for stockpile destruction may be extended once (as in the Chemical Weapons Convention) or even multiple times, where absolutely necessary (as in the Convention on Cluster Munitions).

Often, stockpiles are held of critical parts or components rather than of fully assembled weapons. For example, in the case of munitions, detonators may be stored separately from explosive material, for reasons of safety and security.[27] This practice has no bearing on the overall duty to destroy stockpiles. In specific cases (anti-personnel mines and cluster munitions), the duty excludes a 'minimum number absolutely necessary' for research and training in detection and clearance operations for weapons that have been used.[28]

Prohibitions and controls on transfer

A common element in any arms control or disarmament treaty is a prohibition or restriction on the transfer within its scope. Sometimes the term is explicitly defined in the treaty, but even when it is, the definition of transfer is sometimes ambiguous (this is so under the 1996 Amended Protocol II, the Anti-Personnel Mine Ban Convention, and the Convention on Cluster Munitions). There is also considerable inconsistency in interpretation of the term transfer across the various arms control, disarmament, and non-proliferation treaties. In some instances the concept pertains to export but not to importation, while in others the notion of transfer seemingly requires both movement into the territory of another State of the weapon and transfer of title to it. Uniquely, in the Arms Trade Treaty transfer is defined, in Article 2(2), as meaning export, import, transit, trans-shipment, and brokering.

A transfer of prohibited weapons may be comprehensive and unequivocal in nature, which is the case in the Biological Weapons Convention, the Chemical Weapons Convention, and the TPNW. The Anti-Personnel Mine Ban Convention and the Convention on Cluster Munitions both provide for an exception to the general prohibition on transfer for the purpose of

---

[27] Casey-Maslen and Vestner, *A Guide to International Disarmament Law*, para. 2.3.

[28] Art. 3(1), 1997 Anti-Personnel Mine Ban Convention; Art. 3(6), 2008 Convention on Cluster Munitions.

destruction of anti-personnel mines and cluster munitions, respectively, as well as to facilitate detection, clearance, or destruction techniques.[29] But whereas a State Party to the Anti-Personnel Mine Ban Convention may transfer to any party a minimum number of anti-personnel mines, the corresponding provision in the Convention on Cluster Munitions restricts that transfer to another State Party.

In the NPT the prohibition is also partial, but in the sense that it binds only the five nuclear-weapon States designated by the Treaty. Thus, under Article I of the NPT, a nuclear-weapon State is prohibited from any transfer of nuclear weapons to individuals and non-State actors as well as to all non-nuclear-weapon States (whether or not they are party to the Treaty). Restrictions are imposed on the transfer of nuclear material and related equipment by any non-nuclear-weapon State Party.

Prohibitions on transfer are also included in the 1996 Amended Protocol II and 1995 Protocol IV on blinding laser weapons to the Convention on Certain Conventional Weapons.[30] Although these two Protocols apply primarily in situations of armed conflict, it is understood that the prohibitions on transfer also apply in peacetime.[31]

Prohibitions and controls on use

The concept of use of a weapon is not defined in any arms control or disarmament treaty. According to one definition, use of a weapon means 'at the least, its employment against an adverse party to an armed conflict or other target both outside as well as within a situation of armed conflict'.[32] It is thus broader than a prohibition under IHL, which, as discussed below, governs only use within and associated with an armed conflict. Exceptionally, in the context of the 1997 Anti-Personnel Mine Ban Convention, the prohibition on use may also outlaw taking operational advantage of the presence

---

[29] Art. 3(2), 1997 Anti-Personnel Mine Ban Convention; Art. 3(7), 2008 Convention on Cluster Munitions.

[30] Art. 1, Protocol IV on Blinding Laser Weapons to the Convention on Certain Conventional Weapons; adopted at Vienna, 13 October 1995; entered into force, 30 July 1998, *UNTS* Vol. 1380, Reg. No. 22495.

[31] Art. 1(1), Convention on Prohibitions or Restrictions on the Use of Certain Conventional Weapons which May Be Deemed to Be Excessively Injurious or to Have Indiscriminate Effects; adopted at Geneva, 10 October 1980; entered into force, 2 December 1983, *UNTS* Vol. 1342, Reg. No. 22495. The provision in the Convention refers to Art. 2 common to the four 1949 Geneva Conventions, *UNTS* Vol. 75, Reg. No. 970.

[32] Casey-Maslen and Vestner, *A Guide to International Disarmament Law*, para. 2.14.

of anti-personnel mines previously emplaced by another State or non-State actor.[33]

Where the use of a weapon is prohibited in an arms control or disarmament treaty, the prohibition is usually comprehensive and without exception. That said, while under the Chemical Weapons Convention the use of riot control agents as a method of warfare is explicitly prohibited,[34] a separate provision clarifies that the use of certain chemical agents for the purpose of law enforcement, in particular riot control agents, may not be unlawful.[35] Riot control agents are defined in the Convention as a chemical which 'can produce rapidly in humans sensory irritation or disabling physical effects which disappear within a short time following termination of exposure'.[36] The term 'tear gas' is used to describe a variety of lachrymatory agents used by the police in certain countries. The most widely used chemical irritant dispersed at a distance is CS, which is typically discharged either in the form of projectiles or from grenades shot from a launcher.[37]

Unusually, in the Biological Weapons Convention, the hostile use of biological toxins is not explicitly prohibited. This is explained by the fact that bacteriological warfare had already been outlawed in the 1925 Geneva Protocol, a legally binding instrument adopted under the auspices of the League of Nations.[38]

Assisting or encouraging prohibited activities

Disarmament treaties not only prohibit a State Party from engaging in certain activities, but also preclude them from assisting, encouraging, or inducing others to do so. This is so whether the recipients of assistance or encouragement are party to the treaty in question or not. Assistance is in

---

[33] S. Maslen, *Commentary on the 1997 Anti-Personnel Mine Ban Convention*, Oxford University Press, Oxford, 2003, paras 1.22–1.27.

[34] Art. I(5), 1992 Chemical Weapons Convention.

[35] Art. II(9)(d), 1992 Chemical Weapons Convention.

[36] Art. II(7), 1992 Chemical Weapons Convention.

[37] *United Nations Human Rights Guidance on Less-Lethal Weapons in Law Enforcement*, Office of the UN High Commissioner for Human Rights, New York and Geneva, 2020, at: https://www.ohchr.org/Documents/HRBodies/CCPR/LLW_Guidance.pdf, para. 7.3.1.

[38] Protocol for the Prohibition of the Use of Asphyxiating, Poisonous or Other Gases, and of Bacteriological Methods of Warfare; adopted at Geneva, 17 June 1925; entered into force, 8 February 1928, LNTS Vol. 94, Reg. No. 2138.

the form of material, technical, human, or financial support while encouragement encompasses public or private action that seeks to persuade another State or non-State actor to conduct prohibited actions. The precise scope of the prohibitions on assistance and encouragement is not settled, but it is accepted that they do not forestall all military cooperation with a State not party to the Convention.

In the case of the Anti-Personnel Mine Ban Convention, for example, a number of States entered interpretative declarations upon ratification whereby, for instance:

> the mere participation in the planning or execution of operations, exercises or other military activities by the Armed Forces of the Czech Republic, or individual Czech Republic nationals, conducted in combination with the armed forces of States not party to the [Convention], which engage in activities prohibited under the Convention, is not, by itself, assistance, encouragement or inducement for the purposes of Article 1, paragraph 1 (c) of the Convention.[39]

The prohibition on assistance under a disarmament treaty should be distinguished from the more general (but narrower) prohibition on assisting an internationally wrongful act under international law pertaining to State responsibility.[40] The key distinction to be drawn is that a State Party to a disarmament treaty is prohibited from assisting anyone to engage in conduct that is prohibited to it under the treaty. This is so irrespective of whether the conduct being assisted is *also* unlawful for the recipient of the assistance (notably, if that State is not a party to the Treaty). In contrast, under the law pertaining to State responsibility, the conduct at issue must also be unlawful for both parties: the provider of assistance as well as its recipient. Thus, Draft Article 16 ('Aid or assistance in the commission of an internationally wrongful act') stipulates:

---

[39] Declaration of the Czech Republic, 26 October 1999, on UN Treaty Collection website, Chap. XXVI, No. 5, at: https://treaties.un.org/pages/ViewDetails.aspx?src=TREATY&mtdsg_no=XXVI-5&chapter=26&clang=_en#EndDec.

[40] Art. 16, Draft articles on Responsibility of States for Internationally Wrongful Acts, with commentaries, 2001; text adopted by the International Law Commission (ILC) at its fifty-third session, in 2001, and submitted to the UN General Assembly as a part of the Commission's report covering the work of that session, in UN doc. A/56/10, at: bit.ly/32A30cT.

A State which aids or assists another State in the commission of an internationally wrongful act by the latter is internationally responsible for doing so if:

(a) that State does so with knowledge of the circumstances of the internationally wrongful act; and

(b) the act would be internationally wrongful if committed by that State.

The inter-relationship between arms control and disarmament and *jus ad bellum*

Jus ad bellum—the law on the inter-State use of force—governs when one State may lawfully use force against or on the territory of another State. It is not weapon-specific, and does not per se outlaw the use of any weapon. That said, *jus ad bellum* will restrict the manner in which weapons may lawfully be used.

The primary rules of *jus ad bellum* are found in the 1945 UN Charter. Under the general rule, which is contained in Article 2(4), all UN member States 'shall refrain in their international relations from the threat or use of force against the territorial integrity or political independence of any State, or in any other manner inconsistent with the Purposes of the United Nations'. Although originally directed to UN member States, the general prohibition on use of force extends to all States under customary international law.[41]

The fact that a weapon may be prohibited by an arms control or disarmament treaty will not determine whether action is lawful or not under the law on the inter-State use of force. (There may nonetheless be a violation of disarmament law, and also of IHL, with use of weaponry potentially even amounting to a war crime punishable under international criminal law.) Nonetheless, where force is used in self-defence, it must comply with the principles of necessity and proportionality *ad bellum*. While *jus ad bellum* is not, as a general rule, weapon-specific, in its 1996 Advisory Opinion on the legality of the threat or use of nuclear weapons the International Court of

---

[41] Principle 1, 1970 Declaration on the Principles of International Law. The Declaration on Principles of International Law concerning Friendly Relations and Co-operation among States, annexed to UN General Assembly Resolution 2625, was adopted by the Assembly without a vote on 24 October 1970.

Justice agreed unanimously that a use of force by means of nuclear weapons that is contrary to Article 2(4) of the UN Charter and which fails to meet all the requirements of self-defence is unlawful.[42]

Necessity means that other measures short of the use of force have been unsuccessful in resolving the issue or would inevitably fail. The principle of proportionality acts as a ceiling, restraining the force that may lawfully be employed to that which is required to repel the threat. Nuclear weapons may be a special case. In its 1996 Advisory Opinion, the International Court of Justice held that under existing international law it could not 'conclude definitively whether the threat or use of nuclear weapons would be lawful or unlawful in an extreme circumstance of self-defence, in which the very survival of a State would be at stake'.[43]

With respect to the threat of use of a weapon, the Court declared that 'if the envisaged use of force is itself unlawful, the stated readiness to use it would be a threat prohibited under Article 2, paragraph 4'.[44] Under the TPNW, each State Party undertakes never under any circumstances to threaten to use any nuclear explosive devices.[45] This express and comprehensive prohibition of threatening to use is an exceptional measure in a disarmament treaty, though it had also been incorporated earlier in a number of regional nuclear-weapon-free-zone treaties.[46]

That said, under the Chemical Weapons Convention, each State Party has the right to request assistance and protection against the use or threat of use of chemical weapons if it considers that it is threatened by illegal actions or activities of any State.[47] The Convention obligates the Director-General of the Organisation for the Prohibition of Chemical Weapons (OPCW) 'immediately' to forward the request to States Parties that can provide humanitarian assistance in a situation where the threat of use of chemical weapons is 'serious'.[48]

---

[42] International Court of Justice (ICJ), *Legality of the Threat or Use of Nuclear Weapons*, Advisory Opinion, 8 July 1996, para. 105(2), dispositif C.

[43] Ibid., para. 105(2), dispositif E.

[44] Ibid., para. 47.

[45] Art. 1(1)(d), TPNW.

[46] See, e.g., Additional Protocol II to the Treaty for the Prohibition of Nuclear Weapons in Latin America and the Caribbean; concluded and opened for signature at Tlatelolco, 14 February 1967, entered into force, 22 April 1968, *UNTS* Vol. 634, Reg. No. 9068.

[47] Art. X(8), 1992 Chemical Weapons Convention.

[48] Art. X(9), 1992 Chemical Weapons Convention.

The inter-relationship between arms control and disarmament and international humanitarian law

In earlier decades there was a strict separation between arms control and disarmament, on the one hand, and IHL/the law of armed conflict, on the other. Whereas IHL would prohibit and restrict the use of weapons during and in connection with armed conflict, arms control and disarmament treaties would generally address issues of development and testing, production, stockpiling, and transfer at all times. As noted above, this helps to explain why the 1971 Biological Weapons Convention does not include a prohibition on use: such a prohibition—albeit one that was formally applicable in international armed conflict only—had already been set out in the 1925 Geneva Protocol.[49]

The same approach could, in theory, have been maintained in the Chemical Weapons Convention. But because several States Parties to the 1925 Geneva Protocol had entered a reservation whereby they would use chemical weapons in reprisals to such weapons' use by another State (and in any event were free by the terms of that Protocol to use chemical weapons against States that were not party to the Protocol), it was decided to prohibit explicitly all and any use of chemical weapons in the 1992 Convention. To clarify the status of riot control agents, the Chemical Weapons Convention prohibits their use as a method of warfare but potentially allows their use for law enforcement. (Many States use tear gas during violent protests, for example.)

The strict demarcation between IHL and arms control/disarmament further evolved in the mid-1990s, specifically in the context of the Convention on Certain Conventional Weapons. The Convention (sometimes called the CCW for short) is, at its heart, an IHL treaty. It was negotiated within the United Nations because agreement on the regulation of the use of specific weapons in armed conflict had proved impossible to achieve in the context of the two 1977 Additional Protocols to the Geneva Conventions.[50] The CCW, through a series of weapon-specific Protocols annexed to it,

---

[49] The Protocol stipulates that 'the High Contracting Parties … agree to extend this prohibition [on chemical weapons] to the use of bacteriological methods of warfare and agree to be bound as between themselves according to the terms of this declaration'.

[50] International Committee of the Red Cross (ICRC), Commentary on Article 35 of the 1977 Additional Protocol I to the Geneva Conventions, 1986, at: https://ihl-databases.icrc.org/applic/ihl/ihl.nsf/Comment.xsp?action=openDocument&documentId=2F157A9C651F8B1DC12563CD0043256C, paras 1416, 1421.

prohibits or restricts the use of specific types of weapons that may either cause unnecessary suffering to combatants or have indiscriminate effects (potentially harming protected civilians). There were originally three Protocols when the CCW was adopted in 1980: on undetectable fragments; on landmines and booby-traps; and on incendiary weapons. In 1995, however, when States Parties to the CCW agreed to prohibit the use of blinding laser weapons in a fourth Protocol, they also undertook not to transfer those weapons to any State or to any non-State entity.[51] A year later, in an amended Protocol II on landmines, similar restrictions were included on the transfer of mines whose use was prohibited.[52]

In more recent disarmament treaties, where no IHL prohibition on the use of a weapon as a means or method of warfare existed, a comprehensive prohibition on use at all times and in all circumstances has been included. This is the case with the Anti-Personnel Mine Ban Convention, the Convention on Cluster Munitions, and the TPNW. Use, even as a belligerent reprisal or in response to an act of aggression, is unequivocally unlawful, as is use within a State's own borders for the purpose of 'law enforcement'.

As noted above, one potential benefit that IHL has compared to a disarmament treaty is that it applies to non-State armed groups, at least when the group is a party to an armed conflict. In contrast, disarmament treaties are addressed directly to States. That said, in the 1996 Amended Protocol II on landmines of the Convention on Certain Conventional Weapons, the prohibitions on transfer (in its Article 8) are addressed only to the 'High Contracting Party', meaning a State Party.

The inter-relationship between arms control and disarmament and international criminal law

International criminal law lays down individual criminal responsibility for international crimes such as aggression, genocide, crimes against

---

[51] Art. 1, Additional Protocol to the Convention on Prohibitions or Restrictions on the Use of Certain Conventional Weapons which may be Deemed to be Excessively Injurious or to have Indiscriminate Effects (Protocol IV, entitled Protocol on Blinding Laser Weapons); adopted at Vienna, 13 October 1995; entered into force, 30 July 1998.

[52] According to Art. 8(1): 'In order to promote the purposes of this Protocol, each High Contracting Party: (a) undertakes not to transfer any mine the use of which is prohibited by this Protocol; (b) undertakes not to transfer any mine to any recipient other than a State or a State agency authorized to receive such transfers.'

humanity, and war crimes. War crimes are serious violations of IHL that entail individual criminal responsibility under international law. They are defined in IHL treaties such as the 1949 Geneva Conventions and their two 1977 Additional Protocols.[53] War crimes are also set out in the 1998 Rome Statute of the International Criminal Court[54] and under customary international law.[55]

Until a few years ago, no arms control or disarmament treaty had seen its core prohibition on use incorporated per se in the Rome Statute. Proposals by certain States to include as a war crime the use of anti-personnel mines, prohibited under the 1997 Anti-personnel Mine Ban Convention, had not met with success.[56] The prohibitions on chemical weapons contained in Article 8(2) of the Rome Statute, which apply to all armed conflict, reflect the wording in the 1899 Hague Declaration (IV,2) concerning the Use of Asphyxiating or Deleterious Gases (and subsequently in the 1925 Geneva Protocol).

In 2017, however, language from the definition in Article I of the Biological Weapons Convention was employed in delineating the war crime under the jurisdiction of the International Criminal Court of 'Employing weapons, which use *microbial or other biological agents, or toxins, whatever their origin or method of production*'.[57] This war crime applies in both international and non-international armed conflict.[58] The crime exists even though, as noted above, the Biological Weapons Convention itself does not

---

[53] Protocol Additional to the Geneva Conventions of 12 August 1949 and Relating to the Protection of Victims of International Armed Conflicts (Protocol I); adopted at Geneva, 8 June 1977; entered into force, 7 December 1978, *UNTS* Vol. 1125, Reg. No. 17512; and Protocol Additional to the Geneva Conventions of 12 August 1949 and Relating to the Protection of Victims of Non-international Armed Conflicts (Protocol II); adopted at Geneva, 8 June 1977; entered into force, 7 December 1978, *UNTS* Vol. 1125, Reg. No. 17513.

[54] Rome Statute of the International Criminal Court; adopted at Rome, 17 July 1998; entered into force, 1 July 2002, *UNTS* Vol. 2187, Reg. No. 38544. As of 1 June 2021, 123 States were party to the Rome Statute.

[55] See ICRC Study of Customary International Humanitarian Law, Rule 156: 'Definition of War Crimes', at: https://ihl-databases.icrc.org/customary-ihl/eng/docs/v1_rul_rule156.

[56] In 2017, Belgium suggested incorporating the use of anti-personnel mines as a war crime within the jurisdiction of the ICC both in international armed conflict and in non-international armed conflict. ICC, 'Report of the Working Group on Amendments', ICC doc. ICC-ASP/16/22, 15 November 2017, Annex III: Non-Paper submitted by Belgium: proposal for elements of crimes relating to the proposed amendments to article 8, pp. 9–10.

[57] 'Amendment to Article 8 (Weapons Which Use Microbial or Other Biological Agents, or Toxins)', adopted by Resolution ICC-ASP/16/Res.4 on 14 December 2017 at the Assembly of State Parties to the Rome Statute. The Amendment entered into force on 2 April 2020 in regard to Luxembourg one year after the deposit of its instrument of ratification, in accordance with Art. 121(5) of the Rome Statute.

[58] Art. 8(2)(b)(xxvii) and Art. 8(2)(e)(xvi), respectively, Rome Statute.

formally prohibit use. In 1996, however, States Parties included in the Final Declaration of the Convention's Fourth Review Conference the affirmation that use is 'effectively prohibited under Article I of the Convention'.[59] During the Conference Iran had put forward a formal proposal to amend the Biological Weapons Convention to explicitly prohibit use, but this had not been accepted.[60]

National implementation of arms control and disarmament measures

There is a general principle of law whereby States Parties to any treaty, including one of arms control or disarmament, must both interpret and apply that treaty in good faith. This demands that they take appropriate measures to give effect to their undertakings at domestic level in both law and practice. Thus, as Article 27 of the 1969 Vienna Convention on the Law of Treaties stipulates: 'A party may not invoke the provisions of its internal law as justification for its failure to perform a treaty.'[61]

The implementation of arms control and disarmament treaties often requires the adoption in domestic law of penal sanctions for violations of the prohibited activities. Thus, for example, Article VII(1)(a) of the Chemical Weapons Convention obligates each State Party to prohibit 'natural and legal persons anywhere on its territory or in any other place under its jurisdiction as recognised by international law from undertaking any activity prohibited to a State Party under this Convention, including enacting penal legislation with respect to such activity'. (A natural person is a human being while a legal person is a corporation or other legal undertaking.)

The duties not to develop, produce, retain, or transfer certain weapons clearly demand the issuance of instructions and regulations by the relevant

---

[59] Fourth Review Conference of the Parties to the 1971 Biological Weapons Convention, Geneva, 25 November–6 December 1996, UN doc. BWC/CONF.4/9, Final Declaration, Commentary on Article I(3).

[60] 'A proposal for amending the Convention to incorporate therein the explicit "Prohibition of the Use of Biological Weapons"', Submitted by the Islamic Republic of Iran, Doc. BWC/CONF.IV/COW/WP.02, 1996, at: https://meetings.unoda.org/section/bwc-revcon-1996-documents/. Iran proposed to add the word 'Use' in the title of the Convention and to add 'to use biological weapons' in Art. I of the Convention. The Final Declaration of the Fourth Review Conference took note of the proposal and recommended it for consideration by States Parties.

[61] Vienna Convention on the Law of Treaties; adopted at Vienna, 23 May 1969; entered into force, 27 January 1980, *UNTS* Vol. 1155, Reg. No. 18232.

authorities within a State. Weapons may need to be destroyed in accordance with a duty to eliminate stockpiles. Weapons factories may have to be decommissioned or converted to other usage (this is an explicit requirement under the Chemical Weapons Convention).[62] These actions will often involve ministries, such as ministries of defence, foreign affairs, interior, and trade, along with the armed forces and police service. They will also require the allocation of sufficient funding in the national budget.

In addition to treaty implementation measures, the UN Security Council can require arms control and disarmament actions by UN member States. This includes arms embargoes and broader sanctions not only against States but also against armed groups and individuals, in particular on the basis of their involvement in international terrorism. These measures are typically adopted by the Council acting under Chapter VII of the Charter. With respect to arms embargoes, the Council 'may decide what measures not involving the use of armed force are to be employed to give effect to its decisions'. These measures 'may include complete or partial interruption of economic relations', which includes mandatory arms embargoes.[63] Depending on the text of the resolution, an arms embargo prohibits the transfer of certain or all weapons to the respective State or actor that is the subject of the resolution.

Boko Haram, for instance, has been identified at the international level as a terrorist group and is subject to sanctions. In May 2014, the UN Security Council's Al-Qaida Sanctions Committee added the group to its list of individuals and entities subject to targeted financial sanctions and arms embargo, as set out in paragraph 1 of Security Council Resolution 2083 (2012). As a result of the listing by the Sanctions Committee, any individual or entity that provides financial or material support to Boko Haram, including by providing arms or recruits, is itself eligible to be added to the Al-Qaida Sanctions List and subject to the sanctions measures.

---

[62] Under Art. V(1) of the Convention: 'The provisions of this Article and the detailed procedures for its implementation shall apply to any and all chemical weapons production facilities owned or possessed by a State Party, or that are located in any place under its jurisdiction or control.' Under Art. V(8): 'Each State Party shall destroy all chemical weapons production facilities specified in paragraph 1 and related facilities and equipment, pursuant to the Verification Annex and in accordance with an agreed rate and sequence of destruction ... Such destruction shall begin not later than one year after this Convention enters into force for it, and shall finish not later than 10 years after entry into force of this Convention. A State Party is not precluded from destroying such facilities at a faster rate.'

[63] Art. 41, UN Charter.

UN Security Council Resolution 1540

On 28 April 2004, the Security Council, acting under Chapter VII of the UN Charter, unanimously adopted Resolution 1540. The Resolution declared that the proliferation of nuclear, chemical, and biological weapons and their means of delivery constitute a threat to international peace and security. Under operative paragraph 1 of the Resolution, all States are prohibited from providing any form of support to non-State actors that 'attempt to develop, acquire, manufacture, possess, transport, transfer or use nuclear, chemical or biological weapons and their means of delivery'.

Under paragraph 2 of the Resolution, the Council also decided that

> all States, in accordance with their national procedures, shall adopt and enforce appropriate effective laws which prohibit any non-State actor to manufacture, acquire, possess, develop, transport, transfer or use nuclear, chemical or biological weapons and their means of delivery, in particular for terrorist purposes, as well as attempts to engage in any of the foregoing activities, participate in them as an accomplice, assist or finance them.

In total (though depending on how they are counted), the Resolution was said to create some 200 legally binding obligations for each State.[64] These included the duty to report on measures each has undertaken. Resolution 1540 specifically reserves the 'rights and obligations' of the States Parties to the main arms control and disarmament treaties, in particular the NPT. This has been interpreted by the five NPT nuclear-weapon States as authority to continue to manufacture nuclear weapons, including through the use of private contractors.

A 1540 Committee, functioning as a subsidiary body of the Council, was established to promote effective implementation of the Resolution. Its current mandate is due to expire in 2021 pursuant to Resolution 1977 (2011). The Resolution provides for two comprehensive reviews: one which took place in 2016 and a second 'prior to the renewal of its mandate'. In April 2020, it was stated that the Committee would conduct a Comprehensive

---

[64] R. T. Cupitt, 'Nearly at the Brink: The Tasks and Capacity of the 1540 Committee', *Arms Control Today*, September 2012, available at: https://www.armscontrol.org/act/2012_09/Nearly-at-the-Brink-The-Tasks-and-Capacity-Of-the-1540-Committee.

Review prior to renewal of its mandate on 25 April 2021.[65] A Comprehensive Review planned for December 2020 was delayed due to the COVID-19 pandemic.[66] As of this writing, the planned 2021 Comprehensive Review had not yet been conducted.[67]

[65] UN, '1540 Committee Chair Briefs Security Council on 2021 Comprehensive Review of Implementation Status of Resolution 1540 (2004)', Press release, UN doc. SC/14177, 30 April 2020, at: https://www.un.org/press/en/2020/sc14177.doc.htm.

[66] Kelsey Davenport, 'UN Security Council Resolution 1540 at a Glance', Fact Sheet, Last reviewed February 2021, Arms Control Association, at: https://www.armscontrol.org/factsheets/1540.

[67] See UN, '2021 Comprehensive Review', accessed 10 June 2021, at: https://www.un.org/en/sc/1540/comprehensive-and-annual-reviews/2021-comprehensive-review.shtml.

2
Biological and Chemical Weapons

This chapter addresses the two global WMD disarmament treaties with the broadest participation: the 1971 Biological Weapons Convention,[1] to which 183 States are party, and the 1992 Chemical Weapons Convention,[2] to which 193 of 197 States are party. In turn, the chapter provides a summary of the negotiation of the two treaties along with a description of their content. The operation and implementation of the two is then briefly compared and contrasted. The challenge, given the lack of a formal structure, of verifying compliance with the Biological Weapons Convention is outlined. The operation of the Organization for the Prohibition of Chemical Weapons (OPCW) is also described, with further detail on its role in verifying use in Syria.

The negotiation and entry into force of the 1971 Biological Weapons Convention

The Convention on the Prohibition of the Development, Production and Stockpiling of Bacteriological (Biological) and Toxin Weapons and on Their Destruction was adopted on 16 December 1971, entering into force on 26 March 1975. The Biological Weapons Convention was based on a longstanding prohibition on bacteriological warfare in situations of international armed conflict. Not only did the 1925 Geneva Protocol reaffirm the prohibition on use of certain chemical agents as a means of warfare,

---

[1] Convention on the Prohibition of the Development, Production and Stockpiling of Bacteriological (Biological) and Toxin Weapons and on Their Destruction; adopted at New York, 16 December 1971; opened for signature, 10 April 1972; entered into force, 25 March 1975, *UNTS* Vol. 1015, Reg. No. 14860.

[2] Convention on the Prohibition of the Development, Production and Stockpiling of Development, Production, Stockpiling and Use of Chemical Weapons and on Their Destruction; adopted at Geneva, 3 September 1992; entered into force, 29 April 1997, *UNTS* Vol. 1975, Reg. No. 33757.

which had already been agreed at the First Hague Peace Conference in 1899, but it also imposed, for the first time in an international treaty, a prohibition on the use of 'bacteriological methods of warfare'. This early treaty prohibition is cited in the Preamble to the Biological Weapons Convention.

In its detailed study of the rules of customary international humanitarian law (IHL), published in 2005, the International Committee of the Red Cross (ICRC) concluded that biological weapons may not be used in any armed conflict as a means or method of warfare. Weapons whose effects cannot be limited as required by IHL rules are of an indiscriminate nature. This is so on the basis that although they can be directed at a specific military objective, their effects go far and beyond that objective, often harming civilians. Biological weapons are a generally accepted example of such a weapon. In December 2017, States Parties to the 1998 Rome Statute of the International Criminal Court (ICC) amended the Statute to give the Court potential jurisdiction over the war crime of using biological weapons in international and non-international armed conflict alike.[3]

The Biological Weapons Convention was formally negotiated in the Committee on Disarmament by its then 18 members. Disarmament talks following the end of the Second World War had initially addressed biological and chemical weapons together. But after the conclusion of the NPT in 1968, a United Kingdom initiative helped overcome an impasse in the discussions. The United Kingdom submitted a working paper to the Conference of the Committee on Disarmament in Geneva in which it proposed to separate consideration of biological weapons from that of chemical weapons, and for negotiations to concentrate first on the former. A year later, formal negotiation of what became the Biological Weapons Convention started in Geneva based on a further UK proposal, even though at the time many States were opposed to the idea of a treaty dedicated to biological weapons.[4]

---

[3] As noted in Chapter 1, on 14 December 2017 the Assembly of States Parties to the Rome Statute adopted by Resolution ICC-ASP/16/Res.4 an amendment to Article 8 in order to insert new paragraphs 2(b)(xxvii) (in international armed conflict) and 2(e)(xvi) (in non-international armed conflict) relating to the use of weapons which use microbial or other biological agents, or toxins. The amendment makes it a war crime to employ 'weapons, which use microbial or other biological agents, or toxins, whatever their origin or method of production' in connection with an armed conflict. As of 1 March 2021, seven States Parties had ratified or accepted the amendment: Czechia, Latvia, Luxembourg, the Netherlands, New Zealand, Slovakia, and Switzerland.

[4] UN Office for Disarmament Affairs, *The Biological Weapons Convention: An Introduction*, Geneva, 2017, at: https://www.un.org/disarmament/wp-content/uploads/2017/07/BWS-brochure.pdf, p. 4.

The unilateral renunciation of biological weapons by the United States in 1969 was an important milestone in the negotiations, even though the Soviet Union was sceptical about the sincerity of the US commitment. Accordingly, a Soviet proposal on behalf of the seven Socialist Group nations in March 1971 for a dedicated convention on biological weapons was a further significant development. The United States and the Soviet Union each introduced identical draft treaty texts to the Conference of the Committee on Disarmament in early August. On 28 September 1971, Committee members decided to send a single draft convention to the UN General Assembly, which approved it on 16 December 1971.[5]

As of 1 March 2021, 183 States recognized by the UN Secretary-General were party to the Convention.[6] Four States were signatories (Egypt, Haiti, Somalia, and Syria), while ten had still to sign (Chad, Comoros, Djibouti, Eritrea, Israel, Kiribati, Micronesia, Namibia, South Sudan, and Tuvalu). The three depositaries of the Biological Weapons Convention are Russia (as the successor State to the Soviet Union), the United Kingdom, and the United States. To adhere to the Convention, a State need only deposit its instrument of ratification or accession, as appropriate, with one of the three depositaries.

The content of the 1971 Biological Weapons Convention

The Preamble to the 1971 Convention notes the determination of the States Parties, 'for the sake of all mankind, to exclude completely the possibility of bacteriological (biological) agents and toxins being used as weapons'.[7] The States Parties further declare 'that such use would be repugnant to the conscience of mankind and that no effort should be spared to minimise this risk'.[8]

The States Parties undertake never in any circumstances to 'develop, produce, stockpile or otherwise acquire or retain' biological weapons.[9] Thus, despite the preambular paragraphs, the Convention does not explicitly

---

[5] UN General Assembly Resolution 2826 (XXVI) was adopted on 16 December 1971 by 110 votes to 0, with 1 abstention (France).

[6] This includes the State of Palestine, which is not recognized as such by the United States.

[7] 1971 Biological Weapons Convention, ninth preambular para.

[8] 1971 Biological Weapons Convention, tenth preambular para.

[9] Art. I, 1971 Biological Weapons Convention.

prohibit use. In 1996, however, the Final Declaration of the Convention's Fourth Review Conference stated that use is 'effectively prohibited under Article I of the Convention'. As Chapter 1 observed, during the Convention's Fourth Review Conference, Iran had proposed amending the text of the Convention to incorporate an explicit prohibition on use, but this was not endorsed by the other States Parties.

In its Article 1(1), the 1971 Convention defines bacteriological (biological) and toxin weapons as 'microbial or other biological agents, or toxins whatever their origin or method of production, of types and in quantities that have no justification for prophylactic, protective or other peaceful purposes'. Also prohibited, under Article 1(2), are 'weapons, equipment or means of delivery designed to use such agents or toxins for hostile purposes or in armed conflict'. Thus, the prohibition is on developing the biological agents as well as on their subsequent weaponization.

In November 1969, US President Richard Nixon issued a Statement on Chemical and Biological Defense Policies and Programs, in which he announced an end to all US offensive biological weapons programmes.[10] The United States had begun a biological weapons programme in the spring of 1943. The programme involved weaponizing biological agents such as anthrax, botulism, brucellosis, Q-fever, staphylococcal enterotoxin B, tularaemia, and Venezuelan equine encephalitis virus.[11] President Nixon pledged to confine US biological research to defensive measures such as immunization and safety measures. All production of offensive biological agents ceased, and over the course of the following four years all US biological weapons stockpiles, which were held at Pine Bluff Arsenal in Arkansas, were destroyed.[12]

Russia's compliance with the Biological Weapons Convention is less clear. The First Deputy Chief of the Soviet Biopreparat Programme in the period 1988–92 has acknowledged that tularaemia was used by the Soviet army as early as 1942: against German troops outside Stalingrad.[13] In the

---

[10] President Richard Nixon, Statement on Chemical and Biological Defense Policies and Programs, 25 November 1969, at: https://2001-2009.state.gov/documents/organization/90920.pdf.

[11] See, e.g., D. R. Franz, C. D. Parrott, and E. T. Takafuji, 'The U.S. Biological Warfare and Biological Defense Programs', Chap. 19 in F. R. Sidell and others (eds), *Medical Aspects of Chemical and Biological Warfare*, Office of the Surgeon General (Army), Falls Church VA, 1997.

[12] 'Pine Bluff Chemical Activity (PBCA)', *Global Security*, Last modified on 9 October 2013, at: https://www.globalsecurity.org/wmd/facility/pine_bluff.htm.

[13] S. Hutton Siderovski, *Tularemia*, Chelsea House Publishers, Philadelphia, 2009, p. 82.

early 1990s, Russian President Boris Yeltsin acknowledged the existence of an inherited Soviet biological weapons programme and publicly committed Russia to compliance with the Biological Weapons Convention. The prohibition of Russia's offensive biological weapons in an April 1992 decree prescribed the dismantling of the programme and pledged cooperation with the Convention framework.

The Russian government has subsequently asserted that it does not maintain a stockpile of biological weapons or engage in any illegal development or production activities. However, in a 2019 report on compliance with WMD treaties, including the Biological Weapons Convention, the US Department of State repeated earlier declarations that it could not conclude that Russia had fulfilled its obligations under the Convention to destroy or divert to peaceful purposes prohibited biological weapons.[14]

Exceptionally for a disarmament treaty, the prohibition on transfer in the Biological Weapons Convention is contained in a dedicated provision separate from the other general undertakings. Therein, each State Party 'undertakes not to transfer to any recipient whatsoever, directly or indirectly ... any of the agents, toxins, weapons, equipment or means of delivery' set out in Article I of the Convention.[15] The prohibition on transfer to any recipient pertains only to export. The importation of such weapons or other illegal items is covered by the prohibition on acquisition in Article I.

It is not prohibited to transfer biological agents or toxins where they are of appropriate types and quantities for prophylactic, protective, or other peaceful purposes. The wording of the exception in Article I is reinforced in Article X(1) according to which States Parties 'undertake to facilitate, and have the right to participate in, the fullest possible exchange of equipment, materials, and scientific and technological information for the use of bacteriological (biological) agents and toxins for peaceful purposes'. The term 'exchange' encompasses transfers, including of relevant vaccines and antibiotics and related research. Victims of biological warfare may be given antibiotics orally or intravenously, even before the specific agent is identified. There are already protective vaccines available for anthrax, botulinum toxin, tularaemia, plague, Q-fever, and smallpox. Immune protection

---

[14] US Department of State, *Adherence to and Compliance with Arms Control, Nonproliferation, and Disarmament Agreements and Commitments*, Washington, DC, August 2019, p. 49.

[15] Art. III, Biological Weapons Convention.

against ricin and staphylococcal toxins may also be possible in the near future.[16]

The Biological Weapons Convention was the first global disarmament treaty to provide for stockpile destruction. Under Article II, each State Party 'undertakes to destroy, or to divert to peaceful purposes, as soon as possible but not later than nine months' after the Convention's entry into force all agents, toxins, weapons, equipment, and means of delivery outlawed in Article I. The obligation extends to all such components, means, and equipment 'in its possession or under its jurisdiction or control'. Since the Convention entered into force in late March 1975 (after its ratification by 22 States, including the three depositary States),[17] the treaty deadline for destruction was set just before the end of 1975 for any State Party. There is no possibility of extending the deadline, so any States adhering to the Convention thereafter should have destroyed all prohibited items in their possession or under their jurisdiction or control prior to ratification or accession.

There is a possibility granted to each State Party of withdrawing from the Convention in exceptional circumstances. Thus, a State Party is allowed to withdraw after a three-month period of notice if it decides that extraordinary events related to biological weapons have jeopardized its supreme interests. A withdrawing State Party is required to inform both the other States Parties to the Convention and the UN Security Council, setting out the extraordinary events on which it has based its decision.[18] To date, no State Party has withdrawn from the Biological Weapons Convention.

The negotiation and entry into force of the 1992 Chemical Weapons Convention

The 1992 Convention on the Prohibition of the Development, Production, Stockpiling and Use of Chemical Weapons and on their Destruction was adopted by the Conference on Disarmament in Geneva on 3 September 1992 and 'commended' by the UN General Assembly the same year, entering into force on 29 April 1997. The use of certain chemical agents, such

---

[16] 'Biological Warfare Treatment', *WebMD*, Last reviewed 2 June 2020, at: https://www.webmd.com/first-aid/biological-warfare-treatment.

[17] Art. XIV(3), Biological Weapons Convention.

[18] Art. XIII(2), Biological Weapons Convention.

as chlorine or sulphur mustard, as a means of warfare had first been prohibited almost 100 years earlier, at the First Hague Peace Conference in 1899. The Hague Declaration (IV,2) concerning the Use of Asphyxiating or Deleterious Gases entered into force on 4 September 1900. But it failed to prevent massive use of chemical weapons in the First World War, despite the main protagonists (Belgium, France, Germany, and the United Kingdom, among others) all being party to it.[19] This failure led States after the war to conclude the 1925 Geneva Protocol, which, as its Preamble explains, sought to ensure that the prohibition on chemical warfare 'shall be universally accepted as a part of International Law, binding alike the conscience and the practice of nations'.

The Biological Weapons Convention had been negotiated relatively quickly, particularly owing to the absence of formal and detailed verification measures. The Convention, in its Preamble, had recognized that its conclusion represented 'a first possible step towards the achievement of agreement on effective measures also for the prohibition of the development, production and stockpiling of chemical weapons', noting the determination of its States Parties 'to continue negotiations to that end'. In fact, the elaboration of the Chemical Weapons Convention would be a long and challenging enterprise: one that began with the establishment of an *ad hoc* working group by the Conference on Disarmament in 1980. As the Organization for the Prohibition of Chemical Weapons (OPCW) has observed, the improvement in superpower relations in the late 1980s, the chemical attack by Saddam Hussein's regime on the Kurds in Halabja in 1988, the publicity given to the threat of chemical warfare during the Gulf War, and a bilateral US–Soviet agreement to refrain from further production and to destroy most of their chemical weapon stockpiles 'all gave impetus to the Convention negotiations'.[20]

Challenges in the negotiations concerned the possible linkage sought by some States between the destruction of chemical weapons stockpiles and progress in nuclear disarmament. (Given the complexities of developing nuclear weapons, chemical weapons were often described as the poor man's deterrent.)[21] The protection of trade in chemicals for peaceful

---

[19] During the First World War, approximately 124,000 tonnes of chlorine, mustard gas, and other chemical agents were fired, killing more than 90,000 soldiers and seriously injuring a further million. OPCW, 'Origins of the Chemical Weapons Convention and the OPCW', Fact Sheet No. 1, The Hague, March 2016, at: https://grequim.com/wp-content/uploads/2020/05/Fact_Sheet_History.pdf, p. 1.

[20] Ibid., p. 2.

[21] Casey-Maslen and Vestner, *A Guide to International Disarmament Law*, para. 3.5.

purposes—and consequent economic and technological development—was a major concern for many States. There was also widespread disquiet about the intrusiveness of the Convention's proposed verification regime, particularly the right to undertake 'challenge' inspections. Finally, the United States sought to retain the right to conduct reprisals using chemical weapons in the event that they were used against it until very late in the negotiations. When each of these issues had been resolved, the treaty text was concluded in early September 1992.[22]

After its formal adoption by the Conference on Disarmament, the Chemical Weapons Convention was opened for signature on 13 January 1993 in Paris. During the three-day signing conference, 130 States signed the Convention, a record for a disarmament treaty. As of 1 March 2021, 193 States were party to the Convention, leaving only the Democratic People's Republic of Korea, Egypt, Israel (a signatory), and South Sudan as States not party. The Chemical Weapons Convention is the most widely ratified arms control and disarmament treaty in history.

The content of the 1992 Chemical Weapons Convention

The Convention defines chemical weapons to mean the following: toxic chemicals and their precursors; munitions and devices specifically designed to cause death or other harm through the toxic properties of those toxic chemicals; and equipment specifically designed for use directly in connection with the employment of those munitions and devices.[23] In turn, toxic chemicals are defined as any chemical 'which through its chemical action on life processes can cause death, temporary incapacitation or permanent harm to humans or animals', while precursors are 'any chemical reactant which takes part at any stage in the production by whatever method of a toxic chemical. This includes any key component of a binary or multicomponent chemical system.'[24]

Excluded from the scope of the definition are toxic chemicals where they are intended for purposes not prohibited under the Convention, as long as the types and quantities of those chemicals 'are consistent with

---

[22] OPCW, 'Origins of the Chemical Weapons Convention and the OPCW', p. 2.
[23] Art. I(1), 1992 Chemical Weapons Convention.
[24] Art. II(1), 1992 Chemical Weapons Convention.

such purposes'. Purposes not prohibited include industrial, agricultural, research, medical, and pharmaceutical activities as well as those directly related to protection against toxic chemicals and chemical weapons.[25] This excludes from the scope of the prohibition, among others, all research and development of chemicals and their precursors as long as this is dedicated to peaceful purposes.

The 'General Obligations' of the States Parties are set out in Article I of the Convention, whereunder each State Party undertakes never under any circumstances:

(a) To develop, produce, otherwise acquire, stockpile or retain chemical weapons, or transfer, directly or indirectly, chemical weapons to anyone;

(b) To use chemical weapons;

(c) To engage in any military preparations to use chemical weapons;

(d) To assist, encourage or induce, in any way, anyone to engage in any activity prohibited to a State Party under this Convention.[26]

This broad list of obligations is expanded upon in the remainder of the article. Exceptionally for a disarmament treaty, a specific obligation to destroy chemical weapon production facilities is incorporated in the general obligations.[27] As already noted, and for the avoidance of any future doubt as to the matter, the use of riot control agents as a method of warfare was explicitly outlawed.[28] That said, the use of certain chemical agents, including riot control agents, for the purpose of law enforcement is not prohibited.[29]

The broad prohibition of use of chemical weapons as a method of warfare in the Convention has contributed to the crystallization of a prohibition in customary international law. Use of chemical weapons in connection with an armed conflict is also a war crime. Jurisdiction is given to the ICC under the Rome Statute for the prohibition of 'employing asphyxiating, poisonous or other gases, and all analogous liquids, materials or devices'.[30]

---

[25] Art. II(1)(a) and (9)(a) and (b), 1992 Chemical Weapons Convention.

[26] Art. I(1), 1992 Chemical Weapons Convention.

[27] Art. I(4), 1992 Chemical Weapons Convention.

[28] Art. I(5), 1992 Chemical Weapons Convention.

[29] Art. II(9)(d), 1992 Chemical Weapons Convention.

[30] Art. 8(2)(b)(xviii) and 8(2)(e)(xiv), Rome Statute of the International Criminal Court; adopted at Rome, 17 July 1998; entered into force, 1 July 2002, *UNTS* Vol. 2187, Reg. No. 38544. As of 1 March 2021, 123 States were party to the Rome Statute. Jurisdiction over the war crime of 'employing asphyxiating, poisonous or other gases, and all analogous liquids, materials or devices' in non-international armed conflict was accorded by an amendment adopted at

In accepting the provision in the Statute granting the Court jurisdiction over the war crime when committed in non-international armed conflict, the Czech Republic stated that it interprets the amendment 'in line with the obligations arising from' the Chemical Weapons Convention.[31]

The prohibition on transfer, directly or indirectly, of chemical weapons to anyone renders illegal any export of chemical weapons (importation is covered by the prohibition on acquisition). The ban on indirect transfer outlaws the export of parts and components of chemical weapons, particularly prohibited toxic chemicals and their precursors. The undertaking never under any circumstances to assist, encourage, or induce, in any way, anyone is said to outlaw 'any action which contributes to prohibited activities'.[32] Nevertheless, it is not finally settled whether the scope of this provision extends to curtailing the financing of prohibited activities or to outlawing the transit of weapons across the sovereign territory of a State Party.[33]

States Parties are required to destroy chemical weapons not only that they own or possess but also which are located in any place under their jurisdiction or control.[34] This duty focuses on the location of the weapons rather than necessarily on the exercise of control over the weapons themselves. It is an extremely broad obligation of destruction pertaining not only to stockpiles (narrowly defined) but also to any deployed chemical weapons that have not yet been used.

The Convention obligated all States Parties to destroy their chemical weapons within ten years of the Convention's entry into force, meaning by 2007. Each State Party was permitted to request an extension of the destruction deadline, once only, by up to five years, until 2012, subject to the approval of other States Parties. This extension was, though, not sufficient for both Russia and the United States to complete the destruction of their stockpiles. In late September 2017, Russia announced that it had completed

the Review Conference of the Statute in Kampala in 2010. As of 1 March 2021, the amendment had been ratified or accepted by forty States Parties to the Rome Statute: Andorra, Argentina, Austria, Belgium, Botswana, Chile, Costa Rica, Croatia, Cyprus, Czech Republic, El Salvador, Estonia, Finland, Georgia, Germany, Guyana, Latvia, Liechtenstein, Lithuania, Luxembourg, Malta, Mauritius, Mongolia, the Netherlands, New Zealand, North Macedonia, Norway, Palestine, Panama, Paraguay, Poland, Portugal, Samoa, San Marino, Slovakia, Slovenia, Spain, Switzerland, Trinidad and Tobago, and Uruguay.

[31] Declaration of the Czech Republic, 12 March 2015, at: https://treaties.un.org/pages/ViewDetails.aspx?src=TREATY&mtdsg_no=XVIII-10-a&chapter=18&clang=_en#EndDec

[32] Krutzsch and Trapp, *A Commentary on the Chemical Weapons Convention*, p. 15.

[33] Casey-Maslen and Vestner, *A Guide to International Disarmament Law*, para. 2.20.

[34] Art. I(2), 1992 Chemical Weapons Convention.

destruction of the last of its almost 40,000 metric tons of chemical weapons stockpiles. Whether stocks of Novichok remain has not been clarified.

In contrast, the United States is not expected to complete destruction of its own chemical weapons stocks before late 2023, eleven years after the expiry of its international legal deadline under the Convention. In June 2019 a team began destroying the final stockpile of US chemical weapons at a plant in Kentucky. The aim is to destroy the remaining 523 tonnes of mustard and nerve agents by the end of 2023. Second World War and Cold War-era chemical munitions have been stored at the Blue Grass Army Depot, near the city of Richmond, for decades.[35] In September 2020, the US Department of Defense announced that the Army's Pueblo Chemical Depot in Colorado had completed the destruction of nearly 300,000 155mm projectiles, which each contained 12 pounds (almost 5.5kg) of mustard agent.[36]

Toxic chemicals under the Chemical Weapons Convention include mustard gas, phosgene, ricin, sarin, and VX (venomous agent X). These are set out in Schedules to the Convention. Also addressed are precursors, which comprise, for instance, chlorosarin (for the production of sarin) and methylphosphonyl difluorides (used to produce sarin and soman as a binary chemical weapon). Such agents must be destroyed where they have no legitimate peaceful purpose or, at the least, must be strictly controlled. The dumping of toxic chemicals at sea was widely practised in the past but is now illegal, explicitly prohibited under the Convention,[37] as is burying on land or open burning. The standard method for the destruction of toxic chemicals is closed incineration in specially designed chambers.

Chlorine, which is not a scheduled toxic chemical, is widely used to disinfect tap water, and it is therefore lawful to store and sell it for such purposes. Nonetheless, chlorine can be used as a chemical weapon and even at low concentrations it can cause permanent lung damage.[38] Chlorine was first used in warfare by German forces in the First World War: one third of the 15,000 military casualties of the 1915 gas attack near the town of

---

[35] 'Destruction of Last US Chemical Weapons Stockpile Gets Underway', News, *Army Technology*, 21 June 2019, at: https://www.army-technology.com/news/destruction-us-chemical-weapons/.

[36] D. Vergun, 'DOD Approaches Goal of Destroying All Stockpiled Chemical Weapons', DOD News, 21 September 2020, at: https://www.defense.gov/Explore/News/Article/Article/2354786/dod-approaches-goal-of-destroying-all-stockpiled-chemical-weapons/.

[37] Part IV of the Verification Annex to the Convention.

[38] See, e.g., 'Syria Chlorine Attack Claims: What This Chemical Is and How It Became a Weapon', *The Conversation*, 7 September 2016, at: https://theconversation.com/syria-chlorine-attack-claims-what-this-chemical-is-and-how-it-became-a-weapon-65068.

Ypres died. In Syria, an OPCW fact-finding mission investigating the use of chlorine gas in June 2014 concluded that the chemical agent had been used not only in this instance but also in earlier attacks.[39] In 2015, UN Security Council Resolution 2209 condemned the use of chlorine in attacks in Syria, noting that this was the 'first ever documented instance of the use of toxic chemicals as weapons within the territory' of a State Party to the Chemical Weapons Convention.[40] The use of Novichok in Salisbury in the UK is discussed below and in Chapter 6.

There is, as is the case with the Biological Weapons Convention, the possibility of withdrawing from the Chemical Weapons Convention. Each State Party may withdraw after a 90-day period of notice if it decides that extraordinary events related to chemical weapons have jeopardized its supreme interests. A withdrawing State Party is required to inform the other States Parties, the UN Secretary-General (in his or her capacity as depository), and the UN Security Council of its action, setting out the extraordinary events on which it has based its decision.[41] No State Party has, to date, withdrawn from the Chemical Weapons Convention. According to the OPCW, since its entry into force in 1997 the Convention has been the most successful disarmament treaty ever, eliminating an entire class of WMD.[42]

Comparing and contrasting the two treaties

The absence of an explicit prohibition on use in the Biological Weapons Convention may be seen today largely as a historical curiosity; the understanding reached at the Fourth Review Conference—and repeated subsequently—clarifies that any use of biological weapon as a means or method of warfare would constitute a serious violation of its provisions. Indeed, it is arguable that the declaration from 1996 may constitute an agreement by the States Parties as to the interpretation of Article I of the Biological Weapons Convention.[43]

---

[39] OPCW, 'OPCW Fact Finding Mission: "Compelling Confirmation" that Chlorine Gas Used as Weapon in Syria', The Hague, 10 September 2014, at: https://www.opcw.org/media-centre/news/2014/09/opcw-fact-finding-mission-compelling-confirmation-chlorine-gas-used.

[40] UN Security Council Resolution 2209, adopted on 6 March 2015 by 14 votes to 0, with 1 abstention (Venezuela).

[41] Art. XVI(2), 1992 Chemical Weapons Convention.

[42] OPCW, 'OPCW Director-General Praises Complete Destruction of Libya's Chemical Weapon Stockpile', 11 January 2018, at: https://www.opcw.org/media-centre/news/2018/01/opcw-director-general-praises-complete-destruction-libyas-chemical-weapon.

[43] Art. 31(3)(a), 1969 Vienna Convention on the Law of Treaties.

By far the greatest distinction between the two treaties is found in the realm of verification. While the Biological Weapons Convention similarly obligates the complete destruction of all biological weapons and prohibits future production, in stark contrast to the Chemical Weapons Convention it does not provide for a specific regime of verification or enforcement. In 2001, after six years of negotiations, a proposal was presented for a legally binding protocol to the Biological Weapons Convention that would have established on-site facility visits and procedures for investigating allegations of non-compliance. The United States objected to the protocol, arguing that it would be ineffective while imposing unfair burdens on the US biotechnology industry and national biological defence programmes.[44]

Verification was a primary reason for the decades of discussions and negotiations that were needed to achieve the adoption of the Chemical Weapons Convention. The complexity of the verification procedures laid down by the Convention helps to explain its length: some 160 pages. The Chemical Weapons Convention has the most sophisticated verification system of any global disarmament treaty; the OPCW was created by the Convention as a dedicated institution to oversee the implementation of its obligations.

Verification and compliance mechanisms

Under Article V of the Biological Weapons Convention, the States Parties undertake to consult each other and to 'cooperate in solving any problems which may arise in relation to the objective of, or in the application of the provisions of, the Convention'. Consultation and cooperation may also be undertaken through appropriate international procedures within the framework of the United Nations.

The Convention is an outlier among disarmament treaties in that it does not require either an initial declaration or annual reporting. But at the First Review Conference in 1980, States Parties decided to call for details of national implementation measures to be provided to the United Nations. At the Second Review Conference in 1986, States Parties agreed upon further confidence-building measures (CBMs); these were expanded upon by the Convention's Third Review Conference in 1991. Under these commitments,

---

[44] For one insider's view of the negotiations, see J. Littlewood, *The Biological Weapons Convention: A Failed Revolution*, Ashgate, Aldershot, 2005.

States Parties pledged to provide annual reports, using agreed forms, on research centres and laboratories; on vaccine production facilities; on national biological defence research and development programmes; on past activities in biological research and development programmes; with respect to outbreaks of infectious diseases and similar occurrences caused by toxins; and on legislation, regulations, and other measures. Compliance with these commitments has, however, been 'less than satisfactory', according to the UN Secretary-General, 'with fewer than half of all States Parties regularly providing information'.[45] It continues to be disputed among States Parties whether the measures are legally binding or are merely voluntary in nature. The better view is that they are only politically binding.

The Biological Weapons Convention had made no provision for an Implementation Support Unit (ISU), but in 2006 the Convention's Sixth Review Conference decided to establish one within the Geneva branch of the UN Office for Disarmament Affairs (UNODA). In 2016, the Eighth Review Conference renewed the ISU's mandate until the Convention's Ninth Review Conference in 2021. The ISU of the Biological Weapons Convention provides the following services and support:

- Administrative support and assistance
- National implementation support and assistance
- Support and assistance for confidence-building measures
- Support and assistance for obtaining universality
- Administration of the database for assistance requests and offers, and facilitation of associated exchanges of information; and
- Support for States Parties' efforts to implement the decisions and recommendations of review conferences.

Shortfalls in budgets and accounting problems led to significant cost-cutting measures at UNODA, including for the ISU of the Biological Weapons Convention, in 2019.[46]

---

[45] UN, 'Confidence-Building Measures Supporting Arms Control Extremely Critical, Secretary-General Tells Security Council Meeting on Non-proliferation', UN doc. SG/SM/18858-SC/13167-DC/3755, 18 January 2018, at: https://www.un.org/press/en/2018/sgsm18858.doc.htm.

[46] See, e.g., 'Déclaration sur la situation financière des Conventions de désarmement', Statement by H. E. Amb. Yann Hwang, Permanent Representative of France to the Conference on Disarmament, to the First Committee of the 74th Session of the UN General Assembly, New York, 30 October 2019, at: http://statements.unmeetings.org/media2/22000121/france.pdf.

The Convention is also unusual among disarmament treaties in that it did not provide for regular (annual or biennial) meetings of States Parties, only five-yearly review conferences. In this regard, Article XII of the Convention required that five years after the Convention's entry into force, a conference of States Parties would be held to review the operation of the Convention, with a view to assuring that the purposes of the Convention were being achieved. This First Review Conference was held in Geneva and ran from 3 to 21 March 1980. It was decided that the Second Review Conference would take place five years later (in practice, this turned out to be six). Thereafter, subsequent review conferences have been held every five years (though the Fifth Review Conference, which was suspended in December 2001 following a dispute on possible verification measures and mechanisms, reconvened in 2002).[47] As of this writing, the most recent review conference was the eighth, held in 2016. The 2019 Meeting of States Parties agreed that the Ninth Review Conference would be held on 8–26 November 2021, but with the exact duration and dates still to be determined 'due to continued disagreement among States Parties'.[48]

Although meetings of States Parties were not foreseen in the Convention as adopted, several have since been convened at the request of States Parties. The First Meeting of States Parties, held in 2003, addressed two issues: the adoption of necessary national measures to implement the prohibitions set out in the Convention, including the enactment of penal legislation; and national mechanisms to establish and maintain the security and oversight of pathogenic micro-organisms and toxins. The Second Meeting of States Parties, held in 2004, discussed strengthening institutional efforts and mechanisms for the surveillance, detection, diagnosis, and combating of infectious diseases affecting humans, animals, and plants; and the enhancing of international capabilities for responding to, investigating, and mitigating the effects of cases of alleged use of biological weapons or suspicious outbreaks of disease. Further meetings of States Parties have been held in

---

[47] The monitoring regime contained in a draft Protocol, elaborated in the 1990s, had three basic elements: mandatory declarations of dual-capable activities and facilities; routine visits to declared facilities, without specific evidence of a treaty violation; and short-notice challenge investigations, requested by a State Party, of a suspect facility, an alleged use of biological weapons, or a suspicious outbreak of disease, so as to address concerns about possible non-compliance.

[48] Reaching Critical Will, '2019 Biological Weapons Convention Meeting of States Parties', 2019, at: https://www.reachingcriticalwill.org/news/latest-news/14458-2019-biological-weapons-convention-meeting-of-states-parties#.

most years since then, serving among other things as preparation for the forthcoming review conference.

The UN Secretary-General's Mechanism

In the late 1980s, following use of chemical weapons by Iraq both against Iran and against the Kurds at Halabja, the UN Secretary-General elaborated a mechanism to allow him to investigate alleged use of biological or chemical weapons. The Secretary-General's Mechanism (SGM) was first set out in a UN General Assembly Resolution in 1987, and was reaffirmed the following year by UN Security Council Resolution 620. It was further endorsed by the Assembly in its Resolution 45/57, adopted without a vote on 4 December 1990. The Assembly further noted

> the continuing significance of the Security Council decision to consider immediately, taking into account the investigations of the Secretary-General, appropriate and effective measures in accordance with the Charter of the United Nations, should there be any future use of chemical weapons in violation of international law.[49]

The SGM, which predates the adoption of the Chemical Weapons Convention, involves the UN Secretary-General conducting a prompt investigation into allegations of use of biological or chemical weapons. Triggered by a request from any UN member State, the Secretary-General is authorized to dispatch a fact-finding team to the site of the alleged incident and to report the findings to all UN member States. The purpose is 'to ascertain in an objective and scientific manner facts of alleged violations of the 1925 Geneva Protocol, which bans the use of chemical and biological weapons, or other relevant rules of customary international law'.[50]

The Mechanism was first used in 1992 in both Azerbaijan and Mozambique. More recently, it was applied in Syria in 2013 prior to Syria's adherence to the Chemical Weapons Convention. The mission dispatched by the UN Secretary-General concluded that:

---

[49] UN General Assembly Resolution 45/57, adopted without a vote on 4 December 1990, operative para. 4.

[50] UNODA, 'Secretary-General's Mechanism for Investigation of Alleged Use of Chemical and Biological Weapons', undated but accessed 1 March 2021 at: https://www.un.org/disarmament/wmd/secretary-general-mechanism/.

> On the basis of the evidence obtained during our investigation of the Ghouta incident, the conclusion is that, on 21 August 2013, chemical weapons have been used in the ongoing conflict between the parties in the Syrian Arab Republic, also against civilians, including children, on a relatively large scale.

In particular, the mission found 'clear and convincing evidence that surface-to-surface rockets containing the nerve agent Sarin were used in Ein Tarma, Moadamiyah, and Zamalka in the Ghouta area of Damascus.'[51]

The SGM has not yet been used with respect to alleged use of biological weapons. In 2004, however, at the Second Meeting of States Parties to the Biological Weapons Convention, the States Parties recognized that the SGM 'represents an international institutional mechanism for investigating cases of alleged use of biological or toxin weapons.'[52]

The OPCW

The OPCW has its own mechanism for investigating alleged use of chemical weapons by any State Party to the Chemical Weapons Convention. In response to persistent allegations of chemical weapon attacks in Syria, the OPCW Fact-finding Mission (FFM) was set up in 2014 'to establish facts surrounding allegations of the use of toxic chemicals, reportedly chlorine, for hostile purposes in the Syrian Arab Republic'. The FFM is required to study available information relating to allegations of use of chemical weapons in Syria, including information provided by the Syrian Arab Republic and others. In 2015, the OPCW Executive Council and the UN Security Council endorsed the continuing operation of the FFM.

The FFM confirmed that chemical weapons had been used in Syria. The FFM's findings were the basis for the work of the OPCW–UN Joint Investigative Mechanism (JIM). The purpose of the Mechanism was to identify the perpetrators of the chemical weapon attacks confirmed by the FFM, but the mandate of the Mechanism expired in December 2017

---

[51] UN Mission to Investigate Allegations of the Use of Chemical Weapons in the Syrian Arab Republic, 'Report on Allegations of the Use of Chemical Weapons in the Ghouta Area of Damascus on 21 August 2013', UN docs. A/67/997 and S/2013/553, 16 September 2013, available at: https://digitallibrary.un.org/record/756814?ln=en, paras 27–28.

[52] Biological Weapons Convention Implementation Support Unit, 'Biological Weapons Convention: Background Information', 2012, p. 5.

and was not renewed, following objections from Russia. As of this writing, the work of the FFM was continuing—for despite Syria's accession to the Chemical Weapons Convention in October 2013, chemical weapons (specifically chlorine and sarin, a nerve agent) have continued to be used on many occasions during the armed conflicts that, as of this writing, persisted across the country.

In May 2018, the OPCW Technical Assistance Visit team concluded that the nerve agent found in Salisbury in the United Kingdom—Novichok— was of high purity, persistent, and resistant to weather conditions.[53] The OPCW team worked independently and was not involved in the national investigation by the UK authorities. No State Party was involved in the technical work carried out by the Technical Secretariat.

In November 2018, the 24th Conference of States Parties to the Chemical Weapons Convention agreed to update the list of Schedule 1 chemicals to include Novichok.[54] This was the first time in the history of the Convention that the Annex had been updated. Russia has consistently denied that its agents, including two military intelligence officers, were responsible for the use of the prohibited nerve agent.[55]

Australia Group

The Australia Group is a politically binding regime which, by harmonizing export controls, seeks to ensure that transfers do not contribute to the development of biological or chemical weapons. The Australia Group was established after the use of chemical weapons in the Iran–Iraq war in the 1980s. The 43 members of the Group (42 States and the European Union)[56]

---

[53] OPCW, 'OPCW Spokesperson's Statement on Amount of Nerve Agent Used in Salisbury', News item, The Hague, 4 May 2018, at: https://www.opcw.org/media-centre/news/2018/05/opcw-spokespersons-statement-amount-nerve-agent-used-salisbury.

[54] D. G. Kimball, 'CWC States Update List of Banned Chemicals', *Arms Control Today*, December 2019, at: https://www.armscontrol.org/act/2019-12/news-briefs/cwc-states-update-list-banned-chemicals.

[55] See, e.g., M. Bennetts, 'Novichok Attack: Russia "Has No Reason" to Investigate Suspects', *The Guardian*, 6 September 2018, at: https://www.theguardian.com/uk-news/2018/sep/06/novichok-attack-russia-putin-has-no-reason-to-investigate-uk-named-suspects.

[56] The following States were members as of this writing: Argentina, Australia, Austria, Belgium, Bulgaria, Canada, Croatia, the Republic of Cyprus, Czechia, Denmark, Estonia, Finland, France, Germany, Greece, Hungary, Iceland, India, Ireland, Italy, Japan, Latvia, Lithuania, Luxembourg, Malta, Mexico, the Netherlands, New Zealand, Norway, Poland, Portugal, Romania, Slovakia, Slovenia, South Korea, Spain, Sweden, Switzerland, Turkey, Ukraine, the United Kingdom, and the United States.

aim to ensure that legitimate trade in sensitive dual-use goods and technology is not diverted to biological or chemical weapons production. The members have licensing measures on 63 chemical weapons precursors. They also require licences for the export of specific dual-use chemical manufacturing facilities, equipment, and related technology; plant pathogens; animal pathogens; biological agents; and dual-use biological equipment and related technology.

The Australia Group coordinates national export controls on precursors of biological and chemical weapons. The Group's Common Control Lists define which items should be subject to export controls. The associated Guidelines for Transfers of Sensitive Chemical or Biological Items guide the States in their decision-making:

> [The] evaluation of export applications will take into account the following non-exhaustive list of factors:
>
> a. Information about proliferation and terrorism involving CBW, including any proliferation or terrorism-related activity, or about involvement in clandestine or illegal procurement activities, of the parties to the transaction
> b. The capabilities and objectives of the chemical and biological activities of the recipient State
> c. The significance of the transfer in terms of (1) the appropriateness of the stated end-use, including any relevant assurances submitted by the recipient State or end-user, and (2) the potential development of CBW
> d. The role of distributors, brokers or other intermediaries in the transfer, including, where appropriate, their ability to provide an authenticated end-user certificate specifying both the importer and ultimate end-user of the item to be transferred, as well as the credibility of assurances that the item will reach the stated end-user
> e. The assessment of the end-use of the transfer, including whether a transfer has been previously denied to the end-user, whether the end-user has diverted for unauthorized purposes any transfer previously authorized, and, to the extent possible, whether the end-user is capable of securely handling and storing the item transferred
> f. The extent and effectiveness of the export control system in the recipient State as well as any intermediary States

g. The applicability of relevant multilateral agreements, including the Biological Weapons Convention and the Chemical Weapons Convention
h. The risk of controlled items falling into the hands of terrorist groups and individuals.

States commit to deny transfers 'if the Government judges, on the basis of all available, persuasive information, evaluated according to factors including those [above], that the controlled items are intended to be used in a chemical weapons or biological weapons program, or for CBW terrorism, or that a significant risk of diversion exists'.[57]

---

[57] The Australia Group, *Guidelines for Transfers of Sensitive Chemical or Biological Items*, June 2015, at: https://www.dfat.gov.au/publications/minisite/theaustraliagroupnet/site/en/guidelines.html.

3
Nuclear Weapons and Nuclear Weapon Regimes

Nuclear weapons are by far the most powerful and the most destructive weapons mankind has ever devised. Their energetic effects are measured in terms of explosive yield compared to trinitrotoluene (TNT)—the standard metric for assessing the relative power of a bomb—either in thousands of tons (kilotons; kt) or millions of tons (megatons; MT). As a comparison with conventional ordnance, the largest bomb in the United States (US) armoury, the GBU-43/B Massive Ordnance Air Blast Bomb (MOAB; better known colloquially as the 'mother of all bombs') has an explosive force equating to 11 tons of TNT. Thus, the MOAB, which was first used in anger by the United States in Afghanistan in April 2017, produced an explosive yield that was less than one thousandth of the 15 kt generated by the atomic bomb dropped on Hiroshima in August 1945.

The temperature of a nuclear blast at Ground Zero—the point on the ground directly beneath the point of detonation—can reach several thousand degrees Celsius, matching that on the surface of the Sun. In addition to the tremendous thermal radiation resulting from nuclear fusion or fission, ordinarily huge quantities of radioactive material are diffused. Gamma, neutron, and ionizing radiation are emitted not only at the time of detonation (termed initial radiation) but also for months or years afterwards (residual radiation). Those who are not vaporized by the blast or the heat may be killed by this radiation because high doses of any form of radiation have devastating effects on the human body. If it is not 'shielded' somehow, flesh can literally be cooked. Among the survivors, radiation can lead to loss of fertility, spontaneous abortion, and miscarriage, as well as heritable mutations.

A complex set of multilateral, regional, and bilateral treaties are dedicated to nuclear weapons, some of which have not or did not enter into force and some of which have expired. At the global level, the 1968 Treaty on the

Non-Proliferation of Nuclear Weapons (NPT)[1] is the cornerstone of the nuclear non-proliferation regime. With respect to explosive testing, the 1963 Partial Test-Ban Treaty remains in force[2] while the 1996 Comprehensive Nuclear-Test-Ban Treaty (CTBT) has not yet entered into force.[3] In January 2021, the UN Treaty on the Prohibition of Nuclear Weapons (TPNW) entered into force.[4] The 1987 Intermediate Nuclear Forces (INF) Treaty that removed theatre nuclear missiles from Europe is no longer in force. The 2010 New START treaty between the Russian Federation and the United States was extended *in extremis* until 5 February 2026, when it will formally expire. There are also regional nuclear-weapon-free zone treaties in Africa, the Americas, Central Asia, South Asia, and the Pacific, as well as the 1959 Antarctic Treaty[5] and the 1967 Outer Space Treaty.[6] Describing the content and operation of these instruments—including the International Atomic Energy Agency (IAEA), which works to ensure the peaceful use of nuclear energy—is the focus of this chapter.

Nuclear disarmament is an area of substantial polarization in the international community. In 2019, the United States (US) and Russia announced their withdrawal from the INF Treaty, effectively bringing it to an end in early August 2019 and allowing both States to deploy short and intermediate-range nuclear missiles anywhere in the world. The New START Treaty between the two States, which limits deployable strategic nuclear forces, was all set to expire in February 2021 until the Biden administration entered the White House. The TPNW—derided by the nuclear-armed States and their allies—is a call to implement the duties on every State to negotiate in good faith for nuclear disarmament.

---

[1] Treaty on the Non-Proliferation of Nuclear Weapons; opened for signature at London, Moscow, and Washington, DC, 1 July 1968; entered into force, 5 March 1970, *UNTS* Vol. 729, Reg. No. 10485. As of 1 March 2021, 190 States were party to the NPT.

[2] Treaty Banning Nuclear Weapon Tests in the Atmosphere, in Outer Space and Under Water; concluded at Moscow, 5 August 1963; entered into force, 10 October 1963, *UNTS* Vol. 480, Reg. No. 6964. As of 1 March 2021, 125 States were party to the Partial Test-Ban Treaty.

[3] Comprehensive Nuclear-Test-Ban Treaty; adopted at New York, 10 September 1996; not yet in force. As of 1 March 2021, 170 States had signed and ratified it.

[4] Treaty on the Prohibition of Nuclear Weapons; adopted at New York, 7 July 2017; entered into force, 22 January 2021. As of 1 March 2021, fifty-four States were party to the Treaty.

[5] The Antarctic Treaty; adopted at Washington, DC, 1 December 1959; entered into force, 23 June 1961, *UNTS* Vol. 402, Reg. No. 5778. As of 1 March 2021, fifty-four States were party to it.

[6] Treaty on Principles Governing the Activities of States in the Exploration and Use of Outer Space, including the Moon and Other Celestial Bodies, adopted on 19 December 1966; entry into force, 10 October 1967, UNTS Vol. 610, Reg. No. 23002. As of 1 March 2021, 110 States were party to the Treaty.

The content and status of the Joint Comprehensive Plan of Action (JCPOA, better known as the Iran Nuclear Deal) and the concomitant situation in Iran are also addressed in this chapter, as is the role of the United Nations (UN) Security Council with respect to the Democratic People's Republic of Korea (North Korea). The operation of the Missile Technology Control Regime (MCTR), which seeks to limit the proliferation of missiles and missile technology, is described in Chapter 5. The MTCR was initiated 'by like-minded countries to address the increasing proliferation of nuclear weapons by addressing the most destabilizing delivery system for such weapons'.[7] The chapter begins, however, with a summary of the development (and use) of nuclear weapons, and closes with mention of the new technologies under development for their delivery.

The development and use of nuclear weapons

While the potential for nuclear explosive devices was already understood by scientists early in the twentieth century, it was the Hungarian physicist Leó Szilárd who, in 1933, first conceived of nuclear chain reactions. The subsequent discovery of nuclear fission led Szilárd to draft a warning letter to US President Franklin D. Roosevelt on 2 August 1939; the letter was signed by Albert Einstein. The letter said that 'it may become possible to set up a nuclear chain reaction in a large mass of uranium, by which vast amounts of power and large quantities of new radium-like elements would be generated'. Such a 'phenomenon', the letter continued,

> would also lead to the construction of bombs, and it is conceivable—though much less certain—that extremely powerful bombs of a new type may thus be constructed. A single bomb of this type, carried by boat and exploded in a port, might very well destroy the whole port together with some of the surrounding territory. However, such bombs might very well prove to be too heavy for transportation by air.[8]

---

[7] MCTR, 'Frequently Asked Questions (FAQs)', undated but accessed 1 March 2021 at: https://mtcr.info/frequently-asked-questions-faqs/.

[8] Letter available at Wikisource: 'Albert Einstein to Franklin D. Roosevelt—August 2, 1939', at: https://en.wikisource.org/wiki/Albert_Einstein_to_Franklin_D._Roosevelt_-_August_2,_1939.

Manhattan Project

In the middle of 1942, President Roosevelt authorized the development of just such a nuclear bomb under the 'Development of Substitute Materials' project, better known to the world as the Manhattan Project.[9] One of the greatest challenges for the scientists working on the Manhattan Project was to separate the ^{235}U isotope—used for fission—from the ^{238}U isotope that makes up 99 per cent of naturally occurring uranium. Since the two isotopes are chemically identical, they cannot be separated by chemical means. In parallel with that work, efforts were made to produce plutonium by irradiating ^{238}U, which could then be chemically separated from the uranium and used for a plutonium bomb.

The Manhattan Project's early work focused on 'gun-type' designs whereby one piece of uranium is fired into another to create a critical mass. This is the smallest amount of fissile material necessary for a nuclear chain reaction. The explosive power of the bomb is derived from nuclear fission of the 235 isotope of uranium, during which chain reactions occur as a result of interactions between neutrons and fissile isotopes. When an atom undergoes nuclear fission, neutrons ejected from the reaction are absorbed by other atoms of the fissile material, causing further fissions in a repeating cycle that causes a self-sustaining reaction.

While the gun-type design was promising for uranium-based bombs, it appeared to be less so when plutonium was used. As plutonium was rather easier to obtain than Uranium-235, scientists at the Los Alamos facility in New Mexico began developing an implosion design for a plutonium-based bomb. In an implosion bomb, high explosive surrounding the fissile material is first ignited. A shock wave moves inwards at faster than the speed of sound, creating a large increase in pressure. Compression of the fissile material in the bomb core results in its increased density, leading to the mass becoming supercritical, wherein chain reactions grow in number exponentially. At a certain point, the massive energy released in the fission process is then transferred to the surrounding area.[10]

---

[9] This is because the Corps of Engineers responsible for its development was headquartered on Manhattan Island in New York.

[10] Atomic Archive, 'Implosion-Type Bomb: Detonation Sequence', 2015, at: https://www. atomicarchive.com/science/fission/detonation-sequence.html.

Early on 16 July 1945, a plutonium bomb was test-detonated over the New Mexico desert, marking the dawn of the nuclear age. It was later calculated that the test had released energy equivalent to 21 kt. There was felt to be no need to test the uranium bomb, since the scientists, led by Robert Oppenheimer, were confident of the effectiveness of its design.

The United States would go on to explode nuclear weapons over two Japanese cities. On 6 August 1945 a B-29 bomber, the *Enola Gay*, dropped a 9,700lb uranium gun-type bomb over Hiroshima, a city on Honshu island with a civilian population of almost 300,000 and which was hosting about 43,000 soldiers. Within minutes of the blast, nine of every ten people within almost a kilometre of the centre of the explosion were dead, and about half of the city's entire population were either dead or injured. The many small fires that broke out merged into one large firestorm that engulfed more than four square miles of the city. No one knows how many died as a result of the attack on Hiroshima but at least 70,000 were probably killed in the initial blast and heat, and shortly thereafter by the effects of radiation, while the five-year death toll may have exceeded 200,000 as a result of cancers and other long-term effects. The mushroom cloud reached more than 13 kilometres into the clear morning sky. While the captain of the *Enola Gay* had no qualms about dropping the bomb, Robert Lewis, his co-pilot, wrote in the diary he kept during the flight: 'My God, what have we done?'[11]

Three days later, on 9 August, the US Air Force dropped a plutonium implosion bomb on the city of Nagasaki, an industrial centre and major port on the western coast of Kyushu island. The bomb exploded at 1,650 feet above the city in an explosion whose force was estimated at 21 kt. Everyone within one kilometre of the point of detonation died almost instantly. The best estimate of casualties, according to the US Department of Energy, is that 40,000 people died initially, with 60,000 more injured. By January 1946, the number of deaths may have been as high as 70,000, with perhaps twice that number dying as a consequence over the course of the following four years. Almost all homes within two and a half kilometres were destroyed; less than one in eight of the city's homes escaped unscathed.[12]

---

[11] R. Braithwaite, *Armageddon and Paranoia: The Nuclear Confrontation*, Profile Books, London, 2019, p. 16.

[12] US Department of Energy, 'Manhattan Project: The Atomic Bombing of Nagasaki, August 1945', accessed 1 March 2021 at: https://www.osti.gov/opennet/manhattan-project-history/Events/1945/nagasaki.htm.

Nuclear weapons development during the Cold War

Nazi Germany's own abortive nuclear research programme had come to an end with the nation's military defeat in May 1945. By then the Soviet Union was already stepping up its own development programme. On 29 August 1949 it test-detonated a plutonium implosion bomb at Semipalatinsk in Kazakhstan, making the Soviet Union the world's second nuclear-weapon State.[13] As was the case with the United States, there would be tests, not only of the effectiveness of the bomb, but also of the ability of soldiers to fight in the immediate aftermath of an atomic detonation. On 14 September 1954, near a village in the Ural mountains, the Soviet armed forces air-detonated a 20 kt atomic bomb as part of a military exercise, close to 45,000 Red Army troops and thousands of civilians. The purpose of the exercise, which was filmed, was to assess whether troops could fight a battle in an area just after it had been hit by an atomic bomb. The soldiers were ordered to run through the area with little or no protective equipment.[14]

Some 125,000 nuclear warheads were built between 1945 and 2013, about 97 per cent of which were produced by the United States and the Soviet Union/Russia. More than 2,000 were exploded in test-detonations. In terms of warheads, the Cold War peak was more than 70,000 in the mid-1980s.[15] In addition to the United States and the Soviet Union, by the end of the 1960s at least four other States had developed their own nuclear weapons capability: the United Kingdom (UK) (1952), France (1960), China (1964), and Israel (possibly before the end of 1966). Many other States would initiate research and development programmes to pave the way for the production of nuclear weapons, though the overwhelming majority would renounce their pursuit of nuclear explosive devices and adhere

---

[13] Preparatory Commission for the CTBTO, 'The Soviet Union's Nuclear Testing Programme', accessed 1 March 2021 at: https://www.ctbto.org/nuclear-testing/the-effects-of-nuclear-testing/the-soviet-unionsnuclear-testing-programme/.

[14] M. Simons, 'Soviet Atom Test Used Thousands as Guinea Pigs, Archives Show', *The New York Times*, 7 November 1993, at: https://www.nytimes.com/1993/11/07/world/soviet-atom-test-used-thousands-as-guinea-pigs-archives-show.html?+pagewanted=all.   Pravda reported on the exercise at the time: 'The purpose of the test was to examine the effects of nuclear explosion. Valuable results have been obtained that will help Soviet scientists and engineers to successfully solve the task of protecting the country from nuclear attack.' *Pravda*, 17 September 1954.

[15] H. M. Kristensen and R. S. Norris, 'Global Nuclear Weapons Inventories, 1945–2013', *Bulletin of the Atomic Scientists*, Vol. 69, No. 5 (2013), pp. 75–81, available at: https://www.tandfonline.com/doi/full/10.1177/0096340213501363.

to the NPT (see below). Only the Democratic People's Republic of Korea, India, Pakistan, and South Africa would go on to develop nuclear weapons, with South Africa voluntarily dismantling its six nuclear explosive devices at the end of the 1980s as apartheid was coming to an end.

As of September 2020, according to Hans M. Kristensen and Matt Korda, a total of some 13,410 nuclear weapons remained, of which approximately 9,320 were either in military stockpiles or awaiting dismantlement. Some 3,720 warheads were deployed with operational forces, about half of which were French, Russian, UK, and US warheads on high alert, ready for use at short notice. Nuclear-armed States, they said, 'appear to plan to retain large arsenals for the indefinite future, are adding new nuclear weapons, and are increasing the role that such weapons play in their national strategies'.[16]

The NPT

In 1968, States within the Committee on Disarmament concluded the text of the NPT before forwarding it on to the UN General Assembly for adoption.[17] The preamble refers to 'the devastation that would be visited upon all mankind by a nuclear war' and to the belief 'that the proliferation of nuclear weapons would seriously enhance the danger' of such a war. Under Article I of the NPT, the designated nuclear-weapon States—which, based on the date on which they first detonated a nuclear explosive device, are China, France, Russia (as successor State to the Soviet Union), the United Kingdom, and the United States[18]—are prohibited from transferring nuclear weapons to any non-State actors as well as to 'non-nuclear-weapon States'. Non-nuclear-weapon States are defined as every State except for these five nuclear-weapon States.

The five nuclear-weapon States are not barred from acquiring the material necessary for their nuclear weapons programmes from

---

[16] H. M. Kristensen and M. Korda, 'Status of World Nuclear Forces', Federation of American Scientists, Updated as of September 2020, at: https://fas.org/issues/nuclear-weapons/status-world-nuclear-forces/.

[17] Treaty on the Non-Proliferation of Nuclear Weapons; opened for signature at London, Moscow, and Washington, DC, 1 July 1968; entered into force, 5 March 1970, *UNTS* Vol. 729, Reg. No. 10485. As of 1 March 2021, 190 States were party to the NPT. For detail on the negotiations see M. I. Shaker, *The Nuclear Non-Proliferation Treaty: Origins and Implementation 1959–1979*, 3 vols, Oceana Publications, London/Rome/New York, March 1980.

[18] According to Article IX(3) of the NPT, for the purposes of the Treaty, a nuclear-weapon state 'is one which has manufactured and exploded a nuclear weapon or other nuclear explosive device prior to 1 January, 1967'.

non-nuclear-weapon States. The Treaty does not address the operational deployment of nuclear weapons, although so-called peaceful nuclear explosions are implicitly authorized by Article V of the NPT. All non-nuclear-weapon States Parties are prohibited from acquiring in any manner nuclear weapons (or 'other nuclear explosive devices'),[19] though, as noted in Chapter 1, they are not formally prevented from engaging in preliminary research and development. The NPT does not formally define either *nuclear weapons* or *other nuclear explosive devices* for the purpose of the treaty.

The peaceful use of nuclear energy, such as for the production of electricity or for scientific or medical purposes, is explicitly protected under the NPT. Thus, it is stipulated that nothing in the treaty 'shall be interpreted as affecting the inalienable right of all the Parties to the Treaty to develop research, production and use of nuclear energy for peaceful purposes'.[20] States Parties 'in a position to do so' are obligated to cooperate to promote 'the further development of the applications of nuclear energy for peaceful purposes, especially in the territories of non-nuclear-weapon States Party'.[21]

Most notoriously, under Article VI of the NPT, all States Parties pledge to 'pursue negotiations in good faith on effective measures relating to cessation of the nuclear arms race at an early date and to nuclear disarmament, and on a treaty on general and complete disarmament under strict and effective international control'. The interpretation of this provision remains highly contested, particularly between the five nuclear-weapon States (who assert that they are best placed to judge when the conditions are right for disarmament) and many non-nuclear-weapon States (who wish to see concrete measures towards nuclear disarmament).[22] No specific provision on security assurances to non-nuclear-weapon States was incorporated in the NPT, despite calls from certain States for it to do so.[23] In any event, any

[19] Art. II, NPT.

[20] Art. IV(1), NPT.

[21] Art. IV(2), NPT.

[22] For a useful discussion of this issue, see, e.g., D. Joyner, 'The Legal Meaning and Implications of Article VI of the Non-Proliferation Treaty', Chap. 16 in G. Nystuen, S. Casey-Maslen, and A. G. Bersagel (eds), *Nuclear Weapons under International Law*, Cambridge University Press, Cambridge, 2014.

[23] In April 1995, the five nuclear-weapon States made unilateral commitments on negative security assurances to the non-nuclear-weapon States Parties to the NPT. These declarations were reflected in UN Security Council Resolution 984. France, Russia, the United Kingdom, and the United States reaffirmed that nuclear weapons would not be used against non-nuclear-weapon States Parties to the NPT when they were in compliance with the Treaty, except if one of the nuclear-weapons states were attacked by a non-nuclear weapon State in 'association or alliance' with another nuclear-weapons State.

treaty of nuclear disarmament would be negotiated separately from the NPT, which is an instrument of non-proliferation.

There were 190 States Parties to the NPT as of writing, although a number of authorities suggest that the Democratic People's Republic of Korea is still bound by the treaty under international law. In this regard, the legality of its purported withdrawal from the NPT in 2003 has been questioned.[24] The better view is that it is no longer bound by the treaty and is a State not party.

The other States not party are India, Israel, Pakistan, and South Sudan. The Cook Islands and Niue are not formally States Parties but are considered to be bound by virtue of their administration by New Zealand when it ratified the NPT in 1969. Following the break-up of the Soviet Union, huge numbers of nuclear weapons were left in three of its successor States (Belarus, Kazakhstan, and Ukraine). These States either destroyed the weapons or transferred them to Russia for destruction, with all then adhering to the NPT as non-nuclear-weapon States.

The IAEA

The International Atomic Energy Agency (IAEA) was established by States in 1957. It is mandated to promote peace and international cooperation, in conformity both with 'policies of the United Nations furthering the establishment of safeguarded worldwide disarmament' and 'with any international agreements entered into pursuant to such policies'.[25] Since its inception the IAEA has made a major contribution to peaceful use of nuclear energy. Indeed, although the IAEA is best known for its verification of compliance with the NPT, it was established with a mandate to promote the peaceful exploitation of nuclear power, through the generation of electricity and advances in the medical and scientific spheres.

Under the NPT, each non-nuclear-weapon State Party undertakes to accept safeguards in an agreement with the IAEA 'for the exclusive purpose of verification of the fulfilment' of its NPT obligations 'with a view to preventing diversion of nuclear energy from peaceful uses to nuclear weapons or other nuclear explosive devices'.[26] It is stipulated that the

---

[24] See the note by the UN Office for Disarmament Affairs (UNODA), at: http://disarmament.un.org/treaties/a/npt/democraticpeoplesrepublicofkorea/acc/moscow.

[25] UN, 'Atomic Energy', undated but last accessed 1 March 2021, at: https://www.un.org/en/sections/issues-depth/atomic-energy/.

[26] Art. III(1), NPT.

requisite safeguards 'shall be applied on all source or special fissionable material in all peaceful nuclear activities within the territory of such State, under its jurisdiction, or carried out under its control anywhere'. Each State Party to the Treaty further undertakes not to provide either a source of special fissionable material or specially designed or prepared equipment or material for the processing, use, or production of special fissionable material to any non-nuclear-weapon State for peaceful purposes, unless the source or special fissionable material is subject to the safeguards required by the Treaty.[27]

There are two main agreements between the IAEA and individual States: the Comprehensive Safeguards Agreement (CSA) and the Additional Protocol.[28] A CSA covers plutonium and uranium and other fissile material, along with equipment for their processing, use, or production, seeking to ensure that it does not provide such material or items to any non-nuclear-weapon State other than for peaceful purposes. The IAEA has to date concluded CSAs with 175 States. A Small Quantities Protocol may be concluded in conjunction with a CSA for States that have little or no nuclear material and no nuclear material in a facility; 100 States had already done so as of 1 March 2021.[29]

The more intrusive (and optional) Additional Protocol enhances confidence that nuclear material is not being diverted to the production of nuclear weapons. A CSA can be negated by a failure to declare nuclear material and facilities. This has occurred in Iran, Iraq, and Libya at specific periods over the past fifty years. Under the Protocol, the IAEA is granted expanded rights of access to both information and sites. As of end-2020, 136 States had concluded and brought into force an Additional Protocol with the IAEA.[30] In addition, Iran had been—but had recently, as of writing, had stopped—provisionally applying the Protocol, in compliance with a commitment to do so under the JCPOA.[31]

---

[27] Art. III(2), NPT.

[28] The IAEA concludes three types of safeguards agreements: CSAs with non-nuclear-weapon States Parties to the NPT; voluntary offer safeguards agreements with the nuclear-weapon States Parties to the NPT; and item-specific safeguards agreements with states not party to the NPT.

[29] IAEA, 'Safeguards Legal Framework', undated but last accessed 1 March 2021, at: https://www.iaea.org/topics/safeguards-legal-framework.

[30] IAEA, 'Additional Protocol', 1 February 2021, at: https://www.iaea.org/topics/additional-protocol.

[31] IAEA, 'IAEA Verification in Iran', at: https://www.iaea.org/sites/default/files/18/03/verification-iran-jcpoa.pdf.

The Nuclear Suppliers Group

The Nuclear Suppliers Group (NSG), which first met in 1975, is a group of forty-eight nuclear supplier nations that seek to prevent proliferation of nuclear weapons by implementing two sets of guidelines for nuclear exports and nuclear-related exports. The NSG, which was established after India tested a nuclear explosive device in May 1974, serves to support the implementation of the NPT.[32] The NSG Guidelines contain the so-called Non-Proliferation Principle, which was agreed upon in 1994, whereby a supplier authorizes a transfer only when it is satisfied that it would not contribute to the proliferation of nuclear weapons. The Principle seeks to address situations where adherence to the NPT (or to a nuclear-weapon-free zone treaty) is not a sufficient guarantee that a State will consistently remain in compliance with its Treaty obligation.[33]

Under NSG Guidelines, formal government assurances are required between the exporting and importing governments to assure that the nuclear transfer is for peaceful purposes and will not contribute to the proliferation of nuclear weapons or other nuclear explosive devices. The importing government also has to provide assurance that it will not re-transfer items, material, or technology that it has received to a third government without the exporting government's prior consent. There is also a requirement for physical protection, and an agreement to exercise particular caution when considering the transfer of sensitive facilities (such as enrichment or reprocessing facilities and related equipment and technology), technology, or material usable for nuclear weapons or other nuclear explosive devices.

Separate guidelines (Part II)[34] apply to transfers of nuclear-related dual-use equipment, materials, software, and related technology. The NSG Part 2 Guidelines were adopted in 1992 after the export control provisions then in force had not prevented one State Party to the NPT (the Democratic People's Republic of Korea) from pursuing a clandestine nuclear weapons programme. According to the Guidelines, States should not authorize transfers of equipment, materials, software, or related technology:

---

[32] Nuclear Suppliers Group, 'About the NSG', at: https://www.nsg-online.org/en/about-us.
[33] Ibid.
[34] Nuclear Suppliers Group, Guidelines for transfers of nuclear-related dual-use equipment, materials, software, and related technology (INFCIRC/254, Part 2).

- for use in a non-nuclear-weapon State in a nuclear explosive activity or an unsafeguarded nuclear fuel-cycle activity;
- when there is an unacceptable risk of diversion to such an activity or when the transfers are contrary to the objective of averting the proliferation of nuclear weapons; or
- when there is an unacceptable risk of diversion to acts of nuclear terrorism.

Zangger Committee

The Zangger Committee, also known as the Nuclear Exporters Committee, was established in 1971 with a view to giving effect to Article III(2) of the NPT,[35] which specifies as follows:

> Each State Party to the Treaty undertakes not to provide: (a) source or special fissionable material, or (b) equipment or material especially designed or prepared for the processing, use or production of special fissionable material, to any non-nuclear-weapon State for peaceful purposes, unless the source or special fissionable material shall be subject to the safeguards required by this Article.

The Committee, an informal intergovernmental group with thirty-nine members, including all the nuclear-weapon States, defined which transfers of 'especially designed or prepared equipment or material for the processing, use or production of special fissionable material' covered by Article III(2) of the NPT were to be controlled. It also ensured that items transferred to non-nuclear-weapon States would remain subject to IAEA safeguards. Although both institutions remain formally distinct, the NSG—of which all States of the Zangger Committee are members—has effectively taken over the Committee's activities.

---

[35] The Committee was set up because of France's decision, at the time, not to adhere to the NPT. W. Burr, 'The Making of the Nuclear Suppliers Group, 1974–1976', Wilson Center, 16 April 2014, at: https://www.wilsoncenter.org/publication/the-making-the-nuclear-suppliers-group-1974-1976.

The partial and comprehensive nuclear-test-ban treaties

More than 2,000 test-detonations of nuclear explosive devices, including so-called peaceful nuclear explosions, have occurred since 1945, most recently in 2017 in the Democratic People's Republic of Korea. The United States has reported conducting a total of 1,054 nuclear test-detonations from 1945 until 1992, its last test. Twenty-four of the underground tests were conducted jointly with the United Kingdom.[36] Between January 1951 and July 1962, atmospheric and underground nuclear tests were conducted at the Nevada Test Site.[37] Since then all nuclear tests conducted in the United States have been underground, most at the Nevada Test Site. The United States also carried out 106 test explosions in the Pacific: on Bikini Atoll and Enewetak (part of the Marshall Islands); on Christmas Island (now part of Kiribati); and on Johnston Island (an atoll in the US Minor Outlying Islands), as well as over the Pacific Ocean.[38]

The Soviet Union is said to have conducted 715 nuclear test-detonations between 1949 and 1990 (it ceased to exist a year later). Most of the tests took place at the Semipalatinsk test site in Kazakhstan and the Northern test site at Novaya Zemlya, an archipelago in the Arctic Ocean in northern Russia. A small number of tests were conducted in Turkmenistan, Ukraine, and Uzbekistan.[39] The largest nuclear weapon detonation in history occurred on 30 October 1961 on Severny Island, part of Novaya Zemlya. Code-named Vanya, the Soviet RDS-220 hydrogen bomb had a yield of some 57 MT, equivalent to more than 1,500 times the combined energy of the bombs that were detonated over Hiroshima and Nagasaki. To reduce fallout, a lead tamper was used instead of a Uranium-238 fusion tamper, ensuring that thermonuclear fusion accounted for as much as 97 per cent of the yield. Thus, despite its phenomenal power, the RDS-220 bomb is said not to have generated very large quantities of nuclear fallout.[40]

---

[36] US Department of Energy, *United States Nuclear Tests, July 1945 through September 1992*, Doc. DOE/NV--209-REV 15, December 2000, at: https://www.osti.gov/servlets/purl/10115601, pp. xi, xiii.

[37] Ibid., p. viii.

[38] Ibid., p. xiii.

[39] V. N. Mikhailov (ed.), *USSR Nuclear Weapons Tests and Peaceful Nuclear Explosions: 1949 through 1990*, Ministry of the Russian Federation for Atomic Energy and Ministry of Defense of the Russian Federation, 1996; see: 'Soviet Nuclear Test Summary', Last updated 7 October 1997, at: http://nuclearweaponarchive.org/Russia/Sovtestsum.html.

[40] Atomic Heritage Foundation, 'Tsar Bomba', 8 August 2014, at: https://www.atomicheritage.org/history/tsar-bomba.

The public health and environmental effects of atmospheric (above-ground) tests began to cause alarm as early as the 1950s, including as a result of concern about the radionuclide strontium-90 (a radioactive isotope of strontium produced by nuclear fission) and its effect on mother's milk and babies' teeth. The Russian physicist Andrei Sakharov warned in a journal article in 1958 that millions of people that would die or suffer serious harm as a result of atmospheric nuclear testing. A review of his work in 1990 concluded that his estimate whereby for every megaton of yield in an atmospheric test as many as 10,000 people would ultimately suffer cancers, genetic disorders, and other ill effects remained robust.[41] Atmospheric testing between 1945 and 1980 is estimated to have amounted to a total of 428 MT.

The Treaty Banning Nuclear Weapon Tests in the Atmosphere, in Outer Space and Under Water, better known as the Partial Test-Ban Treaty or PTBT, emerged from a proposal by India in 1954 to elaborate an international agreement to ban nuclear weapons tests. In 1958 the United Kingdom, the United States, and the Soviet Union had initiated discussions at a Conference on the Discontinuance of Nuclear Tests in Geneva, but a treaty was not adopted due to lack of agreement on verification procedures. The Treaty as adopted does not provide for international verification, but each State Party may do so on the basis of its own technical means.

The Treaty requires its States Parties to prohibit, prevent, and abstain from nuclear weapons tests or any other nuclear explosions in the atmosphere, in outer space, or under water, as well as in any other environment where the explosion would cause radioactive debris to be present outside the territorial limits of the State responsible for it.[42] It further obliges States Parties to refrain from causing, encouraging, or in any way participating in any nuclear weapon test explosion or other nuclear explosion that would take place anywhere in any of those environments.[43]

The Partial Test-Ban Treaty was opened for signature at London, Moscow, and Washington DC on 8 August 1963 and entered into force on 10 October 1963. China and France, neither of whom had been invited to participate in the negotiations, did not sign at the time (nor did they do so

---

[41] A. D. Sakharov, 'Radioactive Carbon from Nuclear Explosions and Non-Threshold Biological Effects', *Science & Global Security*, Vol. I (1990), pp. 175–87; and see Appendix reviewing Sakharov's conclusions by Frank von Hippel, all at: http://scienceandglobalsecurity. org/archive/sgs01sakharov.pdf.
[42] Art. I(1), PTBT.
[43] Art. I(2), PTBT.

later), and both continued to conduct atmospheric tests until, respectively, 1980 and 1974.[44] As at 1 March 2021, 125 States were party to the Treaty.

The PTBT did not outlaw all forms of explosive testing of nuclear devices. This was left to the Comprehensive Nuclear-Test-Ban Treaty (CTBT), which was concluded and then adopted by States in controversial circumstances in 1996.[45] Under the CTBT, States Parties undertake not to carry out any nuclear weapon test explosion or any other nuclear explosion, and to prohibit and prevent any such nuclear explosion at any place under their jurisdiction or control.[46] This has arguably become a rule of customary international law. The CTBT further prohibits States Parties from 'causing, encouraging, or in any way participating in the carrying out of any nuclear weapon test explosion or any other nuclear explosion'.[47]

The Treaty includes a Protocol in three parts: Part I detailing the international monitoring system; Part II governing on-site inspections; and Part III relating to confidence-building measures. Under the Treaty, the Comprehensive Nuclear Test-Ban Treaty Organization (CTBTO) is to be established (headquartered in Vienna).[48] As a consequence of a meeting of signatory States in 1996, a Preparatory Commission has been created in Vienna, pending the Treaty's entry into force.[49]

Annexes to the Treaty list States by geographical region for the purposes of elections to the Executive Council (Annex 1), and States that must ratify or accede to the Treaty for it to enter into force (Annex 2).[50] As at 1 March 2021, 170 States had ratified the Treaty and a further 15 had signed but not ratified. Despite this level of adherence, the CTBT has still to enter into force as an instrument of binding international law. To do so would require adherence, as of writing, by China (a signatory), the Democratic People's Republic of Korea, Egypt (a signatory), India, Iran (a signatory), Israel (a signatory), Pakistan, and the United States (a signatory). Prospects for the treaty's early entry into force are extremely slim.

---

[44] CTBTO Preparatory Commission, 'Nuclear Testing: General Overview of the Effects of Nuclear Testing', 2012, at: https://www.ctbto.org/nuclear-testing/the-effects-of-nuclear-testing/general-overview-of-theeffects-of-nuclear-testing/.

[45] See *supra* 'The role of the Conference on Disarmament' in the Introduction to this book.

[46] Art. I(1), CTBT.

[47] Art. I(2), CTBT.

[48] Art. II(1) and (3), CTBT.

[49] Resolution establishing the Preparatory Commission for the Comprehensive Nuclear Test-Ban Treaty Organization; adopted on 19 November 1996 by a Meeting of Signatory States.

[50] Am Annex to the Protocol to the CTBT details the location of various Treaty monitoring assets associated with the International Monitoring System (IMS).

Bilateral nuclear arms control and disarmament treaties

During the late 1960s, the United States learned that the Soviet Union had embarked upon a massive intercontinental ballistic missile (ICBM) build-up with a view to reaching parity in numbers with the United States. In early 1967, after announcing that the Soviet Union had begun to construct a limited anti-ballistic missile (ABM) defence system around Moscow, President Lyndon Johnson called for strategic arms limitation talks with the Soviets; later in the year he would meet with Soviet Premier Alexei Kosygin in New Jersey.[51] These exploratory talks would lead to formal negotiations that culminated in two bilateral nuclear arms control and disarmament treaties in 1972. Many such treaties have since been agreed upon by the United States and the Soviet Union/Russia, but only one is still in force (New START). This sole remaining treaty will formally expire in February 2026.

The ABM Treaty

The first of two bilateral agreements to be concluded in the SALT talks between the United States and the Soviet Union was the 1972 Anti-Ballistic Missile Treaty (ABM Treaty),[52] which was the initial output of the Strategic Arms Limitation Talks that formally started in 1969 with a view to restricting strategic nuclear arsenals. The ABM Treaty in 1972 did not limit nuclear arsenals but prohibited the development, testing, and deployment of weapons that could undermine nuclear deterrence by placing into doubt the effectiveness of retaliatory strikes. In the Preamble of the Treaty, the two parties declared that imposing effective limits on anti-missile systems would be a 'substantial factor in curbing the race in strategic offensive arms'.

The Treaty allowed both parties to deploy two fixed missile defence sites each composed of a maximum of 100 missile interceptors. One site was permitted to protect each of Washington DC and Moscow, while a second site

---

[51] US Department of State, 'Strategic Arms Limitations Talks/Treaty (SALT) I and II', Milestones: 1969–1976 (Archived pages), at: https://history.state.gov/milestones/1969-1976/salt.

[52] Treaty Between the United States of America and the Union of Soviet Socialist Republics on the Limitation of Anti-Ballistic Missile Systems (ABM Treaty); signed at Moscow, 26 May 1972; entered into force, 3 October 1972; United States' withdrawal, 2002.

for each party could be used to guard an ICBM field.[53] No international verification measures were, though, incorporated in the ABM Treaty. It was stipulated instead that 'for the purpose of providing assurance of compliance with the provisions of this Treaty, each Party shall use national technical means of verification at its disposal in a manner consistent with generally recognized principles of international law'.

The 2002 decision by the Administration of President George W. Bush to withdraw from the ABM Treaty, causing the treaty to expire on 13 June 2002, was a significant moment in bilateral relations between the two superpowers. In June 2015, Russian President Vladimir Putin said that the unilateral US withdrawal from the ABM Treaty had pushed Russia towards a new arms race.[54]

The SALT Treaties

The 1972 Interim Agreement (SALT I)[55] was the first bilateral treaty to limit strategic offensive arms. Article I prevented new construction of fixed land-based ICBM launchers after 1 July 1972. Under Article II, no conversion was permitted of land-based launchers for light ICBMs, or, for ICBMs of older types deployed prior to 1964, into land-based launchers for heavy ICBMs. The Parties further undertook in Article III to limit submarine-launched ballistic missile (SLBM) launchers and modern ballistic missile submarines to the numbers operational and under construction on the date of signature of the Treaty. 'For the first time during the Cold War, the United States and Soviet Union had agreed to limit the number of nuclear missiles in their arsenals. SALT I is considered the crowning achievement of the Nixon–Kissinger strategy of *détente*.'[56]

SALT I paved the way for the 1979 US–Soviet Treaty on the Limitation of Strategic Offensive Arms (SALT II Treaty), which set ceilings for both

---

[53] In the Protocol to the ABM Treaty, concluded in 1974, a maximum of 100 interceptors in only one site was permitted. The Soviet Union opted to keep its missile defence system around Moscow, while the United States deployed 100 interceptors to protect an ICBM base in North Dakota.

[54] 'Putin: Unilateral US Withdrawal from ABM Treaty Pushing Russia toward New Arms Race', *RT*, 19 June 2015, at: https://www.rt.com/news/268345-putin-west-russia-relations/.

[55] Interim Agreement Between the United States of America and the Union of Soviet Socialist Republics on Certain Measures with respect to the Limitation of Strategic Offensive Arms (SALT I); adopted at Moscow, 26 May 1972; entered into force, 3 October 1972; expired 3 October 1977.

[56] US Department of State, 'Strategic Arms Limitations Talks/Treaty (SALT) I and II'.

parties on ICBM launchers, SLBMs, heavy bombers, and long-range air-to-surface ballistic missiles. This included a limit of 2,400 on strategic nuclear delivery vehicles (ICBMs, SLBMs, and heavy bombers) for each side; a limit of 1,320 on multiple independently targeted re-entry vehicles (MIRVs); a ban on new land-based ICBM launchers; and limits on deployment of new types of strategic offensive arms.

On 17 June 1979, President Carter and Premier Brezhnev signed the SALT II Treaty in Vienna. Although never ratified by the United States (in part as a consequence of the Russian invasion of Afghanistan), the Treaty was implemented in practice until 1986, when the United States equipped a new heavy bomber with long-range cruise missiles.

The 1987 Intermediate-Range Nuclear Forces Treaty

The 1987 Treaty Between the United States of America and the Union of Soviet Socialist Republics on the Elimination of Their Intermediate-Range and Shorter-Range Missiles, better known as the INF Treaty, required the United States and the Soviet Union to eliminate all nuclear and conventional ground-launched ballistic and cruise missiles (conventional or nuclear) with ranges of between 500 and 5,500 kilometres. The INF Treaty was the first agreement between the two nuclear superpowers that sought to eliminate an entire category of nuclear weapons, backed for a time by extensive on-site inspections to verify compliance. The authority to conduct these inspections ended on 31 May 2001, but use of surveillance satellites continued.[57]

The INF Treaty was signed on 8 December 1987, entering into force on 1 June 1988. The two original parties, the United States and the Soviet Union, destroyed a total of 2,692 short, medium, and intermediate-range missiles, each meeting the Treaty-imposed deadline of 1 June 1991. Most of the missiles were eliminated by detonation while they were unarmed and their stages burnt, or they were cut in half and their wings and tail sections were severed. On 10 February 2007, however, President Vladimir Putin declared that the Treaty no longer served Russia's interests. In July 2014 the United States alleged that Russia, as the primary successor State Party, was

---

[57] Arms Control Association, 'The Intermediate-Range Nuclear Forces (INF) Treaty at a Glance', Last reviewed August 2019, at: https://www.armscontrol.org/factsheets/INFtreaty.

in violation of the Treaty 'not to possess, produce, or flight-test' a ground-launched cruise missile having a range of 500 to 5,500 kilometres or 'to possess or produce launchers of such missiles'.[58] In late November 2017 a senior US national security official stated that the Novator 9M729, a land-based cruise missile, was the weapon that the United States believed was violating the INF Treaty.[59]

For its part, Russia alleged that the United States had violated the Treaty by deploying a component of a missile defence system—the Mark 41 Vertical Launch System (VLS)—that is capable of launching offensive missiles. It also claimed that the United States had used prohibited missiles in defence tests and that some US armed drones are effectively unlawful cruise missiles. A further complicating factor was the perceived threat from China, whose growing nuclear and conventional missile arsenal is mostly composed of weapons in the INF Treaty-prohibited range. The United States formally withdrew from the INF Treaty on 2 August 2019, following a treaty-mandated six-month period of suspension. Russia announced it was doing likewise, putting an effective end to the Treaty.[60]

The START Treaties

The Strategic Arms Reduction Treaties are a set of bilateral treaties between the United States and the Soviet Union/Russia on the reduction and limitation of strategic nuclear weapons. START negotiations, an initiative by US President Ronald Reagan, resulted in the conclusion of the most complex arms control treaty in history: START I.[61] The Treaty, which was originally planned to be called SALT III, was agreed upon in 1991.

---

[58] Ibid.

[59] D. Majumdar, 'Novator 9M729: The Russian Missile that Broke INF Treaty's Back?', *The National Interest*, 7 December 2017, at: https://nationalinterest.org/blog/the-buzz/novator-9m729-the-russian-missile-broke-inf-treatys-back-23547.

[60] Following the dissolution of the Soviet Union in late 1991, the United States sought to ensure that a number of former Soviet republics would succeed to the INF Treaty. Five States in addition to Russia (Belarus, Kazakhstan, Turkmenistan, Ukraine, and Uzbekistan) had inspectable facilities on their territory.

[61] Treaty Between the United States of America and the Union of Soviet Socialist Republics on the Reduction and Limitation of Strategic Offensive Arms (START I); signed at Moscow, 31 July 1991; entered into force, 5 December 1994; expired, 5 December 2009.

START I and New START

START I limited each party to a maximum of 6,000 nuclear warheads on a total of 1,600 ICBMs and bombers. The Treaty, which was signed on 31 July 1991, entered into force on 5 December 1994. By late 2001, about four-fifths of all strategic nuclear weapons then in existence had been eliminated. START I expired on 5 December 2009. On 23 May 1992 the United States, Belarus, Kazakhstan, Russia, and Ukraine signed the START I Protocol (also known as the Lisbon Protocol). Under the Protocol, all five States would become parties to START I, and the three non-Russian former Soviet republics undertook to adhere to the NPT as non-nuclear-weapon States 'in the shortest possible time'.

On 8 April 2010, the replacement for START I, New START, was signed by US President Barack Obama and Russian President Dmitry Medvedev, entering into force on 26 January 2011. The aggregate limits set by New START, whose implementation deadline was 5 February 2018, are as follows:

- 700 deployed ICBMs, deployed SLBMs, and deployed heavy bombers equipped for nuclear arms
- 1,550 nuclear warheads on deployed ICBMs, deployed SLBMs, and deployed heavy bombers equipped for nuclear arms (each heavy bomber is counted as one warhead toward this limit)
- 800 deployed and non-deployed ICBM launchers, SLBM launchers, and heavy bombers equipped for nuclear arms.

Both States reported meeting their obligations under New START by the February 2018 deadline. The Treaty was due to remain in force until at least February 2021. In April 2018 a group of former officials and experts from Europe, Russia, and the United States warned that unless urgent steps were taken to extend the New START treaty the US and Russian nuclear arsenals could be unconstrained by any binding arms control agreements for the first time since 1972, triggering an expensive and dangerous new arms race.[62] The treaty allows for a single five-year extension, by the mutual consent of the two parties.[63]

---

[62] J. Borger, 'US and Russian Nuclear Arsenals Set to Be Unchecked for First Time since 1972', *The Guardian*, 17 April 2018, at: https://www.theguardian.com/world/2018/apr/17/us-russian-nuclear-arsenals-treaty-expire-unconstrained?.

[63] Art. XIV(2), New START.

The United States sought to include China in any extension of the Treaty.[64] In an interview with *The Washington Times*, Marshall Billingslea, who was nominated in May 2020 for the post of Undersecretary of State for Arms Control, said the deal 'does nothing for the United States with respect to our concerns regarding China, and it does nothing for the United States with respect to our concerns regarding what Russia has been doing, which are a series of destabilizing activities outside of—and not constrained by— the treaty'.[65] In May 2020, Billingslea declared that the United States was prepared to spend both Russia and China 'into oblivion' to win a new nuclear arms race.[66]

On 21 January 2021, the day after Joseph Robinette Biden took the oath of office as the forty-sixth president of the United States, the incoming US administration indicated that it would seek a full five-year extension of the Treaty. The same day, a press release by the Russian Ministry of Foreign Affairs declared:

We believe that the treaty can only be extended as it was signed and without any preconditions. The best option would be to extend New START for five years as it is stipulated in the text of the treaty. This would give Russia and the United States enough time to get down to a joint search for answers to the international security and strategic stability questions that are currently emerging. At the same time, this would preserve the current level of transparency and predictability in the sphere of strategic offensive weapons, which will be in the interests of both parties and the rest of the world.[67]

On 3 February 2021, two days before the treaty's expiry, the final exchange of diplomatic notes between Russia and the United States took place, confirming the extension of New START, unamended, until 5

---

[64] Radio Free Europe/Radio Liberty, 'U.S. Holding Off on New START Extension, Hoping to Bring China into Deal', RFE/RL, 15 February 2020, at: https://www.rferl.org/a/us-delays-new-start-decision-giving-china-time-to-join/30435485.html.

[65] B. Gertz, 'EXCLUSIVE: Envoy Says China Is Key to New Arms Deal with Russia', *The Washington Times*, 7 May 2020, at: https://m.washingtontimes.com/news/2020/may/7/marshall-billingslea-says-new-start-fate-hangs-chi/.

[66] Reuters, 'U.S. Prepared to Spend Russia, China "Into Oblivion" to Win Nuclear Arms Race: U.S. Envoy', 21 May 2020, at: https://www.reuters.com/article/uk-usa-armscontrol/u-s-prepared-to-spend-russia-china-into-oblivion-to-win-nuclear-arms-race-u-s-envoy-idUKKBN22X2LS?edition-redirect=uk.

[67] Russian Ministry of Foreign Affairs, 'Press Release on the Future of New START', Moscow, 20 January 2021.

February 2026. The new US Secretary of State, Antony Blinken, publicly welcomed the extension and the continued security that it would ensure.[68] Publishing a series of 'myth-busters' on its website on the day of the exchange of instruments extending the Treaty, the US Department of State declared: 'Without New START, the Russian Federation could significantly increase the number of warheads deployed on its ballistic missiles and our window of transparency into Russian intercontinental-range nuclear forces would shrink. Over time we would have less confidence in our assessments of Russian intercontinental-range nuclear forces and would have less information upon which to base decisions about U.S. nuclear forces.'[69]

START II

The START II Treaty,[70] which prohibited the use of multiple independently targetable re-entry vehicles (MIRVs; multiple warheads) on ICBMs, never formally entered into force. Known popularly as the 'De-MIRV-ing Agreement', it was signed by US President George H. W. Bush and Russian President Boris Yeltsin on 3 January 1993, but on 14 June 2002, despite domestic ratification by both States, Russia denounced the Treaty in response to the US withdrawal from the ABM Treaty.

START III

The abortive START III negotiations never resulted in a signed treaty. Negotiations had begun in 1997 between US President Bill Clinton and Russian President Boris Yeltsin, with Russian officials suggesting that they might accept an upper limit of 1,500 strategic nuclear warheads within the context of the agreement. The 2002 decision by the George W. Bush Administration to withdraw from the ABM Treaty effectively put an end to hopes for START III.

---

[68] 'On the Extension of the New START Treaty with the Russian Federation', Press Statement by Antony J. Blinken, Secretary of State, 3 February 2021, at: https://www.state.gov/on-the-extension-of-the-new-start-treaty-with-the-russian-federation/.

[69] US Department of State, 'Myth: Allowing the New START Treaty to expire does not harm U.S. security', New START Treaty Mythbusters Fact Sheet, 3 February 2021, at: https://www.state.gov/new-start-treaty-mythbusters/.

[70] Treaty between the United States of America and the Union of Soviet Socialist Republics on Strategic Offensive Reductions (START II); signed at Moscow, 3 January 1993; never entered into force.

Regional nuclear-free zones

The NPT stipulates: 'Nothing in this Treaty affects the right of any group of States to conclude regional treaties in order to assure the total absence of nuclear weapons in their respective territories.'[71] UN General Assembly Resolution 3472B (XXX) of 1975 defined a Nuclear-Weapon-Free Zone as any zone that is recognised as such by the General Assembly, and which a group of States, 'in the free exercise of their sovereignty', establish by treaty whereby:

(a) The statute of total absence of nuclear weapons to which the zone shall be subject, including the procedure for the delimitation of the zone, is defined;

(b) An international system of verification and control is established to guarantee compliance with the obligations deriving from that statute.

There are six such regional treaties in force, as well as the 1967 Outer Space Treaty and 1971 Sea-Bed Treaty:[72]

- The 1959 Antarctic Treaty
- The 1967 Treaty of Tlatelolco—Treaty for the Prohibition of Nuclear Weapons in Latin America and the Caribbean
- The 1985 Treaty of Rarotonga—South Pacific Nuclear Free Zone Treaty
- The 1995 Treaty of Bangkok—Treaty on the Southeast Asia Nuclear Weapon-Free Zone (SEANWFZ Treaty)
- The 1996 Treaty of Pelindaba—African Nuclear-Weapon-Free Zone Treaty; and
- The 2006 Treaty of Semipalatinsk—Treaty on a Nuclear-Weapon-Free Zone in Central Asia.

It has not yet been possible to negotiate and adopt a treaty to establish a nuclear-weapon-free zone in the Middle East.

---

[71] Art. VII, NPT.

[72] Treaty on the Prohibition of the Emplacement of Nuclear Weapons and Other Weapons of Mass Destruction on the Sea-Bed and the Ocean Floor and in the Subsoil Thereof; adopted at New York, 7 December 1970; opened for signature at London, Moscow, and Washington, DC, 11 February 1971; entered into force, 18 May 1972, *UNTS* Vol. 955, Reg. No. 13678. As of 1 March 2021, ninety-four States were party to the Treaty.

Antarctic Treaty

Antarctica was declared a nuclear-weapon-free zone under the 1959 Antarctic Treaty: the first formal Cold War-era arms agreement. On 3 May 1958, the United States proposed to the other States participating in the International Geophysical Year of 1957–58—a joint scientific effort by twelve nations[73]—that a diplomatic conference be held to formalize the points of agreement that had been reached in informal discussions. These were: that the legal status of Antarctica would remain unchanged; that scientific cooperation continue; and that the continent be used for peaceful purposes only.

The Washington Conference on Antarctica met from 15 October to 1 December 1959, culminating in the treaty that was signed by all twelve participating nations. The Treaty provides in its Article I that 'Antarctica shall be used for peaceful purposes only'. To this end it prohibits 'any measures of a military nature', including, specifically, any nuclear explosions or the disposal of radioactive waste material.[74] The Treaty provides for the designation of observers to conduct inspections throughout Antarctica (defined as the area south of 60 degrees south latitude), including all stations, installations and equipment, and ships and aircraft at discharge or embarkation points. Each observer has complete freedom of access, at any time, to any or all areas of Antarctica.

The 1959 Antarctic Treaty entered into force on 23 June 1961, after the twelfth ratification was deposited in accordance with its Article XIII(5). As at 1 March 2021 a total of fifty-four States were party to the Treaty, the latest being Slovenia, which adhered in April 2019.[75]

Treaty of Tlatelolco

Costa Rica proposed the negotiation of a Latin American nuclear arms control regime at an Organization of American States (OAS) Council meeting in 1958. The Treaty for the Prohibition of Nuclear Weapons in Latin America and the Caribbean was concluded after two years of negotiations

---

[73] Argentina, Australia, Belgium, Chile, France, Japan, New Zealand, Norway, South Africa, the Soviet Union, the United Kingdom, and the United States.

[74] Arts I(1) and V, Antarctic Treaty.

[75] See the ATS list of States Parties, at: https://www.ats.aq/devAS/Parties?lang=e.

and opened for signature on 14 February 1967. The Treaty of Tlatelolco (as it is popularly known) entered into force for those States Parties that provisionally applied it on 22 April 1968.[76] It prohibits use, testing, production, or acquisition, by any means, of any nuclear weapons by its thirty-three States Parties, as well as the storage, installation, or deployment of any nuclear weapons. The Treaty does not, though, prohibit the detonation of other nuclear explosive devices for peaceful purposes.

Additional Protocol I to the Treaty of Tlatelolco applies the Treaty's provisions to territories for which France, the Netherlands, the United Kingdom, and the United States are internationally responsible, and which lie within the limits of the geographic zone established by the Treaty. The four States are all party to the Protocol. Additional Protocol II effectively obligates the five nuclear-weapon States recognized by the NPT, all of which are party to the Protocol, to respect the status of denuclearization of the relevant geographic zone and commits them not to use or threaten to use nuclear weapons against any party to the Treaty.

Treaty of Rarotonga

In 1975 the South Pacific Forum,[77] a regional organization that promotes cooperation among Pacific nations, responded to a proposal by New Zealand calling for a nuclear-weapon-free zone in the region. This proposal was endorsed by the UN General Assembly the same year,[78] although the conclusion of the South Pacific Nuclear Free Zone Treaty took another ten years to achieve. The Treaty, which was signed at Rarotonga in the Cook Islands on 6 August 1985, entered into force on 11 December 1986. As of 1 March 2021, thirteen States were party to it.[79]

The Treaty of Rarotonga prohibits the manufacture, acquisition, possession, and control of all nuclear explosive devices by its States Parties, as well as the dumping of radioactive waste at sea within a defined zone. Under Annex I, the 'Treaty Zone' covers an extensive part of the South Pacific. The

---

[76] The Treaty fully entered into force only in 2002, after ratification by Cuba.

[77] The South Pacific Forum was renamed the Pacific Islands Forum in 2000.

[78] UN General Assembly Resolution 3477 (XXX), adopted on 11 December 1975 by 110 votes to 0, with 20 abstentions.

[79] Australia, Cook Islands, Fiji, Kiribati, Nauru, New Zealand, Niue, Papua New Guinea, Samoa, Solomon Islands, Tonga, Tuvalu, and Vanuatu.

Treaty further requires States Parties to prevent the testing or stationing of any nuclear explosive devices within their territories.

There are three protocols to the 1985 Treaty of Rarotonga, which are open to adherence by certain nuclear-weapon States. Protocol I, which was open to adherence by France, the United Kingdom, and the United States, obliges each party to apply the prohibitions of the Treaty to territories within the South Pacific Nuclear Free Zone for which it is internationally responsible. France and the United Kingdom are States Parties while the United States is a signatory. Protocol II, which is open to adherence by all five NPT nuclear-weapon States, obliges its States Parties not to use or threaten to use nuclear explosive devices against any party to the Treaty or against each other's territories located within the zone. China, France, Russia, and the United Kingdom are States Parties while the United States is a signatory to Protocol II.

Protocol III obliges the nuclear-weapon States not to test any nuclear explosive devices within the zone established by the Treaty. Again, China, France, Russia, and the United Kingdom are all States Parties while the United States is a signatory. In a statement of reservation and interpretation, however, France affirmed that it did not consider its inherent right to self-defence as set out in the UN Charter to be limited by the Protocols.[80] The United States has stated that its practices and procedures in the South Pacific are not inconsistent with the Treaty and its protocols and that the zone arrangement does not 'impose restrictions on the exercise of rights recognized under international law, particularly the high seas freedoms of navigation and overflight, the right of innocent passage of territorial and archipelagic seas, the right of transit passage of international straits, and the right of archipelagic sea lanes passage of archipelagic waters'.[81] This would allow the United States to move vessels with nuclear weapons through the zone.

---

[80] The Secretary General of the Pacific Islands Forum Secretariat as depositary of the Treaty received France's ratification on 20 September 1996 with the following statement: 'no provision of the Protocols or the articles of the Treaty to which the Protocols refer shall impair the full exercise of the inherent right of self-defence provided for in Article 51 of the United Nations Charter.'

[81] US Department of State, 'South Pacific Nuclear Free Zone Treaty and Protocols', Bureau of International Security and Nonproliferation, at: https://2009-2017.state.gov/t/isn/5189.htm.

Treaty of Bangkok

The idea for the Southeast Asia Nuclear-Weapon-Free Zone was first mooted formally in November 1971, when the original five members of the Association of Southeast Asian Nations (ASEAN) signed a Declaration on a Zone of Peace, Freedom, and Neutrality in Kuala Lumpur. Lack of political will meant that negotiations on a nuclear-weapon-free zone did not start until the mid-1980s, concluding successfully a decade later with the signature of the Treaty by the ten ASEAN members on 15 December 1995.[82] The Treaty of Bangkok entered into force on 28 March 1997; all current ASEAN members are States Parties.

States Parties are obliged not to develop, manufacture, or otherwise acquire, possess, or exercise control over nuclear weapons; station nuclear weapons; or test or use nuclear weapons anywhere inside or outside the treaty zone. They are further prohibited from assisting or encouraging the manufacture or acquisition of any nuclear explosive device by any State and from providing source or special fissionable materials or equipment to any non-nuclear weapon State or any nuclear-weapon State, unless the material is subject to safeguards agreements with the IAEA. States Parties are required to prevent the stationing of any nuclear explosive device in their respective territories and to prevent the testing of any nuclear explosive device. In contrast to other nuclear-weapon-free-zones, the Treaty's zone of application also includes the continental shelves and exclusive economic zones (EEZ) of the States Parties.

A Protocol, open to adherence by the five NPT nuclear-weapon States, would oblige them not to use or threaten to use nuclear weapons against any State Party to the treaty and not to use or threaten to use nuclear weapons within the region. None of the nuclear-weapon States has yet signed it, on the basis that either the zone of application is too broad or its precise scope is unclear. The Nuclear Threat Initiative (NTI) notes the US concern as to the negative security assurances required of the parties to the protocol; alleged ambiguity of the treaty language regarding the permissibility of port calls by ships carrying nuclear weapons; and the procedural rights of the parties to the protocol to be represented before the executive bodies set up by the Treaty to ensure its implementation.[83]

---

[82] Brunei Darussalam, Cambodia, Indonesia, the Lao People's Democratic Republic, Malaysia, Myanmar, the Philippines, Singapore, Thailand, and Viet Nam.

[83] NTI, 'Southeast Asian Nuclear-Weapon-Free-Zone (SEANWFZ) Treaty (Bangkok Treaty)'.

Treaty of Pelindaba

In 1961 the UN General Assembly adopted Resolution 1652 (XVI), which called upon UN member States to respect the continent of Africa as a de-nuclearized zone.[84] In 1964 the Organization of African Unity (OAU) issued the Declaration on the Denuclearization of Africa, which was subsequently endorsed by the General Assembly.[85] The OAU and the UN established a Joint Group of Experts to draft a treaty creating a nuclear-weapon-free zone in Africa, which first met in Addis Ababa in April 1991. The Treaty text was concluded at experts' meetings in South Africa in May and June 1995, and approved by African Heads of State on 23 June 1995. The Treaty of Pelindaba was signed in Cairo on 11 April 1996 by forty-seven States and entered into force on 15 July 2009. As at 1 January 2021, forty-two States were party, including the Sahrawi Arab Democratic Republic, which is a member of the African Union—the successor body to the OAU—but is not recognized as a State by the UN Secretary-General.[86]

States Parties to the Treaty are obligated not to conduct research on, develop, manufacture, stockpile, or otherwise acquire, possess, or have control over any nuclear explosive device by any means anywhere. The contracting parties also undertake to prohibit, in their respective territories, the stationing of any nuclear explosive device. They are explicitly permitted to decide whether to allow visits by foreign ships and aircraft to their ports and airfields; transit of their airspace by foreign aircraft; and navigation by foreign ships in their territorial seas or archipelago waters. The Treaty further prohibits States Parties from testing or allowing testing in their territory, or assisting or encouraging the testing of any nuclear explosive device.

The States Parties undertake to declare any capability for the manufacture of nuclear explosive devices; to dismantle and destroy any nuclear explosive device that they have manufactured prior to the coming into force of this Treaty; to destroy facilities for the manufacture of nuclear explosive devices or, where possible, to convert them to peaceful uses; and to permit the IAEA to verify the processes of dismantling and destruction of the nuclear explosive devices, as well as the destruction or conversion of the

---

[84] UN General Assembly Resolution 1652(XVI) adopted on 24 November 1961 by 55 votes to 0, with 44 abstentions.

[85] UN General Assembly Resolution 45/56A, adopted on 4 December 1990 by 145 votes to 0, with 4 abstentions.

[86] The UN Office for Disarmament Affairs does not list the Sahrawi Arab Democratic Republic as a State Party.

facilities for their production. The parties further undertake not to take, assist, or encourage any action aimed at an armed attack by conventional or other means against nuclear installations in the Treaty's zone of application.

Protocol I to the Treaty of Pelindaba obliges the NPT nuclear-weapon States not to use or threaten to use a nuclear explosive device against any State Party to the Treaty and any territory within the regional zone. China, France, Russia, and the United Kingdom are States Parties, while the United States is a signatory. Neither the United Kingdom nor the United States recognizes Diego Garcia as being subject to the Treaty.[87]

Protocol II calls on the NPT nuclear-weapon States not to test or assist or encourage the testing of any nuclear explosive device anywhere within the regional zone. Again, China, France, Russia, and the United Kingdom are States Parties, while the United States is a signatory. Protocol III calls on each State Party, with respect to the territories for which it is internationally responsible within the region, to apply the provisions of the Treaty to it. It is only open to adherence by France and Spain. France is a State Party to Protocol III. Spain is not a party to the Protocol.

Treaty of Semipalatinsk

The idea of a nuclear-weapon-free zone for Central Asia originated in the 1992 initiative by Mongolia declaring itself a nuclear-weapon-free zone and calling for a regional zone in addition to this. On 27 February 1997 the five presidents of the Central Asian States issued the Almaty Declaration endorsing the creation of a regional nuclear-weapon-free zone. The text was concluded at a meeting in Samarkand in Uzbekistan in September 2002 after five years of discussions and negotiations. On 8 February 2005 the five Central Asian States adopted the treaty text in Tashkent, Uzbekistan. The Treaty of Semipalatinsk was opened for signature on 8 September 2006 and entered into force on 21 March 2009. All five Central Asian republics—Kazakhstan, Kyrgyzstan, Tajikistan, Turkmenistan, and Uzbekistan—are party to it.

Under the 2005 Treaty, the States Parties undertake not to research, develop, manufacture, stockpile, acquire, possess, or have any control over any nuclear weapon or other nuclear explosive device. Each State Party is

---

[87] See, e.g., P. H. Sand, 'Diego Garcia: British–American Legal Black Hole in the Indian Ocean?', *Journal of Environmental Law*, Vol. 21, No. 1 (1 January 2009), pp. 113–37.

further obligated not to carry out nuclear weapon tests or any other nuclear explosion and to prevent any such nuclear explosion at any place under its control. Further, the States Parties are required to maintain effective physical protection of nuclear material, facilities, and equipment. The Treaty does not affect rights and obligations of the parties under other international treaties concluded prior to the entry into force of the Treaty of Semipalatinsk. This is contentious because of the 1992 Collective Security Treaty (CST) to which Kazakhstan, Kyrgyzstan, and Tajikistan have adhered. France, the United Kingdom, and the United States are concerned that the 1992 agreement could allow Russia to deploy nuclear weapons in Central Asian nations that are party to the CST.[88]

Under the Protocol to the 2005 Treaty, each State Party undertakes not to use or threaten to use a nuclear weapon or other nuclear explosive device against any State Party to the Treaty and not to contribute to any act that constitutes a violation of the Treaty. China, France, Russia, and the United Kingdom are States Parties, while the United States is a signatory.

The Outer Space Treaty

The Treaty on Principles Governing the Activities of States in the Exploration and Use of Outer Space, including the Moon and Other Celestial Bodies (1967 Outer Space Treaty) was considered by the Legal Subcommittee of the Committee on the Peaceful Uses of Outer Space in 1966 and concluded and adopted in the General Assembly the same year.[89] The 1967 Outer Space Treaty was largely based on the Declaration of Legal Principles Governing the Activities of States in the Exploration and Use of Outer Space, adopted by the General Assembly in 1963.[90]

As set out in its fourth preambular paragraph, the 1967 Outer Space Treaty reflects the desire of its States Parties to 'contribute to broad international cooperation in the scientific as well as the legal aspects of the exploration and use of outer space for peaceful purposes'. States Parties undertake not to place in orbit around the Earth any objects carrying nuclear weapons or any other weapons of mass destruction, to install such

---

[88] See, e.g., C. Ibragimova, 'Free Zone: Greater Security for the Region?', Russian International Affairs Council, 24 July 2015, at: https://russiancouncil.ru/en/analytics-and-comments/analytics/central-asian-nuclear-weapon-free-zone-greater-security-for-/.

[89] UN General Assembly Resolution 2222 (XXI), 19 December 1966.

[90] UN General Assembly Resolution 1962 (XVIII), 13 December 1963.

weapons on celestial bodies, or to station such weapons in outer space in any other manner.[91] It is further stipulated that the Moon and other celestial bodies shall be used by all States Parties exclusively for peaceful purposes. The establishment of military bases, installations and fortifications; the testing of any type of weapon; and the conduct of military manoeuvres on celestial bodies is forbidden.[92]

What constitutes a weapon of mass destruction is not fully defined in the Treaty, but nuclear weapons are explicitly cited. The use of these weapons in outer space, though, is not specifically prohibited; nor is the launching of weapons from earth into space. The US Department of Defense notes that the Outer Space Treaty also 'does not ban the use of nuclear or other weapons of mass destruction that go into a fractional orbit or engage in suborbital flight'. Thus, for example, ICBMs will travel a portion of their trajectory in outer space, but because this entry into outer space would be only temporary, ICBMs with nuclear warheads 'would not violate this prohibition'.[93]

The second paragraph of Article IV contains both *jus ad bellum* and arms control provisions. It prohibits recourse to all forms of military action on the Moon (and any planet or associated moon or comet or asteroid). This outlaws only the offensive use of any weapons, including conventional weapons, as presumably the provision would not extinguish the inherent right of self-defence of any State. Indeed, according to the US Department of Defense, 'lawful military activities in self-defense (e.g., missile early warning, use of weapon systems) would be consistent with the use of space for peaceful purposes, but aggressive activities that violate the Charter of the United Nations would not be permissible'.[94] In addition, the testing of any type of weapons is prohibited.

The Treaty was opened for signature by the three depositories (the Soviet Union, the United Kingdom, and the United States) in January 1967, entering into force in October 1967. As at 1 March 2021, 110 States were party to the 1967 Outer Space Treaty.

---

[91] Art. IV(1), 1967 Outer Space Treaty.
[92] Art. IV(2), 1967 Outer Space Treaty.
[93] US Department of Defense, *Law of War Manual*, June 2015 (updated December 2016), §14.10.3.1.
[94] Ibid., §14.10.4.

The Treaty on the Prohibition of Nuclear Weapons

Frustration, in particular at the refusal of the five nuclear-weapon States recognized by the NPT to countenance a path towards comprehensive nuclear disarmament, led many States to seek to negotiate a treaty to prohibit all nuclear explosive devices within the United Nations. The mandate for the negotiation of what would become the Treaty on the Prohibition of Nuclear Weapons was given by the UN General Assembly on 23 December 2016. Resolution 71/258 ('Taking forward multilateral nuclear disarmament negotiations'), adopted by 113 votes to 35 with 13 abstentions, decided to convene a UN conference in 2017 'to negotiate a legally binding instrument to prohibit nuclear weapons, leading towards their total elimination'.[95]

The resolution followed the convening of an Open-Ended Working Group on taking forward multilateral nuclear disarmament negotiations, which itself had been mandated by the General Assembly, meeting for three sessions in 2016.[96] Among the Working Group's recommendations had been the convening by the General Assembly of a conference in 2017, open to all States, with the participation and contribution of international organizations and civil society, to negotiate a legally binding instrument to prohibit nuclear weapons, leading towards their total elimination.[97]

After a total of four weeks of negotiations, the TPNW was adopted by UN diplomatic conference on 7 July 2017 by 122 votes to 1 (the Netherlands) with 1 abstention (Singapore), and opened for signature on 20 September 2017. It entered into force on 22 January 2021 following adherence by fifty States. As of 1 March 2021, fifty-four States had ratified or acceded to it[98] and a further thirty-four States were signatories.[99]

---

[95] UN General Assembly Resolution 71/258, operative para. 8.

[96] UN General Assembly Resolution 70/33; and see 'Taking Forward Multilateral Nuclear Disarmament Negotiations. Note by the Secretary-General', UN doc. A/71/371, 1 September 2016.

[97] 'Taking Forward Multilateral Nuclear Disarmament Negotiations. Note by the Secretary-General', para. 67, p. 18.

[98] Antigua and Barbuda, Austria, Bangladesh, Belize, Benin, Bolivia, Botswana, Cambodia, Comoros, Cook Islands, Costa Rica, Cuba, Dominica, El Salvador, Ecuador, Fiji, Gambia, Guyana, Holy See, Honduras, Ireland, Jamaica, Kazakhstan, Kiribati, Lao PDR, Lesotho, Malaysia, Maldives, Malta, Mexico, Namibia, Nauru, New Zealand, Nicaragua, Nigeria, Niue, Palau, Palestine, Panama, Paraguay, Philippines, Saint Kitts and Nevis, Saint Lucia, Saint Vincent and the Grenadines, Samoa, San Marino, South Africa, Thailand, Trinidad and Tobago, Tuvalu, Uruguay, Venezuela, Vanuatu, Viet Nam.

[99] Algeria, Angola, Brazil, Brunei Darussalam, Cabo Verde, Central African Republic, Chile, Colombia, Congo, Côte d'Ivoire, Democratic Republic of Congo, Dominican Republic, Ghana, Grenada, Guatemala, Guinea-Bissau, Indonesia, Libya, Liechtenstein, Madagascar,

It is prohibited for each State Party under any circumstances to use or threaten to use nuclear weapons or other nuclear explosive devices.[100] It is further prohibited to develop, test, produce, manufacture, otherwise acquire, possess, or stockpile such weapons or devices.[101] It is also prohibited for any State Party to transfer nuclear weapons, to receive the transfer of or control over nuclear weapons, or to allow the stationing, installation, or deployment of nuclear weapons in its territory or at any place under its jurisdiction or control.[102] No State Party may, in any way, assist or encourage anyone—State or non-State actor—to engage in any activity that is prohibited by the Treaty.[103]

A State Party that did not possess nuclear weapons on or before 7 July 2017 and which has an existing CSA in force with the IAEA must maintain that agreement in force.[104] Such a State that does not have safeguards obligations in force must conclude the latest form of CSA with the IAEA and ensure that it enters into force within eighteen months of becoming a State Party.[105] A State that had possessed nuclear weapons since 8 July 2017 and destroyed them prior to joining the Treaty must cooperate with an international authority mandated to verify the irreversible elimination of the State's nuclear weapon programme and conclude an advanced safeguards agreement with the IAEA (presumably an Additional Protocol, if one is not yet in force).[106]

Should a nuclear-armed State adhere to the TPNW it must immediately remove its nuclear weapons from operational status and then destroy them as soon as possible, but not later than a deadline to be established by the first Meeting of States Parties.[107] A detailed plan must be concluded for the destruction programme.[108]

Under Article 5 of the TPNW, each State Party is required to take all necessary measures to implement the Treaty's provisions. These measures may be legal, administrative, and/or of other nature, but include the imposition

Malawi, Mozambique, Myanmar, Nepal, Niger, Peru, Sao Tome and Principe, Seychelles, Sudan, Tanzania, Timor-Leste, Togo, Zambia, and Zimbabwe.

[100] Art. 1(1)(d), TPNW.
[101] Art. 1(1)(a), TPNW.
[102] Art. 1(1)(b), (c), and (g), TPNW.
[103] Art. 1(1)(g), TPNW.
[104] Art. 3(1), TPNW.
[105] Art. 3(2), TPNW.
[106] Art. 4(1), TPNW.
[107] Art. 4(2), TPNW.
[108] Art. 4(3), TPNW.

of criminal penalties for violations committed by persons, or on territory, under a State Party's jurisdiction or control.[109] Any State Party with victims of nuclear weapon use or testing who are under its jurisdiction is obligated to provide them with medical care, rehabilitation, and psychological support, and to promote their socio-economic reintegration.[110] A State Party whose territory has been contaminated by nuclear weapon use or testing is required to take measures towards the environmental remediation of affected areas.[111]

Current developments

The situation with respect to nuclear arms control and disarmament is as uncertain now as it has been since the dawn of the nuclear age. There is no agreement among the five nuclear-weapon States as to how—or indeed whether—to proceed to implement Article VI of the NPT, a reality which is putting the NPT itself under strain. The United States had sought a new nuclear arms control agreement to replace the defunct INF Treaty, but this time with China as a member as well as Russia. In mid-February 2020, however, at a meeting in London, Fu Cong, Director-General of the Department of Arms Control of the Chinese Ministry of Foreign Affairs, stated: 'It is neither fair nor reasonable to encourage the Chinese side to join trilateral arms control negotiations.'[112] In a tweet a few days afterwards, Robert Wood, the US Permanent Representative to the Conference on Disarmament in Geneva, claimed that 'Beijing poses a serious threat to strategic security given the trajectory of its nuclear build-up'.

The postponement of the Tenth NPT Review Conference, originally scheduled for April–May 2020—possibly until August 2021 or even beyond, owing to the global COVID-19 pandemic[113]—seemingly averted further dispute among and between the nuclear-weapon States Parties and non-nuclear-weapon States Parties to the NPT.

---

[109] Art. 5(2), TPNW.

[110] Art. 6(1), TPNW.

[111] Art. 6(2), TPNW.

[112] S. Bugos, 'Nuclear Powers Discuss Arms Control', *Arms Control Today*, March 2020, at: https://www.armscontrol.org/act/2020-03/news-briefs/nuclear-powers-discuss-arms-control.

[113] D. G. Kimball, 'NPT Review Conference to Be Postponed', *Arms Control Today*, April 2020, at: https://www.armscontrol.org/act/2020-04/news/npt-review-conference-postponed.

The situation of Iran

Iran's alleged pretensions to becoming a nuclear-armed State have been a concern to a number of other States for several years. In early November 2004, the US Central Intelligence Agency received thousands of pages of information from a 'walk-in' source indicating that Iran was modifying the nose cone of its Shahab-3 medium-range ballistic missile to carry a nuclear warhead.[114]

The 2015 JCPOA, better known colloquially as the Iran Nuclear Deal, was a political agreement concluded on 14 July 2015 between Iran and the P5 + 1 (China, France, Russia, the United Kingdom, and the United States, plus Germany). The JCPOA was endorsed by UN Security Council Resolution 2231 adopted by unanimous vote on 20 July 2015. Iran undertook to eliminate its stockpile of medium-enriched uranium (generally defined as 35 per cent Uranium-235) and to cut its stockpile of low-enriched uranium by 98 per cent, and committed to not enriching uranium above 3.67 per cent ^{235}U. It further pledged to install no more than 5,060 of the oldest and least efficient centrifuges at its reactor plant at Natanz until 2026: ten years after the JCPOA's 'implementation day' on 16 January 2016. Iran further agreed to submit to enhanced IAEA verification of these undertakings. In return, US, European Union, and UN sanctions against Iran would be lifted. Prior to July 2015, Iran had a large stockpile of medium-enriched uranium and almost 20,000 centrifuges, potentially enough fissile material to create up to ten nuclear bombs, according to the Obama administration.

On 8 May 2018 President Trump announced that the United States would withdraw from the JCPOA and reinstate US nuclear sanctions on the Iranian regime. In May 2019, Iran declared that it was suspending its commitments under the agreement and gave the other signatories a 60-day deadline to protect it from US sanctions; otherwise, it said, it would resume production of highly enriched uranium.[115] Iran subsequently reduced its compliance with the JCPOA in five phases: on 1 July 2019, it exceeded 300 kg of uranium hexafluoride; on 8 July 2019, Iran enriched uranium up to 4.5 per cent; and on 8 September 2019, Iran announced that its commitments for research and development under the JCPOA would be

---

[114] 'Implementation of the NPT Safeguards Agreement in the Islamic Republic of Iran', Report by the Director General, IAEA, Vienna, 15 November 2004; see also NTI, 'Iran: Nuclear', Last updated June 2020, at: https://www.nti.org/learn/countries/iran/nuclear/.

[115] BBC, 'Iran Nuclear Deal: Key Details', 11 June 2019, at: https://www.bbc.com/news/world-middle-east-33521655.

completely removed. Iran proceeded to invest in research and development of centrifuge technology that is not compliant with IAEA monitoring and safeguards, and on 16 November 2019 it notified the IAEA that its stockpile of heavy water had exceeded 130 metric tons. On 5 January 2020 Iran announced it was foregoing all agreed-to limits on centrifuges (though it pledged to continue its cooperation with the IAEA).[116]

In March 2020, however, the new IAEA Director General, Rafael Mariano Grossi, stated that the Agency had questions relating to 'possible undeclared nuclear material and nuclear-related activities at three locations that have not been declared by Iran'. He called on Iran 'to cooperate immediately and fully with the Agency, including by providing prompt access to the locations specified by the Agency'.[117]

As of this writing, Iran's future compliance with the IAEA is in serious question.

The situation of the Democratic People's Republic of Korea

One of the most contentious withdrawals from a global weapons treaty in recent years has been that of the Democratic People's Republic of Korea from the NPT. In 1993, one day before the expiration of the three-month notice period, North Korea had suspended its withdrawal from the NPT. Ten years later, on 10 January 2003, it announced publicly that it was withdrawing from the NPT 'effective immediately' and declared that its withdrawal left it free of its CSA with the IAEA.

The current status of the Democratic People's Republic of Korea's nuclear weapons programme is the subject of great international concern. This is especially the case in the United States, but is also so among several States in Asia. On 14 April 2017, the Democratic People's Republic of Korea's vice foreign minister said: 'We have got a powerful nuclear deterrent already in our hands, and we certainly will not keep our arms crossed in the face of a US pre-emptive strike.'[118] In June 2017 the UN Security Council adopted

---

[116] NTI, 'Iran: Nuclear', Last updated June 2020.

[117] IAEA, 'IAEA Director General Calls on Iran to Cooperate Immediately and Fully', Vienna, 9 March 2020, at: https://www.iaea.org/newscenter/news/iaea-director-general-calls-on-iran-to-cooperate-immediately-and-fully.

[118] 'North Korea's Nuclear Weapons: Here Is All We Know', *Aljazeera*, 30 May 2017, at: https://www.aljazeera.com/news/2018/2/20/north-koreas-nuclear-weapons-what-we-know.

Resolution 2356 (2017), in which it reaffirmed its decision 'that the DPRK shall abandon all nuclear weapons and existing nuclear programmes in a complete, verifiable and irreversible manner, and immediately cease all related activities; shall not conduct any further launches that use ballistic missile technology, nuclear tests, or any other provocation.[119]

On 4 July 2017 the Democratic People's Republic of Korea tested, for the first time, an ICBM with the potential to reach the United States mainland.[120] It claimed that its sixth and (as of writing) final nuclear test-detonation, at the beginning of September 2017, was of a thermonuclear device.[121] In late January 2018, then US Central Intelligence Agency (CIA) Director Mike Pompeo predicted that the DPRK would be capable of striking the continental United States with nuclear weapons within 'a handful of months'.[122] Two summits between President Donald Trump and Chairman Kim (on 12 June 2018 and then on 27–28 February 2019) failed to produce a breakthrough in efforts to persuade North Korea to end its nuclear programme and disarm. In June 2020, North Korea accused the Republic of Korea, in the south of the peninsula, of behaving like a 'mongrel dog'. The insults followed the North Korean regime's decision to blow up a liaison office between the two nations, a move that significantly increased tensions.[123]

A new kind of nuclear arms race

It is widely agreed that nuclear-armed States are engaged in a new kind of nuclear arms race. This time, it is one of 'quality' rather than 'quantity', focusing especially on speed but also on autonomy of delivery. That said, there

---

[119] UN Security Council Resolution 2356, 2 June 2017, operative para. 2.

[120] See, e.g., A. Gearan and E. Rauhala, 'North Korea Missile Launch Marks a Direct Challenge to Trump Administration', *The Washington Post*, 4 July 2017, at: https://www.washingtonpost.com/national/north-korea-claims-successful-intercontinental-ballistic-missile-test-defying-international-condemnation/2017/07/04/4f804488-609c-11e7-8adc-fea80e32bf47_story.html?utm_term=.42911fd68ed5.

[121] 'Sixth Nuclear Test Detected at Punggye-Ri, Declared to Be a Hydrogen Bomb', *38 North*, 2 September 2017.

[122] C. Mindock, 'CIA Concerned North Korea Could Hit US with a Missile in a "Handful of Months"', *The Independent*, 30 January 2018, at: https://www.independent.co.uk/news/world/americas/us-politics/cia-north-korea-us-missile-attack-imminent-director-mike-pompeo-trump-kim-jong-un-intelligence-a8183956.html.

[123] J. McCurry, 'North Korea Accuses South of Being Like a "Mongrel Dog" as Relations Worsen', *The Guardian*, 17 June 2020, at: https://www.theguardian.com/world/2020/jun/17/north-korea-raises-tension-with-pledge-to-send-troops-to-border-with-south.

were calls within China in the spring of 2020 for a very significant increase in its nuclear arsenal, as tensions with both the United States and India grew markedly.[124] In June 2020 Singapore's prime minister, Lee Hsien Loong, cautioned China and the United States not to allow their great-power rivalry to force Asian countries to choose between them, fearing a new Cold War, this time in Asia. Lee argued that US efforts to 'contain' China would risk decades of confrontation that would cause economic damage to the whole region. At the same time, he suggested that a US military pullback from east Asia could encourage South Korea and Japan to acquire nuclear weapons.[125] Besides, offensive cyber capabilities are increasing the risk of premature launch of nuclear weapons.

Hypersonic missiles are those travelling faster than Mach 5 (approximately 3,800 miles per hour) and have the ability to manoeuvre during flight.[126] Research and development is focusing on two types of missile technology: a boost-glide vehicle launched from the top of an existing ICBM and a hypersonic cruise missile with its own in-flight propulsion. In December 2019, Russia announced deployment of its Avangard glide missile, claiming that it was capable of carrying a 2 Mt nuclear weapon at twenty-seven times the speed of sound.[127] In March 2020 the United States tested its first hypersonic glide vehicle; the US military said it has the goal 'of fielding hypersonic warfighting capabilities in the early- to mid-2020s'. The speed and manoeuvrability of hypersonic weapons render it well-nigh impossible for existing defence systems to intercept them.[128]

---

[124] On 8 May 2020, Hu Xijin, Editor-in-Chief of *Global Times*, called on the regime to expand its stockpile to 1,000 nuclear weapons. These should, he said, include 100 DF-41s, a newly developed ICBM capable of hitting targets anywhere in the continental United States. 'Three's a Crowd. Donald Trump Wants China to Join a Nuclear-Weapons Pact', *The Economist*, May 2020, at: econ.st/2zQ0gxH.

[125] R. Lloyd Parry, 'New Cold War Risks Nuclear Arms Race in Asia, Singapore PM Warns', *The Times*, 6 June 2020, at: https://www.thetimes.co.uk/article/new-cold-war-risks-nuclear-arms-race-in-asia-singapore-pm-warns-5cw03l7pd.

[126] A. W. Reddie, 'Hypersonic Missiles: Why the New "Arms Race" Is Going Nowhere Fast', *Bulletin of Atomic Scientists*, 13 January 2020, at: https://thebulletin.org/2020/01/hypersonic-missiles-new-arms-race-going-nowhere-fast/.

[127] 'Russia Deploys First Hypersonic Missiles', *The Guardian*, 27 December 2019, at:https://www.theguardian.com/world/2019/dec/27/russia-deploys-first-hypersonic-missiles-nuclear-capable.

[128] T. O'Connor, 'U.S. Tests First Hypersonic Glide Body, Challenging Russia's Advanced Nuclear Weapons Lead', *Newsweek*, 20 March 2020, at: https://www.newsweek.com/us-hypersonic-glide-challenging-russia-lead-1493441.

In November 2015 the Russian Federation revealed that it was developing a nuclear-powered undersea drone designed to carry a thermonuclear warhead. In March 2018, the Russian Ministry of Defence officially named the drone 'Poseidon'. The weapon will have autonomous features incorporated into its design.[129] In January 2019, the Russian Navy announced plans to field more than thirty Poseidon underwater drones.[130] In 2018 the RAND Corporation had published a report on artificial intelligence (AI) noting that a number of experts have expressed the fear that an increased reliance on AI could lead to new types of catastrophic mistakes: 'There may be pressure to use it before it is technologically mature; it may be susceptible to adversarial subversion; or adversaries may believe that the AI is more capable than it is, leading them to make catastrophic mistakes.'[131]

In September 2018, NTI reported on the results of its Cyber-Nuclear Weapons Study Group, established two years earlier. The Study Group, which included high-level former and retired government officials, military leaders, and experts in nuclear systems and policy, concluded that a successful cyberattack on nuclear weapons or related systems could have catastrophic consequences. Cyber threats to nuclear weapons systems increase the risk of use as a result of false warnings or miscalculation and increase the risk of unauthorized use of a nuclear weapon.[132] The report ultimately questions whether, in the age of cyberwarfare, nuclear deterrence has become dangerously obsolete.[133]

Since the publication of the NTI report there have been other warnings of the potential dangers of offensive cyber operations. In Brussels on 18 December 2018, at the European Union Non-Proliferation and Disarmament Conference, it was observed that there are increasing calls within China to move its nuclear arsenal to a 'launch on warning' posture.[134]

---

[129] E. Geist and A. J. Lohn, *How Might Artificial Intelligence Affect the Risk of Nuclear War?*, RAND Corporation, United States, 2018, at: https://www.rand.org/content/dam/rand/pubs/perspectives/PE200/PE296/RAND_PE296.pdf, p. 3.

[130] F.-S. Gady, 'Russia to Deploy Over 30 Nuclear-Capable "Poseidon" Underwater Drones', *The Diplomat*, 14 January 2019, at: https://thediplomat.com/2019/01/russia-to-deploy-over-30-nuclear-capable-poseidon-underwater-drones/.

[131] Geist and Lohn, *How Might Artificial Intelligence Affect the Risk of Nuclear War?*, p. 22.

[132] NTI, *Nuclear Weapons in the New Cyber Age*, September 2018, at: https://media.nti.org/documents/Cyber_report_finalsmall.pdf, p. 7.

[133] Ibid., p. 29.

[134] Remarks by Tong Zhao, Fellow at the Carnegie-Tsinghua Center for Global Policy in Beijing, at the European Union Non-Proliferation and Disarmament Conference, Brussels, 18 December 2018.

This 'hair-trigger' policy has its roots in the Cold War, where US military strategists feared a massive first strike by the Soviet Union, involving hundreds or thousands of nuclear weapons, would compromise its ability to retaliate.[135] Such a change in Chinese nuclear posture would further exacerbate the risk of an accidental or mistaken launch of nuclear weapons.

[135] Union of Concerned Scientists, 'Nuclear Weapons: Hair-Trigger Alert', 3 October 2014, at: https://www.ucsusa.org/resources/what-hair-trigger-alert#.XEhX4JBCfX4.

4
Conventional Weapon Regimes

Arms control during the Cold War focused on the relative numbers of certain conventional weapons between the forces of the North Atlantic Treaty Organization (NATO) and those of the Warsaw Pact. Disarmament by individual States of particularly injurious or indiscriminate conventional weapons was not high on the policy agenda of either military bloc. This situation changed markedly after the end of the Cold War, though achieving consensus on the elimination of any conventional weapons category proved elusive within the United Nations framework. This has meant returning to the approach to regulation that began in the nineteenth century, with one State or a group of States pushing for elimination of specific conventional weapons.

As new regulation of the use of weapons in international humanitarian law (IHL) has fallen into relative disfavour in recent years, States have preferred to outlaw their use and possession outside the auspices of the United Nations (UN) under disarmament law. The two most notable global disarmament treaties with respect to specific conventional weapons are the 1997 Anti-Personnel Mine Ban Convention and the 2008 Convention on Cluster Munitions. In addition to prohibiting use, stockpiling, transfer and development, both treaties not only address stockpile destruction but also require clearance of contaminated areas and the provision of assistance to victims. This marks a new departure for arms control and disarmament. Certain arms control measures are also included in protocols to the UN Convention on Certain Conventional Weapons, although it remains, at its heart, an IHL instrument.

The 1990 Conventional Forces in Europe (CFE) Treaty was a creature of the Cold War and is today moribund, but such was its importance at the time of its elaboration that its key points are recalled in this chapter. The content and effect of the 1992 Open Skies Treaty and the soft-law 2011 Vienna Document, both adopted within the auspices of the Organization for Security and Co-operation in Europe (OSCE), are also summarized in this chapter. In 2020 the United States withdrew from the Open Skies Treaty, followed by Russia in 2021, sounding its death knell.

The 1997 Anti-Personnel Mine Ban Convention

The Convention on the Prohibition of the Use, Stockpiling, Production, and Transfer of Anti-Personnel Mines and on Their Destruction was the first disarmament treaty to be concluded that comprehensively outlawed a conventional weapon. Adopted by a specially convened diplomatic conference in Oslo on 18 September 1997, the 1997 Anti-Personnel Mine Ban Convention entered into force on 1 March 1997. As of 1 June 2021, 164 of 197 States recognized by the depository—the UN Secretary-General—were party to the Convention. Adherence includes two of the five permanent members of the UN Security Council (France and the United Kingdom). The world's largest military powers—China, India, Pakistan, Russia, and the United States—remain formally outside the Convention's purview, although their practice is compliant with its obligations to a certain extent.

The proxy wars of the Cold War and the national liberation struggles for decolonization had seen widespread use of anti-personnel mines, with landmines used by both regular armed forces and non-State armed groups. Many types of anti-personnel mine were designed to maim military personnel rather than to kill them, so that additional human resources would be taken up with the transportation of casualties for medical attention. In fact, very often civilians were the victims (and sometimes the targets). In 1994 the International Committee of the Red Cross (ICRC) estimated, on the basis of its field data and that of other humanitarian organizations, that an average of 2,000 people each month were being killed or injured by anti-personnel mines, terming the global problem of mine injuries 'an epidemic'.[1] As a consequence, supplies of precious blood and medicine in medical facilities were rapidly exhausted, such are the needs of mine victims for transfusions and antibiotics.

As well as the direct humanitarian costs, the negative social and economic impacts were very significant. Land could not safely be used for agriculture or grazing livestock, while refugees and the internally displaced were impeded from safe return. In 1994 the UN Secretary-General called

---

[1] ICRC, 'Anti-personnel Mines: Overview of the Problem', FAQ, Geneva, 2 November 2009, at: https://www.icrc.org/en/doc/resources/documents/faq/mines-fac-cartagena-021109.htm.

for anti-personnel mines to be considered 'in the same legal and ethical category as biological and chemical weapons'.[2]

At the time, the international legal regulation of the use of landmines was set out in a protocol annexed to an IHL treaty adopted under UN auspices in 1980. The Convention on Certain Conventional Weapons[3] (CCW), an instrument that is discussed further below, had a series of Protocols attached to it. The Protocol on Prohibitions or Restrictions on the Use of Mines, Booby-Traps and Other Devices (CCW Protocol II) prohibited the targeting of civilians using anti-personnel (or anti-vehicle) mines as well as such mines' indiscriminate use in line with treaty and customary rules on the conduct of hostilities.[4] But the Protocol did not apply to non-international armed conflicts, in the context of which the overwhelming majority of anti-personnel mines were being used in the early 1990s.

In 1993, France, a State Party to the CCW, called formally for the revision of Protocol II in order to strengthen the regulation of the use of anti-personnel mines in armed conflict. This led to the convening by the UN Secretary-General of the First Review Conference of the CCW in Vienna from 25 September to 13 October 1995. Difficulties in agreeing upon the content of a revised Protocol led to two subsequent sessions in Geneva (from 15 to 19 January 1996 for discussion of the military aspects, and then finally from 22 April to 3 May 1996). On 3 May 1996 a new instrument, the Amended Protocol II, was adopted by the States Parties to the CCW.[5] The Amended Protocol II required that all anti-personnel mines be detectable to a certain standard and that remotely delivered anti-personnel mines self-destruct and self-deactivate within 120 days to a very high combined standard.[6]

While the use of mines was the focus of the 1996 Protocol, Article 8 also outlaws the transfer by a State Party of all mines whose use the Protocol prohibits, as well as any and all transfers to non-State actors. Consonant

---

[2] B. Boutros-Ghali, 'The Land Mine Crisis: A Humanitarian Disaster', *Foreign Affairs*, Vol. 73, No. 5 (September–October 1994), pp. 8–13.

[3] Convention on Prohibitions or Restrictions on the Use of Certain Conventional Weapons which May Be Deemed to Be Excessively Injurious or to Have Indiscriminate Effects; adopted at Geneva, 10 October 1980; entered into force, 2 December 1983, *UNTS* Vol. 1342, Reg. No. 22495. As of 1 March 2021, a total of 125 states were party to the CCW.

[4] Arts 3(2) and (3), Protocol on Prohibitions or Restrictions on the Use of Mines, Booby-traps and Other Devices; adopted at Geneva, 10 October 1980; entered into force, 2 December 1983.

[5] Protocol on Prohibitions or Restrictions on the Use of Mines, Booby-Traps and Other Devices as Amended on 3 May 1996 (hereinafter, 1996 Amended Protocol II).

[6] Arts 4 and 5 and Technical Annex, paras 2 and 3, 1996 Amended Protocol II.

with disarmament treaty rules and the specific provision governing the scope of application of the CCW, this prohibition applies at all times, not only during armed conflict.[7] The previous strict demarcation between IHL and disarmament/arms control had first been overcome the year before, in the adoption of Protocol IV to the CCW on blinding laser weapons. Despite the new Protocol's stricter regulation of anti-personnel mines, its provisions fell short of the total prohibition that was by then being sought by some forty governments. As of 1 June 2021, ninety-seven States were party to the 1980 Protocol II while 106 States were party to the 1996 Amended Protocol II.

The negotiation of the 1997 Anti-Personnel Mine Ban Convention

At the close of the First Review Conference of the CCW on 3 May 1996, the Canadian delegation invited other interested States to come to Canada that autumn in order to discuss the path toward a total global prohibition on anti-personnel mines. The International Strategy Conference: Towards a Global Ban on Anti-Personnel Mines was held in Ottawa on 3–5 October 1996. In the final session, Canada's then Minister of Foreign Affairs, Lloyd Axworthy, surprised the assembled States by inviting them to return to Ottawa before the end of 1997 to sign a treaty comprehensively outlawing anti-personnel mines. Axworthy's initiative would become known as the Ottawa Process.

An early draft of a future ban treaty, focusing mainly on ending the use of anti-personnel mines, had been elaborated by a Geneva-based Austrian diplomat as the negotiations in the CCW were still ongoing. Subsequent Austrian government drafts, however, adopted a disarmament

---

[7] Article 1 ('Scope of application') stipulates that the Convention and its annexed Protocols 'shall apply in the situations referred to in Article 2 common to the Geneva Conventions of 12 August 1949 for the Protection of War Victims'. In turn, Common Article 2 stipulates [with added emphasis] that: '*In addition to the provisions which shall be implemented in peacetime,* the present Convention shall apply to all cases of declared war or of any other armed conflict which may arise between two or more of the High Contracting Parties, even if the state of war is not recognized by one of them.' Article 1(2) of the 1996 Amended Protocol II provides that the Protocol 'shall apply, in addition to situations referred to in Article I of this Convention, to situations referred to in Article 3 common to the Geneva Conventions of 12 August 1949. This Protocol shall not apply to situations of internal disturbances and tensions, such as riots, isolated and sporadic acts of violence and other acts of a similar nature, as not being armed conflicts.'

law approach, using the text of Article I of the 1992 Chemical Weapons Convention as their inspiration. This approach would be reflected in the treaty that was ultimately concluded within the Ottawa Process. To ensure the presence at the planned diplomatic conference of States that were in favour of a total ban on anti-personnel mines, Participating States were required to endorse the concept by signing on to what was termed the Brussels Declaration.[8] More than 150 States attended the conference in Brussels in June 1997,[9] which confirmed that the final Austrian draft of the treaty would be the basis for negotiations at the forthcoming diplomatic conference in Oslo. The agreed rules of procedure allowed a treaty text to be adopted by two-thirds majority if consensus proved impossible.

The Diplomatic Conference on an International Total Ban on Anti-Personnel Mines was held in Oslo on 1–18 September 1997. The Conference was chaired by Ambassador Jacob Selebi of South Africa. The United States, a late entrant to the Ottawa Process, sought to secure a geographical exemption for the use of mines on the Korean peninsula and a specific exception for its remotely delivered anti-personnel mines. It was ultimately unable, despite its lobbying, to attract sufficient support for its proposals among the other negotiating States. A comprehensive prohibition on the development, production, stockpiling, transfer, and use of anti-personnel mines anywhere in the world was incorporated in the treaty text as adopted on 18 September 1997.[10]

The content of the 1997 Anti-Personnel Mine Ban Convention

Reflecting the content and approach of Article I of the 1992 Chemical Weapons Convention, the core of the 1997 Anti-Personnel Mine Ban Convention is its Article 1(1):

---

[8] See, e.g., Belgian Federal Public Service Foreign Affairs, External Trade and Development Cooperation, 'Fight against Anti-Personnel Mines: The Brussels Declaration Is 20 Years Old', 27 June 2017, at: https://diplomatie.belgium.be/en/newsroom/news/2017/fight_against_anti_personnel_mines_brussels_declaration_20_years_old.

[9] J. English, 'The History of the Anti-Personnel Mine Ban Convention', in *The Anti-Personnel Mine Ban Convention: Twenty Years of Saving Lives and Preventing Indiscriminate Harm*, Occasional Papers, No. 34, UN Office for Disarmament Affairs, November 2019, p. 14.

[10] Convention on the Prohibition of the Use, Stockpiling, Production and Transfer of Anti-Personnel Mines and on their Destruction, adopted at Oslo, 18 September 1997, *UNTS* Vol. 2056, Reg. No. 35597.

> 1. Each State Party undertakes never under any circumstances:
>   a) To use anti-personnel mines;
>   b) To develop, produce, otherwise acquire, stockpile, retain or transfer to anyone, directly or indirectly, anti-personnel mines;
>   c) To assist, encourage or induce, in any way, anyone to engage in any activity prohibited to a State Party under this Convention.

The principal change in the order of the prohibitions from that in Article I of the Chemical Weapons Convention involved moving the prohibition on use up to the first sub-paragraph of the article. This change reflected the fact that there had been a pre-existing prohibition in IHL on the use of chemical weapons (at least in international armed conflict), but no equivalent prohibition on the use of anti-personnel mines at that time. The 1997 Convention was therefore instituting a new prohibition on use, as well as on the other activities prior to use.

The prohibition on use

The notion of use is not defined in the Anti-Personnel Mine Ban Convention but the term unquestionably encompasses all new employment of anti-personnel mines (whether that occurs through emplacement by a person or by remote dispersal for artillery or aircraft). The only exception to the prohibition is where new employment occurs, on a State Party's sovereign territory, for the purpose of developing or testing techniques for the detection and clearance of landmines.[11] As the Convention is worded in the form of a disarmament treaty, all of whose provisions apply in all circumstances, and not an IHL treaty primarily limited to situations of armed conflict, the prohibition on use applies also in peacetime, including along an international border. In contradistinction to the Chemical Weapons Convention—and especially its Article II(9)—no exception is allowed for use of the prohibited weapons in law enforcement. This is so even though a number of States were at the time using anti-personnel mines to seek to preclude the passage of smugglers.

During the lifetime of the Convention—twenty-one years since it entered into force, as of this writing—the treaty prohibition on new use has been violated by at least one State Party: Yemen. In 2011–12, at Bani

---

[11] According to Art. 3(1), 'Notwithstanding the general obligations under Article 1, the retention or transfer of a number of anti-personnel mines for the development of and training in mine detection, mine clearance, or mine destruction techniques is permitted.'

Jarmooz, a location north of the capital, Sana'a, Yemen's armed forces used anti-personnel mines during the uprising that led to the ousting of the then President Ali Abdullah Saleh. In November 2013, the office of Yemen's prime minister admitted that a 'violation' of the Convention had occurred in 2011.[12]

In addition, serious accusations of use by State armed forces have been levelled at South Sudan,[13] Turkey,[14] and Ukraine.[15] In its latest monitoring report, issued towards the end of 2019, the International Campaign to Ban Landmines' (ICBL) *Landmine Monitor* publication stated that there had been no allegations of use of anti-personnel mines by States Parties over the preceding three years and that only two States not party (Myanmar and Syria) had used anti-personnel mines.[16] While most States not party have refrained from use of anti-personnel mines in recent years, at the end of January 2020 the United States announced a major reversal of its policy on landmines, declaring that their use outside the Korean peninsula would now be possible.[17]

Extensive use of the weapons has been documented by non-State armed groups over the lifetime of the Convention; most recently this has been by groups operating in Afghanistan, India, Nigeria, Myanmar, Pakistan, and

[12] Human Rights Watch, 'Memo to Delegates: Yemen's Compliance with the Mine Ban Treaty: The Case of Bani Jarmooz', 8 April 2014 at: https://www.hrw.org/news/2014/04/08/memo-delegates-yemens-compliance-mine-ban-treaty.

[13] International Campaign to Ban Landmines (ICBL), 'Concern at Reported Use of Antipersonnel Mines in South Sudan: South Sudanese Authorities Should Confirm or Deny the Claimed Use of Antipersonnel Mines', 31 March 2015, at: http://www.icbl.org/en-gb/news-and-events/news/2015/concern-at-reported-use-of-antipersonnel-mines-in-south-sudan.aspx.

[14] See, e.g., ICBL, 'Spotlight on Turkey', 19 February 2014, at: http://www.icbl.org/en-gb/news-and-events/news/2014/spotlight-on-turkey.aspx.

[15] In 2016, the Office of the UN High Commissioner for Human Rights (OHCHR) reported that the Ukrainian armed forces had used anti-personnel mines. OHCHR, 'Report on the Human Rights Situation in Ukraine 16 February to 15 May 2016', at: https://www.ohchr.org/Documents/Countries/UA/Ukraine_14th_HRMMU_Report.pdf, para. 14. In contrast, the ICBL's *Landmine Monitor* stated in 2019 that it 'has received no credible information that Ukrainian government forces used antipersonnel mines in violation of the Mine Ban Treaty since 2014 and into 2019'. *Landmine Monitor*, 'Ukraine: Mine Ban Policy', Last updated 7 October 2019, at: http://www.the-monitor.org/en-gb/reports/2019/ukraine/mine-ban-policy.aspx.

[16] *Landmine Monitor Report 2019*, ICBL—Cluster Munition Coalition (CMC), Geneva, 2019, at: http://the-monitor.org/media/3074086/Landmine-Monitor-2019-Report-Final.pdf, p. 8.

[17] N. Egel, 'The Trump Administration Approved the U.S. Use of Land Mines. That's a Step Back for Global Campaigns to Ban Their Deployment', *Washington Post*, 11 February 2020, at: https://www.washingtonpost.com/politics/2020/02/11/trump-administration-okd-us-use-landmines-thats-step-back-global-campaigns-ban-their-use/.

Yemen.[18] There has been significant use of mines by forces and groups in Eastern Ukraine. Islamic State forces made massive use of anti-personnel mines in Iraq and Syria.[19]

The mines produced and emplaced by Islamic State gave rise to renewed discussion about the definition of an anti-personnel mine under the 1997 Anti-Personnel Mine Ban Convention. Anti-personnel mines are defined in Article 2(1) as follows: 'a mine designed to be exploded by the presence, proximity or contact of a person and that will incapacitate, injure or kill one or more persons.' In turn, according to Article 2(2), a mine is 'a munition designed to be placed under, on or near the ground or other surface area and to be exploded by the presence, proximity or contact of a person or a vehicle'. The definition focuses on the victim-activated nature of the explosive device. Accordingly, command-detonated devices do not fall within the scope of the 1997 Convention and are thus not prohibited by it. But the method of production of the weapon (factory or artisanal) is not relevant; indeed, during the formal negotiations, the question was asked as to whether improvised anti-personnel mines were covered and it was confirmed by the chair that they were. Subsequent State practice has endorsed this position.[20]

Given the fact that anti-personnel mines are generally long-lasting—many can still be detonated years or even decades after emplacement—the issue also arose as to whether taking military advantage of mines in existing minefields represented a violation of the prohibition on use. State practice on this issue is mixed and inconclusive.[21]

The prohibition on development and production

Both development and production of anti-personnel mines are unequivocally prohibited under the Anti-Personnel Mine Ban Convention. There has been no confirmed unlawful conduct in that regard by any State Party. In late 2019, *Landmine Monitor* suggested that those most likely to be still

---

[18] *Landmine Monitor Report 2019*, ICBL–CMC, Geneva, 2019, p. 8.

[19] See, e.g., Landmine Monitor, 'Syria: Mine Ban Policy', Last updated 24 September 2019, at: http://cwww.the-monitor.org/en-gb/reports/2019/syria/mine-ban-policy.aspx.

[20] ICRC, 'Views and Recommendations on Improvised Explosive Devices Falling Within The Scope of the Anti-Personnel Mine Ban Convention', Working Paper submitted to the Fourth Review Conference of the 1997 Anti-Personnel Mine Ban Convention, Oslo, 25–29 November 2019, p. 2.

[21] S. Maslen, *The Convention on the Prohibition of the Use, Stockpiling, Production, and Transfer of Anti-Personnel Mines and on Their Destruction*, Commentaries on Arms Control Treaties Vol. 1, 1st edn, Oxford University Press, Oxford, 2004, paras 1.19–1.27.

actively producing are India, Myanmar, and Pakistan: all States not party.[22] In contrast, as noted above, non-State armed groups have produced considerable quantities of anti-personnel mines. Most recently, production has concerned groups operating in States Parties Afghanistan, Colombia, Nigeria, Tunisia, and Yemen, as well as States not party Myanmar and Pakistan. Previously, it also concerned groups in State Party Iraq and State not party Syria.[23]

The prohibition on transfer

Transfer of anti-personnel mines is generally but not completely prohibited under the Anti-Personnel Mine Ban Convention. This is because, '[n]otwithstanding the general obligations under Article 1', the transfer of 'a number' of anti-personnel mines 'for the development of and training in mine detection, mine clearance, or mine destruction techniques' is explicitly permitted. The amount transferred must not, however, exceed the 'minimum number absolutely necessary' for those purposes.[24] In contrast, there is no limit to the number of anti-personnel mines that may be transferred for destruction.[25]

Upon the adoption of the 1997 Convention, a number of States that were not ready to support a total prohibition on anti-personnel mines proposed a separate ban on transfers that could be negotiated within the Conference on Disarmament. Although the plan did not materialize, there have been few international transfers over the past twenty years and those that have occurred have typically been for relatively minimal quantities of mines.

There is, though, a lack of clarity as to the precise scope of the notion of transfer under the Anti-Personnel Mine Ban Convention, in particular as to whether transit of mines across the territory of a State Party is prohibited. Repeating the definition in the 1996 Amended Protocol II, the 1997 Anti-Personnel Mine Ban Convention holds that transfer 'involves, in addition to the physical movement of anti-personnel mines into or from national territory, the transfer of title to and control over the mines'.[26] The problem lies in the phrase 'in addition to'. According to one interpretation of the definition, to amount to transfer there must be *both* physical movement of the weapons into or from national territory *and* transfer of title to

---

[22] *Landmine Monitor Report 2019*, p. 15.
[23] Ibid., p. 16.
[24] Art. 3(1), 1997 Anti-Personnel Mine Ban Convention.
[25] Art. 3(2), 1997 Anti-Personnel Mine Ban Convention.
[26] Art. 2(4), 1997 Anti-Personnel Mine Ban Convention.

and control over them. But the wording 'in addition to' may also be read as alternatives: under this interpretation transfer means either physical movement of the weapons into or from national territory, or transfer of title to and control over them. In this latter interpretation, the concept of transfer comprises transit, making the scope of the term broad. This is not the case with the former, which is therefore far narrower in scope.[27] The issue is not settled in international law, with many States seemingly untroubled by the ambiguity of the wording.

The prohibition on assisting prohibited activities

Also of contention has been the prohibition on assisting, encouraging, or inducing prohibited activities in Article 1(1)(c) of the Anti-Personnel Mine Ban Convention. This is language reproduced from Article I of the Chemical Weapons Convention. But while the prohibition's precise scope is debated, it is undoubtedly wide: in particular, the recipient of assistance or encouragement does not need to be a State, and if it is, it does not need to be a party to the 1997 Convention.[28] It is not certain, though, whether the provision outlaws 'any action which contributes to prohibited activities', as commentators on the rule's inclusion in the Chemical Weapons Convention assert.[29] In particular, it is not finally settled whether the scope of the provision in the Convention extends to curtailing the financing of prohibited activities or to outlawing the transit of anti-personnel mines across the sovereign territory of a State Party.[30]

Certain States adhering to the Anti-Personnel Mine Ban Convention, in particular those that are members of NATO, were concerned that they might be prevented from lawfully engaging in military cooperation with the United States, which had expressed its rejection of the Convention. As a consequence several NATO members, when ratifying the Convention,

---

[27] S. Casey-Maslen and T. Vestner, *A Guide to International Disarmament Law*, Routledge, Abingdon, 2019, para. 6.12.

[28] Thus, it must be distinguished from Art. 16 of the 2001 International Law Commission (ILC) *Draft articles on Responsibility of States for Internationally Wrongful Acts*, Text adopted by the ILC at its fifty-third session, in 2001, and submitted to the UN General Assembly in UN doc. A/56/10 (hereinafter, ILC Draft Articles on State Responsibility). This provision, which concerns '[a]id or assistance in the commission of an internationally wrongful act', demands that the act by the recipient of assistance be unlawful, which is not the case under Art. 1(1)(c) of the 1997 Convention.

[29] W. Krutzsch and R. Trapp, *A Commentary on the Chemical Weapons Convention*, Martinus Nijhoff, The Netherlands, 1994, p. 15.

[30] Casey-Maslen and Vestner, *A Guide to International Disarmament Law*, para. 2.20.

provided an explicit interpretation of the provision. Czechia, for instance, stated its understanding as follows:

> that the mere participation in the planning or execution of operations, exercises or other military activities by the Armed Forces of the Czech Republic, or individual Czech Republic nationals, conducted in combination with the armed forces of States not party to the [Convention], which engage in activities prohibited under the Convention, is not, by itself, assistance, encouragement or inducement for the purposes of Article 1, paragraph 1 (c) of the Convention.

Similar declarations of understanding with respect to the 1997 Convention were made by Australia, Canada, Montenegro, Poland, Serbia, and the United Kingdom. Such an interpretation has been tacitly accepted by the other States Parties; certainly, none has opposed the understanding, much less argued that it amounts to a prohibited reservation. Reservations to any of the Convention's provisions are prohibited under its Article 19.

The destruction of stockpiles

Central to any disarmament treaty is the duty to destroy stockpiles.[31] Stockpiling was explicitly prohibited in Article 1(1)(b) of the Anti-Personnel Mine Ban Convention, with the deadline for completion of destruction set out in its Article 4. In addition, States Parties reiterated the duty to destroy anti-personnel mine stockpiles also in Article 1(2) in the following terms: 'Each State Party undertakes to destroy or ensure the destruction of all anti-personnel mines in accordance with the provisions of this Convention.' This is a binding legal obligation, despite occasional suggestions to the contrary by a small number of States. Article 4 obligates every State 'to destroy or ensure the destruction of all stockpiled anti-personnel mines it owns or possesses, or that are under its jurisdiction or control, as soon as possible but not later than four years' after becoming a party to the 1997 Convention.[32]

The fact that the four-year deadline for stockpile destruction for each State Party cannot be extended distinguishes the 1997 Convention from

---

[31] Ibid., para. 2.3.

[32] There is a slight distinction from the corresponding provision in the Chemical Weapons Convention (Art. I(2)) insofar as that treaty referred to weapons 'located in any place under its jurisdiction or control'. In contrast, the 1997 Convention specifies that the *weapons* must themselves be under its jurisdiction or control, which is potentially narrower.

both the Chemical Weapons Convention that preceded it and the 2008 Convention on Cluster Munitions[33] that followed it. Each of those treaties explicitly made provision for a State Party to be able to extend the deadline if it was unable to meet the original date set. In the case of the Chemical Weapons Convention, a single five-year extension for the destruction of chemical weapons was foreseen,[34] which expired in 2012. In the case of the 2008 Convention on Cluster Munitions, as further noted below, in addition to a single four-year extension period, States Parties may seek further extensions of up to four years at a time 'in exceptional circumstances'.[35]

The overwhelming majority of States Parties to the 1997 Anti-Personnel Mine Ban Convention met their international legal obligations for anti-personnel mine stockpile destruction. According to *Landmine Monitor*, as of late 2019 at least 160 of the 164 States Parties did not stockpile anti-personnel mines. Of these, ninety-three had formally declared completion of stockpile destruction while the other sixty-seven had declared never possessing anti-personnel mine stockpiles.[36] Collectively, States Parties are said to have destroyed more than 55 million stockpiled anti-personnel mines.[37]

Article 3(1) of the 1997 Convention explicitly allows the retention of the minimum number absolutely necessary of anti-personnel mines 'for the development of and training in mine detection, mine clearance, or mine destruction techniques'. Following proposed retention by several States Parties of huge numbers of mines, States Parties collectively reiterated at a formal meeting in 2001 that it would only be acceptable to retain hundreds or thousands, not tens of thousands.[38]

As of late 2020, two States Parties remained in serious violation of the Anti-Personnel Mine Ban Convention, and specifically its Article 4, having failed to complete destruction of stockpiles by their due date. Ukraine still had a huge stockpile of more than 3 million anti-personnel mines while Greece still held several hundred thousand mines.[39] Greece, which should

---

[33] Convention on Cluster Munitions; adopted at Dublin, 30 May 2008; entered into force, 1 August 2010.

[34] Chemical Weapons Convention, Part IV (A) (Destruction of Chemical Weapons and its Verification Pursuant to Article IV), para. 26.

[35] Art. 3(3), Convention on Cluster Munitions.

[36] *Landmine Monitor Report 2019*, p. 18.

[37] Ibid.

[38] Third Meeting of the States Parties to the 1997 Anti-Personnel Mine Ban Convention, Final Report, Doc. APLC/MSP.3/2001/1, 10 January 2002, 'Report of the Standing Committee on the General Status and Operation of the Convention to the Third Meeting of States Parties', at: https://www.apminebanconvention.org/fileadmin/APMBC/MSP/3MSP/Reports/3MSP_Final_Report_E.pdf, para. 19.

[39] *Landmine Monitor Report 2019*, p. 19.

have completed destruction by 1 March 2008, had pledged to complete destruction by the end of 2019;[40] it did not meet this new target date. In its Article 7 transparency report for 2019, Greece reported that it had 343,413 anti-personnel mines to destroy as of 31 December 2019.[41] Ukraine's deadline expired on 1 June 2010. It reported that as of end-2019, 3,364,889 mines remained to be destroyed.[42] It is not known as of this writing when Ukraine will fulfil its obligations in this regard.

The obligations in Article 8(1), wherein the States Parties 'agree to consult and cooperate with each other regarding the implementation of the provisions of this Convention, and to work together in a spirit of cooperation to facilitate compliance', have been employed regularly during the Convention's lifetime. This pertains to stockpile destruction as it does to allegations of use or fundamental respect for other provisions. To date, however, no fact-finding mission, as foreseen in the remaining paragraphs of Article 8, has been undertaken. The monitoring of compliance has been done by States Parties during meetings of States Parties and review conferences (governed by Articles 11 and 12 of the Convention), which are influenced by annual reports by every State Party (under Article 7) and broader monitoring from civil society.

Clearance of mined area

By far the most expensive and demanding obligations under the 1997 Convention are those upon each State Party to clear all emplaced anti-personnel mines on territory under its jurisdiction or control. No precedent for clearance of contaminated areas was contained in the Chemical Weapons Convention, but many of the negotiating States and other stakeholders believed that the future Convention must have a humanitarian component as well as a disarmament focus. A range of deadlines were proposed during the preliminary discussions and final negotiations. States settled on an initial ten-year deadline with the possibility of securing additional deadlines of up to ten years at a time. Thus, according to Article 5(1) each State 'undertakes to destroy or ensure the destruction of all anti-personnel mines

---

[40] Implementation Support Unit, 'Greece a Step Closer to Meeting Stockpile Destruction Obligation', Press Release, 24 May 2019, at: https://www.apminebanconvention.org/newsroom/press-release-archives/archives-2019/detail/article/1558594955-greece-a-step-closer-to-meeting-stockpile-destruction-obligation/.

[41] Greece Article 7 Report (covering calendar year 2019), at: https://geneva-s3.unoda.org/artvii-database-dump/Greece/2020.pdf, Form B.

[42] Ukraine Article 7 Report (covering calendar year 2019), at: https://geneva-s3.unoda.org/artvii-database-dump/Ukraine/2020.pdf, Form B.

in mined areas under its jurisdiction or control, as soon as possible but not later than ten years' after becoming a party to the Convention. The notion of 'jurisdiction' over geographical area concerns, first and foremost, sovereign territory (whether metropolitan or non-metropolitan), whereas 'control' concerns other territory that a State occupies abroad, irrespective of whether that control is lawful or unlawful under *jus ad bellum* rules.[43]

In the twenty years since the entry into force of the Convention, a total of at least 2,880 square kilometres of mined area has been cleared and more than 4.6 million emplaced anti-personnel mines destroyed.[44] What was in the 1990s a humanitarian crisis is now largely a developmental challenge. Over the same period, thirty-two States Parties to the Convention[45] and one State not party (Nepal), as well as one other territory (Taiwan), have completed mine clearance on their territory.[46]

But progress in mine clearance among States Parties has been uneven. As of March 2021, thirty-four States Parties to the 1997 Convention still had to fulfil their clearance obligations.[47] In March 2020 Chile reported publicly that it had completed its clearance,[48] while the United Kingdom completed clearance of the Falkland Islands/Malvinas in November 2020.[49] A further twenty-two States not party were also mine-affected.[50]

---

[43] Ibid., p. 44.

[44] Mine Action Review, *Clearing the Mines 2019*, Norwegian People's Aid, October 2019, p. 1.

[45] Albania, Algeria, Bhutan, Bulgaria, Burundi, Republic of Congo, Costa Rica, Denmark, Djibouti, France, The Gambia, Germany, Greece, Guatemala, Guinea-Bissau, Honduras, Hungary, Jordan, Mauritania, Malawi, Montenegro, Mozambique, Nicaragua, North Macedonia (previously known as the former Yugoslav Republic of Macedonia), Palau, Rwanda, Suriname, Swaziland, Tunisia, Uganda, Venezuela, and Zambia.

[46] Mine Action Review, *Clearing the Mines 2019*, p. 1.

[47] Afghanistan, Angola, Argentina, Bosnia and Herzegovina, Cambodia, Cameroon, Chad, Chile, Colombia, Croatia, Cyprus, the Democratic Republic of Congo, Ecuador, Eritrea, Ethiopia, Iraq, Mauritania, Niger, Nigeria, Oman, Palestine, Peru, Senegal, Serbia, Somalia, South Sudan, Sri Lanka, Sudan, Tajikistan, Thailand, Turkey, Ukraine, Yemen, and Zimbabwe.

[48] See, e.g., Anti-Personnel Mine Ban Convention Implementation Support Unit, 'Chile Ends Mine Clearance Operations, the Americas a Step Closer to Becoming a Mine-Free Region', Press Release, 3 March 2020, at: https://www.apminebanconvention.org/fileadmin/APMBC/press-releases/PressRelease-Chile_free_of_all_known_minefields-2020-03-03.pdf.

[49] Agence France-Presse, 'Falkland Islands Cleared of Mines 38 Years after War', Courthouse News, 10 November 2020, at: https://www.courthousenews.com/falkland-islands-cleared-of-mines-38-years-after-war/; and Statement by Ambassador Liddle of the United Kingdom, Seventeenth Meeting of States Parties to the Anti-Personnel Mine Ban Convention, Geneva, 16–20 November 2020, at: https://www.apminebanconvention.org/fileadmin/APMBC/MSP/18MSP/statements/9b-United_Kingdom.pdf.

[50] Armenia, Azerbaijan, China, Cuba, Egypt, Georgia, India, Iran, Israel, Kyrgyzstan, Lao People's Democratic Republic, Lebanon, Libya, Morocco, Myanmar, North Korea, Pakistan, Russia, South Korea, Syria, Uzbekistan, and Vietnam.

Mine Action Review has estimated that global contamination from anti-personnel mines now covers no more than 2,000 square kilometres in total.[51] On average, a single manual deminer can clear about 20 square metres of land a day.[52]

The Third Review Conference of the Convention, held in Maputo, Mozambique, had set the objective of global clearance of anti-personnel mines by the end of 2025. As of March 2021, though, relatively few States Parties were on course to meet that objective. A particular concern arose in the case of Eritrea. The Convention's informal standing Committee on Article 5 Implementation announced to the Eighteenth Meeting of States Parties in September 2020 that 'the Committee reached out to Eritrea on several occasions to discuss matters related to its upcoming Article 5 deadline of 31 December 2020 and its requirement to submit an extension request'. The Committee regretted that Eritrea had

> failed to comply with its Article 5 obligations and that it did not make use of the process collectively agreed to by the Seventh Meeting of the States Parties. The decisions taken by the Fifteenth and Sixteenth Meetings of the States Parties confirm that a failure to submit an extension request in accordance with the Convention and the agreed processes established by the States Parties constitutes a case of non-compliance under the Convention. The failure of Eritrea to request and receive an extension on its deadline prior to that date represents a matter of serious concern, which will unfortunately lead to Eritrea falling into a state of non-compliance by its upcoming deadline of 31 December 2020.[53]

Victim assistance

Victim assistance may be, in legal respects, one of the weakest substantive components of the 1997 Anti-Personnel Mine Ban Convention. This is despite the Convention's preamble, which records the desire of the States Parties 'to do their utmost in providing assistance for the care and rehabilitation, including the social and economic reintegration of mine

---

[51] Mine Action Review, *Clearing the Mines 2019*, at: www.mineactionreview.org, p. 1.

[52] Mechanical clearance is far faster, but is expensive, is often unwieldy, and can only be used in certain areas. Dogs and increasingly rats are also used for mine detection, but are also not cheap to secure or apply, largely because of the demanding training requirements.

[53] Committee on Article 5 Implementation, 'Eritrea', November 2020, at: https://www.apminebanconvention.org/fileadmin/APMBC/MSP/18MSP/statements/8-Committee-Chair-Eritrea-en.pdf.

victims'. But there is no general obligation to assist mine victims under the Convention, despite calls for the inclusion of such in the lead-up to the diplomatic conference in Oslo. Instead, under Article 6(3), those States Parties 'in a position to do so' are obliged to provide international cooperation and assistance for the care and rehabilitation of mine victims in other affected countries. These provisions do, though, complement States' obligations towards their own citizens,[54] in particular under international human rights law. Moreover, State practice and international support have combined to fill the legal gap in the treaty on assistance to victims.

Those who lose a limb as a result of an anti-personnel mine blast will need lifelong care: after emergency medical care most will require physical rehabilitation, including physiotherapy, prosthetics, and assistive devices, as well as psychological support and social reintegration. Thirty States Parties[55] have indicated that they have significant numbers—hundreds or thousands—of landmine survivors for whom they must care. Many of these countries face significant challenges in fulfilling their responsibilities.

International cooperation and assistance

From the outset of the discussions about its content, the 1997 Anti-Personnel Mine Ban Convention had been seen as a balance between humanitarian and disarmament obligations, with each underpinned by the willingness of donors to foot a large part of the bill. In addition to requiring support for victim assistance, Article 6 obligates each State Party in a position to do so to provide assistance for mine clearance and related activities and for the destruction of stockpiled anti-personnel mines. Total financial support for demining (meaning survey of mined areas and clearance) has amounted to more than US$10 billion over the past twenty years, the majority of which was international aid.[56] Other support, albeit in far smaller amounts, has been provided for stockpile destruction and victim assistance in dozens of countries.

---

[54] ICRC, '1997 Anti-Personnel Mine Ban Convention', Fact Sheet, Geneva, September 2019, p. 2.

[55] Afghanistan, Albania, Angola, Bosnia and Herzegovina, Burundi, Cambodia, Chad, Colombia, Croatia, Democratic Republic of Congo, El Salvador, Eritrea, Ethiopia, Guinea-Bissau, Iraq, Jordan, Mozambique, Nicaragua, Peru, Senegal, Serbia, Somalia, South Sudan, Sri Lanka, Sudan, Tajikistan, Thailand, Uganda, Yemen, and Zimbabwe. Implementation Support Unit, 'Assisting the Victims', undated but accessed 1 March 2021 at: https://www.apminebanconvention.org/status-of-the-convention/assisting-the-victims/.

[56] Mine Action Review, *Clearing the Mines 2019*, p. 2.

The 2008 Convention on Cluster Munitions

Cluster munitions were originally developed and used before the Second World War, but it was their use on an unprecedented scale by the United States during the Vietnam War—especially during its bombing of Laos, where 260 million submunitions were dropped over the country—that marked out the weapons as being especially hazardous to civilians. Also heavily affected were—and still are—Cambodia and Vietnam. More recently, Soviet forces used air-dropped and rocket-delivered cluster munitions on a wide scale in Afghanistan in the 1980s. Israel fired several million submunitions into southern Lebanon during its invasion of the country in 2006. These explosive munitions are designed to kill personnel or destroy vehicles, including tanks. Whereas anti-personnel mines are often designed to maim, submunitions are typically designed to kill.

In 1974 a group of countries led by Sweden had called for the prohibition of a number of anti-personnel weapons, including 'cluster warheads', and these proposals were subsequently discussed in the diplomatic conferences that resulted in the two 1977 Additional Protocols and the CCW. When the CCW was adopted in 1980, however, it contained no measures on cluster munitions. Renewed use of the weapons in Afghanistan in 2001–02—this time by the United States—and then in Iraq in 2003 underlined problems associated with the accuracy and reliability of a weapon intended to saturate areas with explosive force, and increased disquiet among national policy-makers in a number of States Parties to the CCW.[57] Israel's use of the weapons in Lebanon proved to be a tipping point in the decisions by many States.

In a process led by Norway, the Convention on Cluster Munitions was adopted in Dublin on 30 May 2008, entering into force on 1 August 2010. As was the case with the 1997 Anti-Personnel Mine Ban Convention, the 2008 Convention on Cluster Munitions was negotiated at an ad hoc diplomatic conference convened outside UN auspices, as agreement to prohibit those weapons within the global organization's consensus-based framework proved impossible. As of 1 March 2021, 110 States were party to the Convention on Cluster Munitions.

---

[57] V. Wiebe, J. Borrie, and D. Smyth, 'Introduction', in G. Nystuen and S. Casey-Maslen (eds), *The Convention on Cluster Munitions: A Commentary*, Oxford University Press, Oxford, 2010, paras 0.21, 0.22.

Similar to the 1997 Anti-Personnel Mine Ban Convention, States adhering to the Convention on Cluster Munitions must never under any circumstances use, develop, produce, acquire, stockpile, retain, or transfer cluster munitions. They are also generally prohibited from assisting, encouraging, or inducing anyone to undertake any activity prohibited by its provisions.

The Convention on Cluster Munitions defines a cluster munition as 'a conventional munition that is designed to disperse or release explosive submunitions each weighing less than 20 kilograms, and includes those explosive submunitions'.[58] Cluster munitions are typically deployed by aircraft or artillery with a canister or dispenser that disperses explosive submunitions. The Convention applies also to explosive bomblets that are specifically designed to be dispersed or released directly from dispensers fixed to aircraft.[59] All mines are excluded from the scope of the Convention on Cluster Munitions, as are munitions or submunitions designed to dispense flares, smoke, pyrotechnics, or chaff, as well as munitions or submunitions designed to produce electrical or electronic effects.[60]

The Convention requires that States destroy all stockpiles within eight years of becoming party to it. But, uniquely for disarmament treaties, a potentially unlimited number of extensions could be granted to that obligation, albeit for a maximum period of four years at a time.[61] A meeting of States Parties or a review conference assesses the request and decides by a majority of votes of States Parties present and voting whether to grant the request for an extension.[62] The States Parties may decide to grant a shorter extension than that requested and may propose benchmarks for the extension.[63] The Ninth Meeting of States Parties assessed a request by Bulgaria for an extension of its deadline for completing destruction of its cluster munitions stockpiles, agreeing to grant an extension of 12 months up to 1 October 2020, pending the provision of a detailed project management and workplan to be included in an updated extension request to be considered at the Second Review Conference in 2020.[64] As of end-2019, Bulgaria

---

[58] Art. 2(2), Convention on Cluster Munitions.
[59] Art. 1(2), Convention on Cluster Munitions.
[60] Art 2(2)(a) and (b), Convention on Cluster Munitions.
[61] Art. 3(3), Convention on Cluster Munitions.
[62] Art. 3(5), Convention on Cluster Munitions.
[63] Ibid.
[64] Final Report of the Ninth Meeting of States Parties to the Convention on Cluster Munitions, Doc. CCM/MSP/2019/13, 18 September 2019, para. 29. In fact, the Second Review Conference was due to take place only in November 2020.

reported that more than 180,000 explosive submunitions were awaiting destruction.[65] In November 2020 Bulgaria sought an additional extension of twenty-four months, setting the deadline for the ultimate destruction of all cluster munitions and related submunitions on Bulgarian territory as October 2022.[66]

As is the case with the 1997 Anti-Personnel Mine Ban Convention, the Convention on Cluster Munitions requires that clearance and destruction of unexploded submunitions be completed within ten years of its entry into force for the affected State, although in both cases it is possible to request extensions to the deadline from the other States Parties. In total, clearance operations around the world have destroyed at least 844,000 unexploded submunitions in 2010–19, returning more than 638 square kilometres of land to communities, enabling resettlement, reconstruction, and development to occur. In 2018 alone more than 128 square kilometres of cluster munition-contaminated area was released through clearance, with the destruction of more than 135,000 submunitions. This total was the highest ever recorded for a single year's clearance, bettering by nearly 35 per cent the previous high set in 2017 (95 square kilometres).[67]

As of 1 September 2020, twenty-five States and three other areas were confirmed or strongly suspected to have areas containing cluster munition remnants on their territory. Affected States Parties were Afghanistan, Bosnia and Herzegovina, Chad, Chile, Germany, Iraq, Laos, Lebanon, Mauritania, and Somalia. In 2019 Germany was granted an extension of five years for clearance of cluster munition remnants, until 1 August 2025.[68] Laos was granted a similar extension—although it was expected that multiple extension periods would be necessary, such is the massive contamination that remains in Laotian territory.[69]

Signatory States Angola and DR Congo were also suspected to have still cluster munition remnants. Affected States not party were Azerbaijan, Cambodia, Georgia, Iran, Libya, Serbia, South Sudan, Sudan, Syria,

---

[65] Bulgaria CCM Article 7 Report (covering 2019), at: https://geneva-s3.unoda.org/artvii-ccm-database-dump/Bulgaria/2020.pdf, Form B.

[66] Presentation by the delegation of the Republic of Bulgaria to the 2nd Review Conference of the State Parties to the Convention on Cluster Munitions, Ref.: CCM Art.3 Extension Request Update, November 2020, at: https://www.clusterconvention.org/wp-content/uploads/2020/11/Presentation-Text-BG-CCM-ART-3-25-NOV-2020-1300hrs-Part-I-Clean-24112020-.pdf.

[67] Mine Action Review, *Clearing Cluster Munition Remnants 2020*, Norwegian People's Aid, London, 2020, at: mineactionreview.org, p. 1.

[68] Final Report of the Ninth Meeting of States Parties to the Convention on Cluster Munitions, Doc. CCM/MSP/2019/13, 18 September 2019, para. 34.

[69] Ibid., para. 42.

Tajikistan, Ukraine, Vietnam, and Yemen, along with the territories of Kosovo, Nagorno-Karabakh, and Western Sahara. Eleven States had completed cluster munition survey and clearance on their territory since 2010: Colombia, the Republic of Congo, Croatia, Grenada, Guinea-Bissau, Montenegro, Mozambique, Norway, Thailand, the United Kingdom, and Zambia.[70]

The most detailed obligations on victim assistance of any disarmament treaty are set out in the Convention on Cluster Munitions. Article 5 of the Convention allocates clear responsibility to each State Party to 'adequately' provide age- and gender-sensitive assistance to cluster munition victims in areas under its jurisdiction or control. The required assistance includes medical care, rehabilitation, and psychological support, as well as provision for victims' social and economic inclusion. Article 5 also sets out in detail how a State Party is to implement these obligations.

The Convention on Certain Conventional Weapons

The Convention on Prohibitions or Restrictions on the Use of Certain Conventional Weapons Which May Be Deemed to Be Excessively Injurious or to Have Indiscriminate Effects (CCW)[71] was an offshoot of the failure of negotiating States to agree upon prohibitions and restrictions of specific conventional weapons in the context of the elaboration of the two 1977 Additional Protocols to the four Geneva Conventions. The Convention on Certain Conventional Weapons is composed of a framework ('chapeau') treaty with six annexed protocols that regulate specific categories of weapons. It contains detailed rules for the use—and in certain cases also the transfer and even the production—of specific weapons that raise humanitarian concerns. It is primarily an IHL treaty, but it also comprises arms control elements.

The Convention's scope of application has been expanded to cover all types of armed conflicts. When adopted in 1980, Protocols I to III applied only to international armed conflicts. However, the 1996 Amended

---

[70] Mine Action Review, *Clearing Cluster Munition Remnants 2020*, p. 1.

[71] Convention on Prohibitions or Restrictions on the Use of Certain Conventional Weapons which May Be Deemed to Be Excessively Injurious or to Have Indiscriminate Effects; adopted at Geneva, 10 October 1980; entered into force, 2 December 1983, *UNTS* Vol. 1342, Reg. No. 22495. As of 1 March 2021, a total of 125 states were party to the CCW.

Protocol II specifically applies also to non-international armed conflicts. In 2001, the Second Review Conference of the CCW expanded the scope of all the Protocols to non-international armed conflicts. As of 1 June 2021, 86 States had accepted this extension of scope.[72]

CCW Protocol I prohibits the use of any weapon whose *primary* effect is to injure, by fragments that are not detectable in the human body, by X-rays. The use of such weapons is defined as a war crime under the Statute of the International Criminal Court (ICC).[73] There is in fact no known weapon whose primary effect falls within the scope of the Protocol or the corresponding war crime.

CCW Protocol II and Amended Protocol II, as discussed above, focus on the regulation of landmines and include arms control elements, particularly on transfer but also on the production of certain anti-personnel mines, to ensure that they are detectable by mine detectors. The two Protocols are the only treaties that regulate anti-vehicle mines, though they do not generally prohibit their use.

CCW Protocol III applies to incendiary weapons. Incendiary weapons are those that are primarily designed to set fire to objects or to burn persons, such as by napalm or flame throwers (Article 1). It is prohibited in all circumstances to use incendiary weapons against civilians. It is also prohibited to make any military objective located within a concentration of civilians the object of attack by air-delivered incendiary weapons. Finally, it is prohibited to make forests or other kinds of plant cover the object of attack by incendiary weapons unless they are being used to conceal combatants or other military objectives (Article 2). The Protocol does not regulate the transfer of incendiary weapons.

CCW Protocol IV prohibits the use of laser weapons specifically designed to cause permanent blindness. The Protocol also prohibits the transfer of such weapons to any State or non-State entity (Article 1). The inclusion of this provision in the 1995 Protocol marked the first time that

---

[72] Amendment to Article I of the Convention on Prohibitions or Restrictions on the Use of Certain Conventional Weapons which May Be Deemed to Be Excessively Injurious or to Have Indiscriminate Effects; adopted at Geneva, 21 December 2001, *UNTS* Vol. 2260, Reg. No. 22495.

[73] Art. 8(2)(b)(xxviii) and (e)(xvii), Rome Statute of the International Criminal Court; adopted at Rome, 17 July 1998; entered into force, 1 July 2002, *UNTS* Vol. 2187, Reg. No. 38544. As of 1 March 2021, 123 States were party to the Rome Statute. Of these, seven had ratified or accepted the amendment for this specific war crime in all armed conflict: the Czech Republic, Latvia, Luxembourg, Netherlands, New Zealand, Slovakia, and Switzerland. The amendment entered into force on 2 April 2020.

the CCW and its annexed protocols had regulated an activity other than use in armed conflict of weapons within its purview. The use of laser weapons specifically designed to cause permanent blindness to unenhanced vision has been added as a war crime under the Rome Statute.[74]

CCW Protocol V requires the parties to a conflict to take measures to reduce the dangers posed by explosive remnants of war (defined as unexploded ordnance and abandoned explosive ordnance linked to an armed conflict).[75]

The 1990 Conventional Forces in Europe (CFE) Treaty

The 1990 Treaty on Conventional Armed Forces in Europe (ordinarily known as the CFE Treaty) is a binding arms control agreement that was negotiated during the final years of the Cold War. Signed on 19 November 1990, it entered into force on 9 November 1992 and formally has thirty States Parties.[76] It is nominally still in force, but see below concerning the suspension of the Treaty's implementation by and with respect to Russia.

Once described as the 'cornerstone of European security', since it had both set weapons limits and provided for a detailed inspection regime, the CFE Treaty had provided 'an unprecedented degree of transparency on military holdings'. The Treaty had eliminated the overwhelming numerical advantage the Soviet Union had enjoyed in conventional weapons, by setting equal limits on the number of tanks, armoured combat vehicles, heavy artillery, combat aircraft, and attack helicopters that NATO and the Warsaw Pact could deploy in Europe. The CFE Treaty was designed to prevent a

---

[74] Art. 8(2)(b)(xxix) and (2)(e)(xviii), Rome Statute. The amendment entered into force on 2 April 2020. As of 1 March 2021, seven States Parties to the Statute had ratified or accepted the amendment for this specific war crime in all armed conflict: the Czech Republic, Latvia, Luxembourg, Netherlands, New Zealand, Slovakia, and Switzerland.

[75] Protocol on Explosive Remnants of War to the Convention on Prohibitions or Restrictions on the Use of Certain Conventional Weapons Which May Be Deemed to Be Excessively Injurious or to Have Indiscriminate Effects (Protocol V); adopted at Geneva, 28 November 2003; entered into force, 12 November 2006, *UNTS* Vol. 2399, Reg. No. 22495.

[76] Armenia, Azerbaijan, Belarus, Belgium, Bulgaria, Canada, Czechia, Denmark, France, Georgia, Germany, Greece, Hungary, Iceland, Italy, Kazakhstan, Luxembourg, Moldova, the Netherlands, Norway, Poland, Portugal, Romania, Russia, Slovakia, Spain, Turkey, Ukraine, the United Kingdom, and the United States.

lightning offensive that could have triggered the use of nuclear weapons in response.[77]

Article IV(1) of the CFE Treaty set limits for both NATO and Warsaw Pact forces across Europe at 20,000 battle tanks, 30,000 armoured combat vehicles, 20,000 artillery pieces, 6,800 combat aircraft, and 2,000 attack helicopters. Weapons systems not in active units were required to be placed in designated permanent storage sites. Article XIV stipulated that States Parties had the right to conduct inspections and were required to accept such inspections, in accordance with a Protocol on Inspection. The Treaty established a Joint Consultative Group to address questions relating to compliance with the Treaty.

A revised treaty text was adopted at a diplomatic conference in Istanbul in 1999 to reflect the reality of the dissolution of the Warsaw Pact, but this 'Adapted Treaty' never entered into force. At the conference Russia had pledged, in what are known as the Istanbul Commitments, to withdraw its remaining military forces and equipment from both Georgia and Moldova. NATO members refused to ratify the 1999 Adapted Treaty until Russia complied with those commitments. In December 2007, Russia announced it was suspending its implementation of the original Treaty. On 22 November 2011 the United States announced that, along with its NATO allies as well as Moldova and Georgia, it would no longer carry out certain obligations under the original CFE Treaty with regard to Russia.[78] As of writing, the CFE Treaty appeared moribund.

The 1992 Open Skies Treaty

US President Dwight D. Eisenhower first proposed that the United States and the Soviet Union allow aerial reconnaissance flights over each other's territory in 1955. Fearing that the initiative would be used for espionage rather than confidence-building, the Soviet Union rejected Eisenhower's proposal. In May 1989, however, President George H. W. Bush revived the idea

---

[77] D. Kimball and K. Reif, 'The Conventional Armed Forces in Europe (CFE) Treaty and the Adapted CFE Treaty at a Glance', Fact Sheet, Arms Control Association, Last reviewed August 2017, at: https://www.armscontrol.org/factsheet/cfe.

[78] NTI, 'Treaty on Conventional Armed Forces in Europe (CFE)', Last updated 31 August 2020, at: https://www.nti.org/learn/treaties-and-regimes/treaty-conventional-armed-forces-europe-cfe/.

and negotiations between NATO and the Warsaw Pact began in February 1990.[79]

The 1992 Treaty on Open Skies establishes confidence and security-building measures among OSCE member States. The Treaty, which entered into force on 1 January 2002, has thirty States Parties[80] and one signatory State (Kyrgyzstan). The Treaty allows States Parties to conduct unarmed reconnaissance flights over other States' entire territories at short notice to collect data on military forces and activities. The treaty allows participation in overflights by States other than the overflying State. All of a State Party's territory can be overflown and no territory can be declared off-limits by the host nation.[81]

Although States Parties are permitted to overfly all of a member's territory, the Open Skies Treaty sets specific points of entry and exit as well as specific refuelling airfields. The Treaty also establishes ground resolution thresholds for the onboard still and video cameras. The aircraft and its sensors must undergo a certification procedure before being allowed to be used for Open Skies, in order to confirm that they do not exceed the allowed resolutions.[82]

In May 2020 it was reported that the United States had decided to withdraw from the Treaty. Secretary of State Mike Pompeo formally announced that the administration would initiate the six-month notice period, although he also declared that 'We may, however, reconsider our withdrawal should Russia return to full compliance with the Treaty'. What was meant by 'full compliance' was unclear. Christopher Ford, US Assistant Secretary of State for International Security and Nonproliferation, told reporters there were 'many variables' as to what that would entail, particularly as a number of American complaints about Russian activities involved behaviour that, Ford acknowledged, was 'not in fact violations of the treaty'.[83]

---

[79] D. Kimball, 'The Open Skies Treaty at a Glance', Fact Sheet, Arms Control Association, Last reviewed November 2020, at: https://www.armscontrol.org/factsheets/openskies.

[80] Armenia, Azerbaijan, Belarus, Belgium, Bulgaria, Canada, Czechia, Denmark, France, Georgia, Germany, Greece, Hungary, Iceland, Italy, Kazakhstan, Luxembourg, Moldova, the Netherlands, Norway, Poland, Portugal, Romania, Russia, Slovakia, Spain, Turkey, Ukraine, the United Kingdom, and the United States.

[81] Kimball, 'The Open Skies Treaty at a Glance', Fact Sheet.

[82] Ibid.

[83] A. Mehta and J. Gould, 'Trump Administration Prepares to Leave Open Skies Treaty', *Defense News*, 21 May 2020, at: https://www.defensenews.com/global/europe/2020/05/21/trump-admin-to-withdraw-from-open-skies-treaty/.

The 1990 Vienna Document

The Vienna Document is a soft-law instrument that was also elaborated within the OSCE. Originally concluded in 1990 in parallel to the CFE Treaty, and subsequently revised several times, its latest iteration is from 2011. This politically binding agreement, which is now considered the most important confidence and security-building measure in the OSCE, provides for the exchange and verification of information about armed forces and military activities. It requires Participating States to provide each other annually with information on their military forces, including with respect to manpower and major conventional weapon and equipment systems as well as deployment plans and budgets.

Participating States must also notify each other in advance about major military activities such as exercises; accept up to three inspections of their military sites per year (though some sensitive areas are excluded); and consult and cooperate in case of unusual military activity or increasing tensions. The Vienna Document encourages Participating States to, for example, voluntarily host military visits with a view to dispelling any concerns that may exist among the concerned States.[84]

---

[84] See, e.g., OSCE, 'Ensuring Military Transparency—The Vienna Document', undated but accessed 1 March 2021 at: https://www.osce.org/fsc/74528.

5

Arms Transfer Regimes

The principal global treaty governing the transfer of conventional weapons is the 2013 United Nations (UN) Arms Trade Treaty. More than half of the world's States are party to the Treaty, including many major exporters of arms (though not three of the world's biggest: China, Russia, and the United States). The UN Arms Trade Treaty prohibits the transfer of conventional weapons falling within its scope in a series of set circumstances. Although the UN informally classifies the Treaty as a disarmament instrument, it is better understood as an arms control treaty.

Regional legally binding regimes include the European Union Common Position (made binding on all EU member States in 2008), the 2006 Economic Community of West Africa (ECOWAS) Convention on Small Arms and Light Weapons (SALW), and the 2010 Kinshasa Convention on SALW. The subject and the operation of politically binding regimes, in particular the Wassenaar Arrangement and the Missile Technology Control Regime, are also described in this chapter, as is the voluntary reporting regime of the UN Register of Conventional Arms.

The Arms Trade Treaty

The annual value of the trade in conventional arms is counted in tens of billions of dollars. In 2019, exports of conventional weapons amounted to more than US$27 billion, according to the Stockholm International Peace Research Institute (SIPRI) (see below for further data on this issue). In addition, domestic military expenditure adds tens of billions of dollars more to this amount, including with respect to nuclear weapons. In December 2019, SIPRI reported that sales of arms and military services by the sector's largest 100 companies (excluding those in China) had totalled US$420 billion in 2018 (an increase of 4.6 per cent compared with 2017).[1] In July 2012, during

---

[1] SIPRI, 'Global Arms Industry Rankings: Sales Up 4.6 Per Cent Worldwide and US Companies Dominate the Top 5', 9 December 2019, at: https://www.sipri.org/media/

the UN diplomatic conference that was negotiating the Arms Trade Treaty, the UN Secretary-General observed that sixty years of UN peacekeeping operations had cost less than six weeks of global military spending.[2]

The Arms Trade Treaty was ultimately adopted by the UN General Assembly in New York on 2 April 2013,[3] a few days after three States (Democratic People's Republic of Korea, Iran, and Syria) had blocked its adoption by the final session of the diplomatic conference established to negotiate the Treaty. The Arms Trade Treaty entered into force on 24 December 2014, ninety days after its fiftieth ratification, in accordance with its Article 22. As of 1 March 2021, 110 States were party to the Treaty, including China, a major exporter of conventional arms.[4]

Until the adoption of the Treaty, international legal regulation of conventional arms transfers existed particularly under disarmament treaties prohibiting or restricting the transfer of certain conventional weapons (particularly the 1997 Anti-Personnel Mine Ban Convention[5] and the 2008 Convention on Cluster Munitions),[6] as well as in accordance with Amended Protocol II and Protocol IV to the Convention on Conventional Weapons. In addition, arms embargoes, imposed by the UN Security Council under Chapter VII of the UN Charter or declared by regional organizations, restricted export to certain States or non-State actors. In 1986 the International Court of Justice (ICJ) had declared that 'in international law there are no rules, other than such rules as may be accepted by the State

press-release/2019/global-arms-industry-rankings-sales-46-cent-worldwide-and-us-companies-dominate-top-5.

[2] UN Department of Public Information (DPI), 'Secretary-General, in Remarks to Conference on Arms Trade Treaty, Calls Absence of Global Instrument Dealing with Conventional Weapons "a Disgrace"', UN doc. SG/SM/14394, 3 July 2012, at: https://www.un.org/press/en/2012/sgsm14394.doc.htm.

[3] UN General Assembly Resolution 67/234B, adopted on 2 April 2013 by 154 votes to 3, with 23 abstentions.

[4] In a communication received on 18 July 2019, the United States informed the UN Secretary-General that 'the United States does not intend to become a party to the treaty. Accordingly, the United States has no legal obligations arising from its signature on September 25, 2013.' The full declaration is available on the UN Treaty Collection Series website, at: https://treaties.un.org/pages/ViewDetails.aspx?src=TREATY&mtdsg_no=XXVI-8&chapter=26&clang=_en#3.

[5] Convention on the Prohibition of the Use, Stockpiling, Production and Transfer of Anti-Personnel Mines and on Their Destruction; adopted at Oslo, 18 September 1997; entered into force, 1 March 1999, *UNTS* Vol. 2056, Reg. No. 35597. As of 1 March 2021, 164 States were party to the Convention.

[6] Convention on Cluster Munitions; adopted at Dublin, 30 May 2008; entered into force, 1 August 2010, *UNTS* Vol. 2699, Reg. No. 47713. As of 1 March 2021, 110 States were party to the Convention.

concerned, by treaty or otherwise, whereby the level of armaments of a sovereign State can be limited, and this principle is valid for all States without exception'.[7]

The non-governmental campaign Control Arms was launched in October 2003 with a view to mobilizing support for a global arms trade treaty. In 2006 the UN General Assembly recognized in Resolution 61/89 that 'the absence of common international standards on the import, export and transfer of conventional arms' was a 'contributory factor to conflict, the displacement of people, crime and terrorism' and further that this absence undermined peace, reconciliation, safety, security, stability, and sustainable development.[8]

The content of the Arms Trade Treaty

Under Article 2(1), the Treaty 'shall apply to all conventional arms' within the categories set out in that provision (see below). While the term is not defined in the Treaty, as discussed in the Introduction to this book, 'conventional arms' is understood to include all arms other than weapons of mass destruction. According to Article 2(2): 'For the purposes of this Treaty, the activities of the international trade comprise export, import, transit, transshipment and brokering, hereafter referred as "transfer"'. Trade is generally defined as 'the action of buying and selling goods and services', whereas transfer would also be expected to include gifts, leases, and loans.[9]

Article 2 delineates the scope of the Arms Trade Treaty, identifying the categories of conventional arms and types of activities that are formally subject to its provisions, while also specifying certain acts which are excluded from the treaty's purview. Paragraph 1 describes the categories of arms to which the provisions of the treaty apply. Therein it is determined that the following arms fall within the scope of the Treaty: battle tanks; armoured

---

[7] ICJ, *Case Concerning Military and Paramilitary Activities In and Against Nicaragua* (*Nicaragua* v. *United States*), Judgment (Merits), 27 June 1986, para. 269.

[8] UN General Assembly Resolution 61/89 ('Towards an arms trade treaty: establishing common international standards for the import, export and transfer of conventional arms'), adopted on 6 December 2006 by 153 votes to 1 (United States), with 24 abstentions, preambular para. 9.

[9] Liechtenstein, for instance, when adhering to the Arms Trade Treaty, declared its understanding 'that the terms "export", "import", "transit", "transshipment" and "brokering" in Article 2, paragraph 2, include, in light of the object and purpose of this Treaty and in accordance with their ordinary meaning, monetary or non-monetary transactions, such as gifts, loans and leases, and that therefore these activities fall under the scope of this Treaty.'

combat vehicles; large-calibre artillery systems; combat aircraft; attack helicopters; warships; and missiles and missile launchers.[10] These were derived from the main categories used in the UN Register of Conventional Arms (UNROCA),[11] to which is added the category of small arms and light weapons.[12]

The list in Article 2(1) is not, however, exhaustive. Articles 3 and 4 identify two other categories—ammunition/munitions and parts and components—that are subject to some of the treaty's provisions. Whether or not to regulate ammunition in the Treaty was one of the most contentious issues during the negotiations. For certain States, the inclusion of ammunition raised practical obstacles to treaty implementation, particularly with regard to record-keeping and reporting on transfers, while for many others a treaty designed to regulate arms trade would be of little value if it did not encompass ammunition. The wording in Article 3 sought to balance the concerns of different States.

Article 2(2) identifies the activities that comprise international trade in conventional arms for the purpose of the treaty (export, import, transit, trans-shipment, and brokering), and introduces the term 'transfer' as a collective concept for these activities. This paragraph contains the only definition of a term in the entire Treaty. Excluded from the Treaty's application is the international movement of conventional arms by, or on behalf of, a State Party for its own use as long as the State continues to own the arms in question.[13] Arms that are moved across State borders under such circumstances are not transfers for the purposes of the Arms Trade Treaty—unless and until there is a change in ownership—and thus need not be subjected to the transfer controls the Treaty establishes.

There is a general obligation imposed on each State Party to implement the Treaty at national level, in particular by establishing and maintaining a national control system for the transfer of conventional arms, integral parts and components, and ammunition.[14] Article 5 further requires each State Party to regulate, at a minimum, battle tanks, armoured combat vehicles, large-calibre artillery systems, combat aircraft, attack helicopters, warships, and missiles and missile launchers, in accordance with the definitions

---

[10] Art. 2(1)(a) to (g), 2013 Arms Trade Treaty.

[11] UNODA, 'UN Register of Conventional Arms', undated but accessed 1 March 2021, at: https://www.un.org/disarmament/convarms/register/.

[12] Art. 2(1)(h), 2013 Arms Trade Treaty.

[13] Art. 2(3), 2013 Arms Trade Treaty.

[14] Art. 5, 2013 Arms Trade Treaty.

under UNROCA that existed on 24 December 2014 (the date of entry into force of the Arms Trade Treaty).

The Treaty's application to small arms and light weapons is made indirectly subject to the definition in the 2005 International Tracing Instrument (ITI).[15] The Arms Trade Treaty stipulates that SALW shall not cover less than the descriptions used in relevant UN instruments at the time of entry into force of the Treaty.[16] According to the ITI, which is the most relevant UN instrument in this regard:

> For the purposes of this instrument, 'small arms and light weapons' will mean any man-portable lethal weapon that expels or launches, is designed to expel or launch, or may be readily converted to expel or launch a shot, bullet or projectile by the action of an explosive, excluding antique small arms and light weapons or their replicas. Antique small arms and light weapons and their replicas will be defined in accordance with domestic law. In no case will antique small arms and light weapons include those manufactured after 1899:
>
> > 'Small arms' are, broadly speaking, weapons designed for individual use. They include, inter alia, revolvers and self-loading pistols, rifles and carbines, sub-machine guns, assault rifles and light machine guns;
> >
> > 'Light weapons' are, broadly speaking, weapons designed for use by two or three persons serving as a crew, although some may be carried and used by a single person. They include, inter alia, heavy machine guns, hand-held under-barrel and mounted grenade launchers, portable anti-aircraft guns, portable anti-tank guns, recoilless rifles, portable launchers of anti-tank missile and rocket systems, portable launchers of anti-aircraft missile systems, and mortars of a calibre of less than 100 millimetres.[17]

This is a broad definition that encompasses not only conventional firearms but also certain less lethal weapons, such as those that expel tear gas

---

[15] International Instrument to Enable States to Identify and Trace, in a Timely and Reliable Manner, Illicit Small Arms and Light Weapons (ITI).

[16] Art. 5(3), 2013 Arms Trade Treaty.

[17] Art. II(4), ITI.

canisters or kinetic impact projectiles. Conducted electrical weapons, such as the TASER brand, are not covered, on the basis that the dart probes from such weapons are ordinarily expelled by means of compressed gas, not explosive.

Article 6 (Prohibitions) and Article 7 (Export and Export Assessment) are the core provisions that govern when a transfer or, in the case of Article 7, just the export of conventional arms, ammunition, and integral parts or components falling within the scope of the treaty must be prohibited.

Transfers that would violate a State Party's obligations pertaining to UN Security Council measures adopted under Chapter VII of the UN Charter are prohibited.[18] These relate, in particular, to arms embargoes. Also prohibited are transfers that would violate obligations under treaties to which the transferring State is a party, in particular those relating to conventional arms, such as disarmament treaties.[19]

Article 6(3) is a critical provision, prohibiting transfers where the State Party 'has knowledge at the time of authorization' that the arms or items would be used in the commission of genocide, crimes against humanity, or certain war crimes, including attacks against civilians, or the murder or torture of prisoners of war. These prohibitions apply not only to transfers from a State-owned entity but also to privately incorporated companies operating from or within the jurisdiction of a State Party.

The crime of genocide may be committed in peacetime as well as during armed conflict. Article II of the 1948 Genocide Convention defines genocide as

> any of the following acts committed with intent to destroy, in whole or in part, a national, ethnical, racial or religious group, as such:
> (a) Killing members of the group
> (b) Causing serious bodily or mental harm to members of the group
> (c) Deliberately inflicting on the group conditions of life calculated to bring about its physical destruction in whole or in part
> (d) Imposing measures intended to prevent births within the group
> (e) Forcibly transferring children of the group to another group.[20]

---

[18] Art. 6(1), 2013 Arms Trade Treaty.
[19] Art. 6(1), 2013 Arms Trade Treaty.
[20] Art. II, Convention on the Prevention and Punishment of the Crime of Genocide; adopted at Paris, 9 December 1948; entered into force, 12 January 1951, *UNTS* Vol. 78, Reg. No. 1021. As of 1 March 2021, 152 States were party to the Convention.

The requirement for specific intent (*dolus specialis*) means that mass killings do not, per se, constitute genocide; there must be the intent to eliminate, partially or entirely, a minority group.

Crimes against humanity are not defined in a dedicated treaty as is genocide, but their punishment under international criminal law is addressed in the 1998 Rome Statute of the International Criminal Court. Therein, they mean the following acts 'committed as part of a widespread or systematic attack directed against any civilian population, with knowledge of the attack':

(a) Murder

(b) Extermination

(c) Enslavement

(d) Deportation or forcible transfer of population

(e) Imprisonment or other severe deprivation of physical liberty in violation of fundamental rules of international law

(f) Torture

(g) Rape, sexual slavery, enforced prostitution, forced pregnancy, enforced sterilization, or any other form of sexual violence of comparable gravity

(h) Persecution against any identifiable group or collectivity on political, racial, national, ethnic, cultural, religious, gender . . .

(i) Enforced disappearance of persons

(j) The crime of *apartheid*

(k) Other inhumane acts of a similar character intentionally causing great suffering, or serious injury to body or to mental or physical health.[21]

With respect to war crimes, Article 6(3) details three categories of crime that are encompassed by the prohibition: grave breaches of the 1949 Geneva Conventions; attacks directed against civilian objects or civilians protected as such; and other war crimes defined by international agreements to which a State Party to the Arms Trade Treaty is bound.

Grave breaches of the 1949 Geneva Conventions include acts of violence against protected persons, for example, wounded members of the armed

---

[21] Art. 7(1), Rome Statute of the International Criminal Court; adopted at Rome, 17 July 1998; entered into force, 1 July 2002, *UNTS* Vol. 2187, Reg. No. 38544. As of 1 March 2021, 123 States were party to the Rome Statute.

forces (Geneva Convention I), prisoners of war (Geneva Convention III), or civilians in the power of the enemy (Geneva Convention IV). Grave breaches apply only to situations of international armed conflict. In contrast, the reference to 'attacks directed against civilian objects or civilians protected as such' applies in all armed conflicts, including those of a non-international character. Whether this comprises indiscriminate attacks as well as direct attacks is unsettled.[22]

The reference to war crimes 'defined by international agreements' covers several treaties in addition to the grave breaches of the 1949 Geneva Conventions: serious violations of the 1899/1907 Hague Regulations; grave breaches under 1977 Additional Protocol I; and all other war crimes included in the Rome Statute. These include serious violations of Common Article 3 to the 1949 Geneva Conventions, which protects detainees held in connection with a non-international armed conflict.[23]

If a proposed export (but not other forms of transfer) is not already prohibited under Article 6, in accordance with Article 7 the exporting State Party must, before deciding whether or not to authorize any export of conventional arms, ammunition, or parts or components within the scope of the Arms Trade Treaty, assess the possibility that the export concerned would contribute to or undermine peace and security. If the exporting State Party assesses that the proposed export would undermine peace and security, the request for authorization must be denied.

If, however, the exporting State Party determines that the proposed export would contribute to peace and security, the exporting State Party's assessment must then consider the potential for the arms or items to be exported to be used to commit or facilitate a serious violation of international humanitarian law (IHL) or international human rights law or an act of terrorism or transnational organized crime.[24]

The term 'serious violation of IHL' is not a synonym for a war crime—it is broader. It would certainly include all indiscriminate attacks as well as the use of prohibited weapons in non-international as well as international armed conflicts, along with a failure to take all feasible precautions in attack. With respect to international human rights law, serious violations include those acts that violate human rights that are peremptory norms of

---

[22] See on this issue the commentary by Andrew Clapham on Article 6(3) in S. Casey-Maslen et al., *The Arms Trade Treaty: A Commentary*, Oxford University Press, Oxford, 2016, para. 6.160 et seq.

[23] Ibid., para. 6.169 et seq.

[24] Art. 7(1)(b), 2013 Arms Trade Treaty.

international law (*jus cogens*), such as arbitrary deprivation of life, torture, slavery, or enforced disappearance.[25] Violations of other human rights may need to be widespread, gross, or systematic to give rise to a duty to prohibit a transfer in a particular context.

According to paragraph 3 of Article 7, an exporting State must deny authorization if its assessment concludes that, despite any mitigating measures that can be taken, the risk of any of the negative consequences listed in the Arms Trade Treaty is 'overriding'. The interpretation of this term is disputed, potentially resulting in a lack of clarity as to the meaning of the provision. Some believe that it is a balance between the positive effects on peace and security and the risk of the negative consequences, while others argue that whenever the risk of negative consequences is serious, a proposed export must be denied.[26]

In addition: 'If, after an authorization has been granted, an exporting State Party becomes aware of new relevant information, it is encouraged to reassess the authorization after consultations, if appropriate, with the importing State.'[27] Authorizations for export are typically valid for between one and five years, but may be renewed automatically if they have not been used and if no change of circumstance has occurred. Under this provision, States Parties are encouraged to reassess authorization if new information indicates that the situation in the State of final destination or its surrounding region has changed or generated important risks.[28] But while reassessment may lead a State Party to suspend or revoke its export authorization, it is not obligated to do so.

There are also certain less far-reaching obligations upon importing States where they are a party to the Arms Trade Treaty. When importing conventional arms, the State of final destination for those arms (i.e., the importing State) must provide information to the State that is proposing to export arms to it, upon request, in order to assist the exporting State to conduct the export assessment contemplated in Article 7.[29] The obligation to provide information is not absolute, and importing States may limit the information they provide in order to protect national security or commercial interests.

---

[25] See the commentary in Casey-Maslen et al., *The Arms Trade Treaty: A Commentary*, para. 7.52.

[26] For a detailed discussion of these issues see, e.g., Casey-Maslen et al., *The Arms Trade Treaty: A Commentary*, para. 7.90 et seq.

[27] Art. 7(7), 2013 Arms Trade Treaty.

[28] Casey-Maslen et al., *The Arms Trade Treaty: A Commentary*, paras 7.125–7.126.

[29] Art. 8, 2013 Arms Trade Treaty.

It is, though, in their interest to provide as much as possible of the information sought, since this may facilitate the granting of export authorization.[30]

Article 11 of the Arms Trade Treaty sets out a series of obligations with a view to preventing the diversion of conventional arms. Although the term 'diversion' is not defined in the Treaty, it is generally understood as either delivery of arms to an unauthorized end user or supply for an unauthorized use by an authorized end user. Paragraph 2 obligates each exporting State Party to seek to prevent the diversion of conventional arms through its national control system by assessing the risk of diversion prior to authorizing an export. Cooperation and assistance, and in particular information-sharing among States Parties, are central to the provisions in Article 11, highlighting that the diversion of conventional arms is not something that States can prevent or address in isolation from each other.[31]

The implementation of the Arms Trade Treaty

Article 12 of the Arms Trade Treaty sets out the obligations upon each State Party to keep records of certain information pertaining to their international transfers of conventional arms. States Parties are required to keep records of export authorizations or actual exports of conventional arms for a minimum of ten years and are given guidance on the information that States Parties should include in those records.

Article 13 establishes transparency measures, obliging each State Party to submit an initial report on measures taken to implement the Treaty within the first year of being a party. Thereafter, States Parties are required to report to the Secretariat on new measures taken to implement the treaty on an ad hoc basis, 'when appropriate'. States Parties are also encouraged to report on measures taken that have proven effective in addressing the diversion of transferred conventional arms on an ad hoc basis. Finally, States Parties are obliged to report annually by 31 May on their authorized or actual exports and imports of conventional arms for the preceding calendar year. They may, though, exclude from their reports commercially sensitive or national security information. Reports on implementation and transfers

---

[30] Casey Maslen et al., *The Arms Trade Treaty: A Commentary*, para. 8.01.
[31] Ibid., para. 11.01.

must be made generally available, and distributed to States Parties, by the Arms Trade Treaty Secretariat established under Article 18 of the Treaty.[32]

The Arms Trade Treaty Secretariat, which is headquartered in Geneva, comprises a team of four staff. The Secretariat manages the collection of information, including reports submitted by States Parties, nominated points of contact in connection with the Treaty, and their national control lists. The Secretariat also supports the Treaty process by helping to organize conferences of States Parties and intersessional work. The Secretariat also administers the Voluntary Trust Fund established by States Parties under Article 16(3) of the Treaty to assist in the implementation of the Treaty. In addition, the Fourth Conference of States Parties entrusted the Secretariat with the administration of the Treaty Sponsorship Programme, established to facilitate the participation of State representatives in Treaty meetings.[33]

Under Article 17 of the Treaty, a Conference of States Parties was to be convened within one year of the entry into force of the Treaty 'and thereafter at such other times as may be decided by the Conference of States Parties'. The First Conference of States Parties was held at Cancun in Mexico in August 2015. The Conference decided to hold the next Conference of States Parties in 2016, and subsequently sessions of the Conference have been held annually. The 2020 session of the Conference was held virtually in August 2020 as a result of the global COVID-19 pandemic.[34] The Seventh Conference of States Parties was also due to be held virtually, on 30 August to 3 September 2021.

The mandate of the Conference of States Parties is broad. According to an exhaustive (and mandatory) list set out in the Treaty, the Conference is required to:

- Review the implementation of the Treaty, including developments in the field of conventional arms
- Consider and adopt recommendations regarding the Treaty's implementation and operation, particularly effort to promote universality of adherence

---

[32] The reports are available at: https://thearmstradetreaty.org/annual-reports.html?templateId=209826.

[33] Arms Trade Treaty Secretariat, 'Role of the Secretariat', undated but last accessed 1 March 2021, at: https://thearmstradetreaty.org/role-of-the-secretariat.html.

[34] Arms Trade Treaty, Sixth Conference of States Parties, Geneva, 17–21 August 2020, Final Report, at: https://thearmstradetreaty.org/hyper-images/file/CSP6%20Final%20Report%20-%2021%20August%202020/CSP6%20Final%20Report%20-%2021%20August%202020.pdf?templateId=1335658.

- Consider proposed amendments to the Treaty
- Consider issues arising from the interpretation of the Treaty
- Consider and decide the tasks and budget of the Treaty Secretariat
- Consider the establishment of any subsidiary bodies necessary to improve the functioning of the Treaty; and
- Perform 'any other function consistent' with the Treaty.[35]

Under Article 14, which deals with issues of Treaty enforcement, each State Party is required to 'take appropriate measures to enforce national laws and regulations that implement the provisions' of the Arms Trade Treaty. Such enforcement is typically achieved by a range of legislative and administrative measures, policies, and programmes, including penal sanctions. A range of State agencies and bodies are responsible for enforcing controls on arms trade, such as law enforcement agencies, border guards, customs, the judiciary, and immigration authorities.[36]

Regional transfer regimes

A number of regional, legally binding regimes exist within Europe and Africa with respect to the transfer of conventional weapons. Each predates the adoption of the Arms Trade Treaty.

The European Union Common Position

The European Union (EU) Common Position 2008/944/CFSP of 8 December 2008 defines common rules governing control of exports of military technology and equipment. The Common Position is binding on all EU member States. As of 1 March 2021, there were twenty-seven EU members: Austria, Belgium, Bulgaria, Croatia, Cyprus, Czechia, Denmark, Estonia, Finland, France, Germany, Greece, Hungary, Ireland, Italy, Latvia, Lithuania, Luxembourg, Malta, the Netherlands, Poland, Portugal, Romania, Slovakia, Slovenia, Spain, and Sweden. The Position was most recently updated on 17 December 2019.[37]

---

[35] Art. 17(4), 2013 Arms Trade Treaty.
[36] Casey-Maslen et al., *The Arms Trade Treaty: A Commentary*, para. 14.18.
[37] Available at: https://eur-lex.europa.eu/legal-content/EN/TXT/PDF/?uri=CELEX: 02008E0944-20190917&from=EN.

The Common Position sets out eight criteria for determining whether a request for export authorization should be denied.

Criterion One concerns respect for international obligations and commitments by EU member States, in particular sanctions adopted by the UN Security Council or the EU and agreements on non-proliferation and other subjects, as well as other international obligations. The EU has arms embargoes in place with respect to Belarus, China, Egypt, Eritrea, Iran, Libya, Myanmar, North Korea, Somalia, South Sudan, Sudan, Syria, Venezuela, Yemen, and Zimbabwe. It also has embargoes on al-Qaeda and the Taliban as well as non-State actors in the Democratic Republic of Congo, Iraq, and Lebanon.[38]

Criterion Two concerns respect for human rights in the country of final destination as well as respect by that country of IHL.

Criterion Three concerns the internal situation in the country of final destination, as a function of the existence of tensions or armed conflicts.

Criterion Four refers to the preservation of regional peace, security, and stability.

Criterion Five addresses the national security of EU member States and of territories whose external relations are the responsibility of a member State, as well as that of friendly and allied countries.

Criterion Six looks at the behaviour of the buyer country with regard to the international community, as regards in particular its attitude to terrorism, the nature of its alliances, and respect for international law.

Criterion Seven assesses the existence of a risk that the military technology or equipment will be diverted within the buyer country or re-exported under undesirable conditions.

Criterion Eight concerns the compatibility of the exports of the military technology or equipment with the technical and economic capacity of the recipient country, taking into account the desirability that States should meet their legitimate security and defence needs with the least amount of diversion of human and economic resources for armaments.

---

[38] For a list of embargoes in place under EU auspices, see, e.g., Stockholm International Peace Research Institute (SIPRI), 'SIPRI Databases: Arms Embargoes', undated but accessed 1 March 2021 at: https://www.sipri.org/databases/embargoes.

The 2006 ECOWAS Convention on Small Arms and Light Weapons

The preamble to the 2006 ECOWAS Convention notes the deep concern of its States Parties 'about the uncontrolled flow of small arms and light weapons into Africa in general and West Africa in particular', and refers to 'the need to effectively control the transfer of arms by suppliers and arms brokers'.[39] Fourteen of the fifteen member States of ECOWAS are party to the Convention: Benin, Burkina Faso, Cape Verde, Côte d'Ivoire, Ghana, Guinea, Guinea-Bissau, Liberia, Mali, Niger, Nigeria, Senegal, Sierra Leone, and Togo.

Under the 2006 Convention, the term transfer is defined broadly as 'import, export, transit, transhipment and transport or any other movement whatsoever of small arms and light weapons, ammunition and other related materials from or through the territory of a State'.[40] In turn, States Parties are obligated to 'ban the transfer of small arms and light weapons and their manufacturing materials into their national territory or from/through their national territory'.[41] An exemption from this prohibition can be sought in order to meet legitimate national defence and security needs, or to participate in peace support or other operations in accordance with the decisions of the UN, the African Union, ECOWAS, or another regional or sub-regional body of which it is a member.[42] A separate prohibition applies to transfers of small arms and light weapons to non-State actors unless they are 'explicitly authorised' by the importing State Party.[43]

The 2010 Kinshasa Convention on Small Arms and Light Weapons

The 2010 Central African Convention for the Control of Small Arms and Light Weapons[44] (better known as the 2010 Kinshasa Convention) follows

---

[39] ECOWAS Convention on Small Arms and Light Weapons, Their Ammunition and Other Related Materials; adopted at Abuja, 14 June 2006; entered into force, 29 September 2009 (2006 ECOWAS Convention on Small Arms and Light Weapons).

[40] Art. 1(9), 2006 ECOWAS Convention on Small Arms and Light Weapons.

[41] Art. 3(1), 2006 ECOWAS Convention on Small Arms and Light Weapons.

[42] Art. 4, 2006 ECOWAS Convention on Small Arms and Light Weapons.

[43] Art. 3(2), 2006 ECOWAS Convention on Small Arms and Light Weapons.

[44] Central African Convention for the Control of Small Arms and Light Weapons, Their Ammunition and all Parts and Components that can be used for Their Manufacture, Repair

the approach laid down in the 2006 ECOWAS Convention. Under the Convention, small arms and light weapons, their ammunition, and parts and components thereof may only be lawfully transferred where they are necessary in order to:

a. Maintain law and order, or for defence or national security purposes
b. Participate in peacekeeping operations conducted under the aegis of the UN, the African Union, the Economic Community of Central African States or other regional or sub-regional organisations of which the State Party concerned is a member.[45]

States parties are required to prohibit any transfer of small arms and light weapons, their ammunition, and parts and components thereof to non-State armed groups.[46]

As of 1 March 2021, there were eight States Parties to the Kinshasa Convention and three signatory States.[47]

Politically binding transfer regimes

The most important politically binding transfer regime is the Wassenaar Arrangement, which has forty-two exporting States as members. Also significant is the Missile Technology Control Regime (MTCR), to which thirty-five States have adhered. For the purpose of transparency in conventional arms transfers, the voluntary UNROCA is a valuable confidence-building measure.

and Assembly; adopted at Kinshasa, 30 April 2010; entered into force, 8 March 2017, Reg. No. 54327.

[45] Art. 3(2), 2010 Kinshasa Convention.
[46] Art. 4, 2010 Kinshasa Convention.
[47] Angola, Cameroon, the Central African Republic, Chad, Congo, Equatorial Guinea, Gabon, and Sao Tome and Principe are States Parties. Burundi, Democratic Republic of the Congo, and Rwanda are signatories.

The Wassenaar Arrangement

The Wassenaar Arrangement on Export Controls for Conventional Arms and Dual-Use Goods and Technologies is a multilateral export control regime with forty-two Participating States, including all the major exporters of conventional weapons. The Wassenaar Arrangement arose out of the end of the Cold War. The Coordinating Committee for Multilateral Export Controls (CoCom) was an informal multilateral organization through which the United States and its allies sought to coordinate national controls over export of strategic materials and technology to the Soviet bloc. Following the end of the Cold War, CoCom's members recognized that a new mechanism was needed to address risks related to the spread of conventional weapons and dual-use goods and technologies.[48]

On 19 December 1995, States agreed to establish the Wassenaar Arrangement and that Vienna would host the Arrangement's Secretariat. At the first plenary meeting on 2–3 April 1996, the founding members adopted the 'Initial Elements', including the List of Dual-Use Goods and Technologies and the Munitions List, which became active on 1 November 1996.[49] All Wassenaar Arrangement documents are adopted by the plenary meeting, which convenes every December in Vienna. Guiding documents such as the Elements for Objective Analysis and Advice concerning Potentially Destabilising Accumulations of Conventional Weapons and the Best Practices for Effective Legislation on Arms Brokering support the implementation of national export controls and export decisions by Participating States. They are developed and updated by the General Working Group, which typically meets twice a year.

The Munitions List and the List of Dual-Use Goods and Technologies are regularly updated by the Expert Group. Military items are divided into twenty-two categories, ranging from small arms to heavy weapons systems and ammunition. Nine categories are covered by the List of Dual-Use Goods and Technologies:

1. Special Materials and Related Equipment
2. Materials Processing

---

[48] Wassenaar Arrangement, 'Genesis of the Wassenaar Arrangement', Last updated 17 December 2020, at: https://www.wassenaar.org/about-us/.

[49] The latest versions of the Wassenaar Arrangement's List of Dual Use Goods and Technologies and Munitions List are available at: https://www.wassenaar.org/control-lists/.

3. Electronics
4. Computers
5. Telecommunications (Part 1) and Information Security (Part 2)
6. Sensors and Lasers
7. Navigation and Avionics
8. Marine
9. Aerospace and Propulsion.

Some of the items contained in the nine categories are listed on a Sensitive List while others are included on a Very Sensitive List; the latter items require the application of heightened vigilance prior to any export.

Missile Technology Control Regime

The Missile Technology Control Regime (MTCR) is an informal political understanding among States that seeks to limit proliferation of missiles and missile technology. It was established in 1987 by the Group of Seven (G-7) industrialized nations: Canada, France, Germany, Italy, Japan, the United Kingdom, and the United States. Thirty-five States are members of the MTCR (called 'Partners'): Argentina, Australia, Austria, Belgium, Brazil, Bulgaria, Canada, Czechia, Denmark, Finland, France, Germany, Greece, Hungary, Iceland, India, Ireland, Italy, Japan, Luxemburg, the Netherlands, New Zealand, Norway, Poland, Portugal, the Republic of Korea, Russia, South Africa, Spain, Sweden, Switzerland, Turkey, Ukraine, the United Kingdom, and the United States. The MTCR was created with a view to addressing the proliferation of nuclear weapons by controlling the most 'destabilizing' delivery system for such weapons.[50]

In 1992, the MTCR's original focus on missiles for nuclear weapons delivery was extended to a focus on the proliferation of missiles for the delivery of all types of weapons of mass destruction (WMD). The MTCR comprises Guidelines for Sensitive Missile-Relevant Transfers and a list of dual-use items of particular concern: the Equipment, Software, and Technology Annex. The MTCR Annex is the regime's list of controlled items, which includes virtually all key equipment, materials, software, and technology needed for missile development, production, and operation.

[50] Missile Technology Control Regime, 'Frequently Asked Questions (FAQs)', undated but last accessed 1 March 2021, at: https://mtcr.info/frequently-asked-questions-faqs/.

These are the items that are controlled by the MTCR Partners. The Annex is divided into two parts: Category I and Category II items.

The Guidelines set out the purpose of the MTCR and call for particular restraint to be exercised in the consideration of 'Category I' transfers, regardless of their purpose. Indeed, there exists a strong presumption to deny altogether such transfers, which concern complete rocket systems (including ballistic missiles, space launch vehicles, and sounding rockets) and unmanned air vehicle systems (including cruise missiles systems and target and reconnaissance drones) with capabilities exceeding a 300 km/500 kg range/payload threshold; production facilities for such systems; and major sub-systems including rocket stages, re-entry vehicles, rocket engines, guidance systems, and warhead mechanisms.[51]

Particular restraint must also be exercised with regard to possible transfers of any items in the Annex, or of any missiles (whether or not in the Annex), if the government adjudges 'on the basis of all available, persuasive information' that they are intended to be used for the delivery of weapons of mass destruction (WMD). Again, there is a strong presumption to deny such transfers. Until further notice, the transfer of Category I production facilities is not to be authorized.[52] This is the only activity prohibited absolutely by the Guidelines.

While still undertaking to exercise 'restraint', partners have greater flexibility in the treatment of Category II transfer applications. Category II items include other less sensitive and dual-use missile related components, as well as other complete missile systems capable of a range of at least 300 km, regardless of payload. Their export is subject to licensing requirements taking into consideration the non-proliferation factors specified in the MTCR Guidelines. Exports judged by the exporting country to be intended for use in WMD delivery are to be subjected to a strong presumption of denial.

In general, the MTCR Guidelines propose that the following factors be taken into account by States when assessing transfer applications of the items in the MTCR Annex:

A: Concerns about the proliferation of WMD

---

[51] Missile Technology Control Regime, 'MTCR Guidelines and the Equipment, Software and Technology Annex', undated but last accessed 1 March 2021, at: https://mtcr.info/mtcr-guidelines/.
[52] MTCR Guidelines for Sensitive Missile-Relevant Transfers, para. 2.

B: The capabilities and objectives of the missile and space programs of the recipient State

C: The significance of the transfer in terms of the potential development of delivery systems (other than manned aircraft) for WMD

D: The assessment of the end use of the transfers, including the relevant assurances of the recipient States

E: The applicability of relevant multilateral agreements

F: The risk of controlled items falling into the hands of terrorist groups and individuals.[53]

The UN Register of Conventional Arms

The UNROCA is a voluntary but 'key' confidence-building measure. Under the Register, which was established in 1992, UN member States are requested to provide data on the number of items under the seven listed categories of conventional arms when they are either imported into or exported from their territory. As of March 2021, UNROCA had received reports from more than 170 States. On average, more than sixty States report annually to UNROCA, including virtually all major arms exporting States. According to the UN Office for Disarmament Affairs (UNODA), the vast majority (well over 90 per cent) of official arms transfers are captured by it.[54]

The UNROCA has a two-tier system of reporting. The primary tier regards transfers under the seven pre-defined categories of heavy weapons, plus small arms. Additionally, however, States can report on military holdings, procurement through national production, and national legislation or policies. The seven categories are as follows:

I. Battle tanks

These are tracked or wheeled self-propelled armoured fighting vehicles with high cross-country mobility and a high-level of self-protection, weighing at least 16.5 metric tons unladen weight, with a high muzzle velocity direct fire main gun of at least 75 millimetres calibre.

---

[53] Ibid., para. 3.

[54] UNODA, 'UN Register of Conventional Arms', at: https://www.un.org/disarmament/convarms/register/; and 'Transparency in Armaments', at: https://www.un.org/disarmament/convarms/transparency-in-armaments/.

II. Armoured combat vehicles

These are tracked, semi-tracked or wheeled self-propelled vehicles, with armoured protection and cross-country capability, either: (a) designed and equipped to transport a squad of four or more infantrymen, or (b) armed with an integral or organic weapon of at least 12.5 millimetres calibre or a missile launcher.

III. Large-calibre artillery systems

These are guns, howitzers, artillery pieces combining the characteristics of a gun or a howitzer, mortars, or multiple-launch rocket systems, capable of engaging surface targets by delivering primarily indirect fire, with a calibre of 75 millimetres and above.

IV. Combat aircraft and unmanned combat aerial vehicles

These include fixed-wing or variable-geometry wing aerial vehicles as defined below:

(a) Manned fixed-wing or variable-geometry wing aircraft, designed, equipped or modified to engage targets by employing guided missiles, unguided rockets, bombs, guns, cannons or other weapons of destruction, including versions of these aircraft which perform specialized electronic warfare, suppression of air defence or reconnaissance missions.

(b) Unmanned fixed-wing or variable-geometry wing aircraft, designed, equipped or modified to engage targets by employing guided missiles, unguided rockets, bombs, guns, cannons or other weapons of destruction.

The terms 'combat aircraft' and 'unmanned combat aerial vehicles (UCAV)' do not include primary trainer aircraft, unless designed, equipped or modified as described above.

V. Attack helicopters

These are rotary-wing aircraft designed, equipped or modified to engage targets by employing guided or unguided anti-armour, air-to-surface, air-to-subsurface, or air-to-air weapons and equipped with an integrated fire control and aiming system for these weapons, including versions of these aircraft which perform specialized reconnaissance or electronic warfare missions.

VI. Warships

These are vessels or submarines armed and equipped for military use with a standard displacement of 500 metric tons or above, and those with a standard displacement of less than 500 metric tons, equipped for launching missiles with a range of at least 25 kilometres or torpedoes with similar range.

VII. Missiles/missile launchers

This category comprises the following:

(a) Guided or unguided rockets, ballistic or cruise missiles capable of delivering a warhead or weapon of destruction to a range of at least 25 kilometres, and means designed or modified specifically for launching such missiles or rockets, if not covered by categories I through VI. For the purpose of the Register, this sub-category includes remotely piloted vehicles with the characteristics for missiles as defined above but does not include ground-to-air missiles.

(b) Man-Portable Air-Defence Systems (MANPADS).

Small arms

The additional category of small arms does not enjoy an agreed definition, according to the UN, though it is noted that usually included are revolvers and self-loading pistols, rifles and carbines, sub-machine guns, assault rifles, and light machine guns. Light weapons typically include heavy machine guns, hand-held under-barrel and mounted grenade launchers, portable anti-tank guns, recoilless rifles, portable anti-tank missile launchers and rocket systems, and mortars of calibres less than 75 mm.[55]

Data on the arms trade

The SIPRI Arms Transfers Database is a valuable source of information on transfers of major conventional weapons by calendar year. As of this

---

[55] Ibid.

writing, the latest version was published on 9 March 2020.[56] In 2019 the largest importer by value was Saudi Arabia (almost US$3.7 billion), with India second (at more than US$2.9 billion). During the same year the largest exporter by value was the United States (at more than US$10.7 billion), with Russia second (at more than US$4.7 billion).

---

[56] See: https://www.sipri.org/databases/armstransfers.

6

Verification of Arms Control and Disarmament Agreements

Introduction

In his negotiations in the 1980s with Soviet Premier Mikhail Gorbachev, United States (US) President Ronald Reagan famously quoted a Russian proverb which in English translates as 'Trust, but verify'. Indeed, verification is integral to the success of both arms control and disarmament agreements, for, as is the case in times of war, 'where little is known much is feared'.[1] This chapter discusses the nature and extent of verification measures in arms control and disarmament. It considers thematic areas where verification is generally required, as well as weapon-specific issues within those areas. Examples are provided of verification measures in both bilateral and multilateral agreements, including but not limited to legally binding treaties.

Transparency is a critical first step towards building confidence among parties and other stakeholders as to the implementation of arms control and disarmament agreements. But disclosure of relevant information is rarely sufficient to build the requisite confidence among concerned States in and of itself, especially where weapons of mass destruction are concerned. For instance, weapons, their parts and components, and weapons development, production, and storage facilities may be inadvertently—or deliberately—omitted from States' declarations and annual progress reports. For this reason, other measures such as satellite imagery or reconnaissance overflights (often considered within the category of 'national technical measures') and inspections (by personnel from other States Parties or dedicated inspectors from duly mandated international organizations) are integral to verification of compliance.

---

[1] T. Powers, *Heisenberg's War: The Secret History of the German Bomb*, Jonathon Cape, London, 1993, p. 205.

Thematic areas where verification is especially important

Verification measures can address a wide set of thematic areas within arms control and disarmament. These areas comprise weapons development and production, testing, deployment and stockpiling, stockpile destruction, and use. These issues are discussed in turn.

Verification of the prohibitions on development and production

Disarmament agreements typically prohibit the development and production of any weapon that they outlaw. This is explicitly the case in the 1971 Biological Weapons Convention, the 1992 Chemical Weapons Convention, the 1997 Anti-Personnel Mine Ban Convention, the 2008 Convention on Cluster Munitions, and the 2017 Treaty on the Prohibition of Nuclear Weapons. The 1968 Treaty on the Non-Proliferation of Nuclear Weapons (NPT)[2] does not explicitly outlaw development of nuclear weapons, but under Article II each non-nuclear-weapon State Party is obligated 'not to manufacture or otherwise acquire' any nuclear explosive device. In accordance with Article III, the non-nuclear-weapon States Parties are further required to accept safeguards under an agreement with the International Atomic Energy Agency (IAEA) 'for the exclusive purpose of verification of the fulfilment' of their obligations under the Treaty 'with a view to preventing diversion of nuclear energy from peaceful uses to nuclear weapons or other nuclear explosive devices'.

There is no formal verification system instituted under the 1971 Biological Weapons Convention and attempts to instigate one have failed, particularly given US concern about industrial espionage. Article VI(1) of the Convention stipulates, however, that any State Party 'which finds that any other State Party is acting in breach of obligations deriving from the provisions of the Convention' may lodge a complaint with the United

---

[2] Treaty on the Non-Proliferation of Nuclear Weapons; opened for signature at London, Moscow, and Washington, DC, 1 July 1968; entered into force, 5 March 1970, *UNTS* Vol. 729, Reg. No. 10485. As of 1 March 2021, 190 States were party to the NPT.

Nations (UN) Security Council. The Council may in theory investigate the complaint, 'but this power has never been invoked'.[3]

No formal verification regime is instituted under either the 1997 Anti-Personnel Mine Ban Convention or the 2008 Convention on Cluster Munitions, though provision is made for possible fact-finding missions in case of an allegation of non-compliance with the treaty provisions,[4] which could potentially include the development of prohibited weapons. There are also civil society mechanisms—*Landmine Monitor*[5] and Mine Action Review[6]—that provide non-governmental monitoring and analysis of implementation of the two conventional disarmament treaties.

The inspections regime under the Chemical Weapons Convention

The 1992 Chemical Weapons Convention has extensive verification provisions to ensure that its States Parties do not develop or produce prohibited chemical weapons, while permitting States to develop and produce chemical agents for peaceful purposes. The centrepiece of verification, which is entrusted to the Organisation for the Prohibition of Chemical Weapons (OPCW), is the inspections regime. This regime comprises two types of inspections with respect to development and production: *routine inspections* of chemical weapons-related facilities and chemical industry facilities using certain dual-use chemicals; and short-notice *challenge inspections*, which can be conducted at any location in any State Party about which another State Party has compliance concerns. To conduct these inspections, the OPCW has an Inspectorate of around 100 inspectors.[7]

Routine inspections

Routine inspections are 'cooperative events'. This means that the inspection teams seek to verify the contents of declarations by States Parties to the Convention; they do not adopt 'an investigative approach'. Between April 1997 and October 2017, the OPCW conducted more than 6,600 inspections on the territory of eighty-six States Parties.[8]

---

[3] D. Kimball, 'The Biological Weapons Convention (BWC) at a Glance', Last Reviewed March 2020, Fact Sheets & Briefs, Arms Control Association, Washington DC, at: https://www.armscontrol.org/factsheets/bwc.

[4] See Art. 8(8), 1997 Anti-Personnel Mine Ban Convention; Art 8(6), 2008 Convention on Cluster Munitions.

[5] At: https://www.the-monitor.org.

[6] At: https://www.mineactionreview.org.

[7] OPCW, 'Three Types of Inspections', Fact Sheet 5, The Hague, November 2017, p. 1.

[8] Ibid.

The frequency of inspections at chemical industry facilities depends on the chemicals those facilities produce. Schedule 1 chemicals, which include mustard gas, ricin, and sarin (and now Novichok, following a decision in 2018 by the Conference of States Parties), are particularly hazardous and pose a high risk to life and health. They have been developed, produced, stockpiled, and used as chemical weapons in the past and have little or no use in activities not prohibited by the Convention. Use of Schedule 1 chemicals is restricted to pharmaceutical, research, medical, and protective purposes related to protection against toxic chemicals. For such purposes, the Convention limits all production above 100 grams to a Single Small-Scale Facility within each State Party.[9] This Single Small-Scale Facility is visited by OPCW inspectors twice a year on average. In the case of the United Kingdom (UK), its Single Small-Scale Facility is the Ministry of Defence's Defence Science and Technology Laboratory, better known as Porton Down, which is located a few miles outside Salisbury in southern England.[10]

Inspections of facilities producing Schedule 2 chemicals, which include Amiton (a V-series nerve agent chemically similar to VX) and BZ (an odourless chemical incapacitant), are limited to two a year per site. Visits are based on a risk assessment after an initial inspection and facility agreement. The visits must be unimpeded, not only to the plant but also within the entire plant site. At Schedule 2 plant sites, inspections include quantitative checks of certain facility records. Following an inspection, the OPCW team draws up a preliminary factual findings report, which is discussed with the facility management and the National Authority of the State Party at a debriefing which must occur within twenty-four hours of the time at which the inspection finished. 'The inspection team is then transported to the point of exit as quickly as possible.'[11]

Challenge inspections

Challenge inspections, which are designed to resolve allegations of non-compliance with the Chemical Weapons Convention, are said by the OPCW to be one of the treaty's 'most innovative features'. Under Article IX of the Convention, any State Party can request the OPCW Secretariat to conduct

---

[9] United Kingdom Government, 'Chemical Weapons Convention Guidance', Last updated 8 January 2021, at: https://www.gov.uk/guidance/chemical-weapons-convention-guidance.

[10] See, e.g., F. Gardner, 'Porton Down: What's Inside the UK's Top-Secret Laboratory?', BBC, 13 June 2019, at: https://www.bbc.co.uk/news/uk-48540653.

[11] OPCW, 'Three Types of Inspections', Fact Sheet 5, pp. 2, 3.

an on-site challenge inspection anywhere in the territory of any other State Party (and anywhere else under its jurisdiction or control). Challenge inspections are characterized by the 'any time, any place' concept: they are intended to be launched at very short notice and can be conducted at both declared and undeclared facilities and locations.[12]

As is the case in routine inspections, the inspection team can take samples, which are either analysed on-site or transferred off-site for analysis at an OPCW-designated laboratory. The duration of an inspection cannot exceed eighty-four hours in total without the consent of the territorial State Party.[13]

A challenge inspection request must be submitted to the OPCW Executive Council and the Director-General. A requested State Party cannot refuse a challenge inspection, regardless of the nature of the site at which it is to take place, although Article IX of the Convention encourages concerned States Parties to seek to resolve compliance concerns through a consultative process before proceeding to request a challenge inspection.[14] In addition, the Council may block an inspection within twelve hours of receiving a request if supported by a three-quarters majority of Council members. This opportunity exists where the request is deemed frivolous, abusive, or clearly beyond the scope of the Convention.

To date, no challenge inspections have been requested.[15] A number of test inspections have, though, been organized by the OPCW in States Parties 'to test the Organisation's readiness to conduct a challenge inspection'.[16]

Safeguards against the development and production of nuclear weapons

The backbone of verification in both the NPT and the 2017 Treaty on the Prohibition of Nuclear Weapons is the system of safeguards within the IAEA. As noted in earlier chapters, there are two main forms of safeguards agreements: the basic agreement—somewhat misleadingly referred to as

---

[12] OPCW, 'Preventing the Re-Emergence of Chemical Weapons', 2021, at: https://www.opcw.org/work/preventing-re-emergence-chemical-weapons.

[13] OPCW, 'Three Types of Inspections', Fact Sheet 5, pp. 3, 4.

[14] Ibid., p. 3.

[15] Ibid. See also, e.g., T. Abe, 'Challenge Inspections under the Chemical Weapons Convention: Between Ideal and Reality', *The Nonproliferation Review*, Vol. 24, Nos 1–2 (2017), pp. 167–84, available at: https://www.tandfonline.com/doi/abs/10.1080/10736700.2017.1380429?src=recsys&journalCode=rnpr20.

[16] See, e.g., OPCW, 'OPCW Launches Challenge Inspection Exercise 2011', 28 October 2011, at: https://www.opcw.org/media-centre/news/2011/10/opcw-launches-challenge-inspection-exercise-2011.

the Comprehensive Safeguards Agreement (CSA)— and the Additional Protocol.

Comprehensive Safeguards Agreement

A CSA focuses on assessments by the IAEA of the correctness and completeness of a State's *declared* nuclear material and nuclear-related activities. Verification measures include on-site inspections, visits, and ongoing monitoring and evaluation.[17] In 2015, for instance, a combined total of 709 facilities and 577 locations outside facilities in 181 States were under the various IAEA safeguards, making them subject to verification by IAEA inspectors. IAEA inspectors performed a total of 2,118 inspections of power plants, uranium mines, nuclear fuel fabrication plants, enrichment facilities, research reactors, and waste facilities. Inside the reactor hall of a power plant, verification of the spent fuel pond's contents is particularly important. Inspectors determine the presence of the spent nuclear fuel assemblies stored inside the pool and check that the plant operator has as much fuel as was reported by the relevant State. Depending on the size and age of the reactor, the total number of spent fuel assemblies can number in the thousands.[18]

Nuclear material 'accountancy' is complemented by measures of containment and surveillance, such as through the use of seals and of cameras and detectors installed at a relevant nuclear facility. These measures help to provide 'continuity of knowledge' over nuclear material and facilities between inspections, preventing undetected access to nuclear material or any undeclared operation of the facility.[19] Under its safeguards programme, the IAEA has established more than 100 measurement and monitoring systems.[20] Some of these are specifically intended for monitoring of plutonium and highly enriched uranium encountered in the peaceful use of nuclear energy in non-nuclear-weapon States Parties to the NPT.[21] This nuclear

---

[17] IAEA, 'IAEA Safeguards Overview', 2019, at: https://www.iaea.org/publications/factsheets/iaea-safeguards-overview.

[18] S. Henriques, 'A Day in the Life of a Safeguards Inspector', IAEA Office of Public Information and Communication, Vienna, 27 July 2016.

[19] IAEA, *IAEA Safeguards: Serving Nuclear Non-Proliferation*, Vienna, 2015, at: https://www.iaea.org/sites/default/files/safeguards_web_june_2015_1.pdf, p. 16.

[20] IAEA, *International Target Values 2010 for Measurement Uncertainties in Safeguarding Nuclear Materials*, IAEA doc. STR-368, Vienna, 2010.

[21] IAEA, *Safeguards Techniques and Equipment*, International Nuclear Verification Series No. 1 (Rev.2), Vienna, 2011; see also T. Shea, *Verifying Nuclear Disarmament*, 1st edn, Routledge, Abingdon, 2019, para. 3.5.1.

material can be diverted away from peaceful purposes and is integral to the development of a nuclear explosive device.

In Iraq, the Tuwaitha Nuclear Research Centre, located about 30 kilometres south of Baghdad, was a site used for clandestine nuclear weapons-related activities in the 1970s and 1980s in violation of the country's obligations under the NPT. In 1981 Israel bombed a materials test reactor (MTR) at the site formally called Tammuz-1, but better known as Osirak. Israel had feared the reactor would produce weapon-grade plutonium in secret.[22] Despite this setback, Saddam Hussein continued to pursue a nuclear weapons programme, though ultimately no nuclear weapon could be built.[23] The Tuwaitha site was extensively damaged during the Allied bombing campaign in early 1991 during the Gulf War. Subsequently, Iraq razed several buildings to the ground with a view to concealing evidence of secret uranium enrichment activities from the IAEA inspectors.

In the early 1990s, the IAEA identified inconsistencies between nuclear activities declared by the Democratic People's Republic of Korea (DPRK) under its CSA and information available 'through inspections and other sources'. The IAEA had not been permitted since 1994 to conduct the necessary safeguards activities provided for in the DPRK's CSA. Since April 2009, when IAEA inspectors were formally requested by DPRK authorities to leave the country, the IAEA has not implemented any measures under the ad hoc monitoring and verification arrangement agreed between the IAEA and North Korea. So-called Six-party Talks between China, the DPRK, Japan, the Republic of Korea, Russia, and the United States did not succeed in resolving the situation.[24] Today, the DPRK is a nuclear-armed State.

On 11 September 2017, following the DPRK's sixth nuclear test on 3 September (see below), the UN Security Council unanimously adopted Resolution 2375 in which it called upon all UN member States to inspect vessels, with the consent of the flag State, on the high seas if they have information that provides reasonable grounds to believe that the cargo of such vessels contains items the supply, sale, transfer, or export of which is prohibited by earlier resolutions on the DPRK. If a suspected vessel refuses

---

[22]   D. Albright, C. Gay, and K. Hamza, 'Development of the Al-Tuwaitha Site: What If the Public or the IAEA Had Overhead Imagery?', Institute for Security and International Studies, 26 April 1999, at: https://isis-online.org/publications/iraq/tuwaitha.html.

[23]   Federation of American Scientists, 'Iraqi Nuclear Weapons', 31 May 2012, at: https://fas.org/nuke/guide/iraq/nuke/program.htm.

[24]   IAEA, *IAEA Safeguards: Serving Nuclear Non-Proliferation*, p. 12; see also IAEA, Fact Sheet on DPRK Nuclear Safeguards, 2009.

inspection, the flag State must direct the ship to a port for inspection or risk being designated for an asset freeze or denied port access.

In March 2020, the IAEA Director General declared before the Agency's Board of Governors that the Agency was 'investing considerable effort in ensuring that we are ready to resume verification of the DPRK's nuclear programme if a political agreement is reached among countries concerned. If and when such an agreement is achieved, we will be ready to deploy our inspectors from day one. The Agency will have an indispensable role to play.'[25] Director General Rafael Mariano Grossi called on the DPRK 'to comply fully with its obligations under Security Council resolutions, to co-operate promptly with the Agency, and to resolve all outstanding issues, including those that have arisen during the absence of Agency inspectors from the country'.[26]

Additional Protocol

The IAEA's experience in Iraq and the DPRK in the early 1990s had demonstrated that, although IAEA safeguards had worked well with respect to declared nuclear material and facilities, it was not well equipped to detect *undeclared* nuclear material and activities in States with CSAs. At the end of 1993 the IAEA embarked on a programme to strengthen safeguards implementation by enhancing the Agency's ability to detect such undeclared material or activities. Some of the measures, known as 'Part 1' measures (comprising actions such as environmental sampling and the use of satellite imagery), could be implemented under the authority provided by existing CSAs. But other 'Part 2' measures, such as access to all parts of a State's nuclear fuel cycle, from mines to nuclear waste, demanded new legal authority. This led to the development and formal approval of the Model Additional Protocol in 1997.

Under the Additional Protocol, the IAEA is granted expanded rights of access to information and locations in the contracting States. This expanded access covers all the constituent elements of a State's nuclear fuel cycle, and grants the Agency access at short notice to all buildings on a site. The IAEA is also authorized to collect environmental samples beyond declared locations when it deems it necessary to do so. Under an Additional

---

[25] 'IAEA Director General's Introductory Statement to the Board of Governors', Vienna, 9 March 2020, at: https://www.iaea.org/newscenter/statements/iaea-director-generals-introductory-statement-to-the-board-of-governors-9-march-2020.
[26] Ibid.

Protocol, the IAEA may also confirm that a facility or location outside nuclear facilities but where nuclear material was customarily used, such as in hospitals, has indeed been decommissioned.

Although not yet a State Party to an Additional Protocol, under the 2015 Joint Comprehensive Plan of Action[27] Iran agreed to permit the IAEA equivalent rights of access, and in 2016 it provisionally applied the terms of the Protocol. Cumulatively with the CSA, this placed eighteen nuclear facilities and nine other facilities in Iran under IAEA safeguards. Initially, the IAEA did not doubt Iran's compliance with its undertakings. On 8 July 2019, however—a year after the United States' withdrawal from the politically binding Joint Comprehensive Plan of Action (JCPOA; known familiarly as the Iran Nuclear Deal)—the Agency verified that Iran had begun enriching uranium up to 4.5 per cent Uranium-235.[28] The IAEA reported further in early March 2020 that it had detected natural uranium particles of anthropogenic origin at a location in Iran not declared to the Agency. 'Interactions between the Agency and Iran to resolve the matter continue', in the words of a March 2020 IAEA report.[29] Later in March, Director General Grossi called on Iran to cooperate immediately and fully with the IAEA and to provide prompt access to three locations which it has refused to let Agency inspectors visit, as well as to resolve questions related to possible undeclared nuclear material.[30]

Verification of the prohibition on testing of nuclear weapons

A number of treaties specifically prohibit the explosive testing of nuclear weapons or other nuclear explosive devices. Under the 1963 Partial Nuclear-Test-Ban Treaty, States Parties undertake 'to prohibit, to prevent, and not to carry out any nuclear weapon test explosion' above ground, in

---

[27] On 14 July 2015, China, France, Germany, Russia, the United Kingdom, and the United States, along with the High Representative of the European Union for Foreign Affairs and Security Policy, agreed with Iran on the text of the JCPOA. On 8 May 2018, then-US President Donald Trump announced the United States' withdrawal from the Iran nuclear deal.

[28] 'Verification and Monitoring in the Islamic Republic of Iran in Light of United Nations Security Council Resolution 2231 (2015): Report by the Director General', IAEA doc. GOV/2020/5, 3 March 2020, para. 12.

[29] Ibid., para. 32.

[30] N. Jawerth, 'IAEA Director General Calls on Iran to Cooperate Immediately and Fully', IAEA, 9 March 2020.

outer space, or under water.[31] But no verification provisions were incorporated in the Treaty. The same applies with respect to the 1979 Moon Treaty, which provides that testing of any type of weapons on the Moon shall be forbidden.[32]

In the 1959 Antarctic Treaty, however, which not only outlawed the testing of any type of weapons in Antarctica but also explicitly prohibited any nuclear explosions in that region,[33] specific provision was made for inspections, setting an important precedent. All areas of Antarctica, including all stations, installations, and equipment within those areas, and all ships and aircraft at points of discharging or embarking cargoes or personnel in Antarctica, shall be open at all times to inspection by any duly designated observers.[34] In addition, aerial observation may be carried out 'at any time over any or all areas of Antarctica by any of the Contracting Parties having the right to designate observers'.[35]

In 1996, the Comprehensive Nuclear-Test-Ban Treaty imposed on each State Party the obligation 'not to carry out any nuclear weapon test explosion or any other nuclear explosion'.[36] This extended the prohibition under the Partial Nuclear-Test-Ban Treaty to underground testing. It also provided for a detailed verification system designed to detect any nuclear explosion anywhere in the world.

Although the Treaty has not entered into force, the Preparatory Commission for the Comprehensive Nuclear-Test-Ban Treaty Organization (CTBTO) has already implemented a series of measures foreseen by the Treaty as part of an International Monitoring System (IMS). Key to these is seismic monitoring, one of the three waveform technologies used by the verification regime to monitor compliance with the Treaty. The objective of seismic monitoring is to detect and locate *underground* nuclear explosions. Data resulting from seismic monitoring are used to distinguish between an underground nuclear explosion and the numerous natural and man-made seismic events that occur every day, such as earthquakes and

---

[31] Art. I(1), Treaty Banning Nuclear Weapon Tests in the Atmosphere, in Outer Space and Under Water; opened for signature at London, Moscow, and Washington, DC, 8 August 1963; entered into force, 10 October 1963.

[32] Art. 3(4), Agreement Governing the Activities of States on the Moon and Other Celestial Bodies; opened for signature at New York, 18 December 1979; entered into force, 11 July 1984.

[33] Arts I(1) and V(1), The Antarctic Treaty; adopted at Washington, DC, 1 December 1959; entered into force, 23 June 1961.

[34] In accordance with Art. IX(3) of the Treaty.

[35] Art. IX(4), The Antarctic Treaty.

[36] Comprehensive Nuclear-Test-Ban Treaty; adopted at New York, 10 September 1996.

mining explosions. Seismic waves travel so fast that an event creating these waves can be registered by seismic stations distributed worldwide in a time span ranging from a few seconds to about ten minutes.[37]

The IMS has been designed to detect nuclear explosions, anywhere around the globe, of at least a 1 kt explosive yield. This is not a Treaty threshold but a practical means of monitoring the prohibition on explosive testing, which can be cost-effective. Negotiating States for the CTBT had decided to rule out satellite and electromagnetic pulses (EMP) monitoring due to financial restraints.[38]

Seismic monitoring is significant in preparation for an on-site inspection (OSI). The analysis of seismic data identifies the location of a suspected underground nuclear explosion, 'which is a prerequisite for the identification of an inspection area'. On 3 September 2017, at 03:30 (UTC), CTBTO's monitoring stations picked up an unusual seismic event in the DPRK.[39] More than 100 of its stations worldwide contributed to the analysis, which concluded that the event was 'consistent with a man-made explosion'. An initial magnitude estimate of 5.8 was later revised upwards to 6.1. The location estimate showed that the event took place in the area of the DPRK's nuclear test site.[40]

Radionuclide technology complements the three waveform verification technologies—seismic, infrasound, and hydroacoustic—employed by the CTBTO verification regime. This technology 'is the only one that is able to confirm whether an explosion detected and located by the others is indicative of a nuclear test'. The radionuclide monitoring technology measures the abundance of radioactive particles and noble gases, that is, radionuclides, in the air. Radionuclides (also called radioisotopes) may occur naturally, but they can also be artificially produced.[41]

---

[37] Preparatory Commission for the CTBTO, 'The Seismic Network and How It Works', undated but accessed 1 March 2021 at: https://www.ctbto.org/verification-regime/monitoring-technologies-how-they-work/seismic-monitoring/.

[38] Preparatory Commission for the CTBTO, '1994–96: Monitoring and Inspection', undated but accessed 1 March 2021 at: https://www.ctbto.org/the-treaty/1993-1996-treaty-negotiations/1994-96-monitoring-and-inspection/.

[39] The primary seismic stations are located at Yellowknife, Northwest Territories, Canada; Tahiti, France; Makanchi, Kazakhstan; Wonju, Republic of Korea; Petropavlovsk-Kamchatskiy, Russia; and Lajitas, Texas, in the United States.

[40] Preparatory Commission for the CTBTO, 'DPRK Sept. 2017 Unusual Seismic Event', 3 September 2017, at: https://www.ctbto.org/press-centre/press-releases/2017/ctbto-executive-secretary-lassina-zerbo-on-the-unusual-seismic-event-detected-in-the-democratic-peoples-republic-of-korea/.

[41] Preparatory Commission for the CTBTO, 'Radionuclide Monitoring', at: https://www.ctbto.org/verification-regime/monitoring-technologies-how-they-work/radionuclide-monitoring/.

There is a narrow time window during which some of the conclusive evidence for a Treaty violation can be obtained. The occurrence of seismic aftershocks after an event declines each day. Equally, radionuclides dissipate quickly due to their relatively short half-lives. An OSI should therefore start as soon as possible after a suspicious event to gather the respective data. While no on-site visit was possible at the Punggye-ri Nuclear Test Facility (because of lack of access granted by the DPRK authorities), the independent Norwegian Research Organization (NORSAR) calculated that the yield of the test device would have been about 120 kt.[42]

The DPRK test of September 2017 was, as of this writing, the most recent recorded nuclear explosion anywhere in the world.

Verification of the prohibition on stockpiling and deployment of weapons

The US–Soviet Strategic Arms Reduction Treaty, better known as START I, was signed in July 1991 by US President George H. W. Bush and Soviet Premier Mikhail Gorbachev. START I was the first treaty to impose deep reductions of US and Soviet/Russian strategic nuclear weapons. Reductions mandated by the treaty—down to a maximum of 6,000 warheads—were to be completed no later than seven years after its entry into force, but in fact, both the United States and Russia continued reductions after reaching START I mandated limits. By the time of the treaty's expiry (December 2009), their strategic nuclear arsenals were significantly below those stipulated in the Treaty. The Treaty's transparency and verification provisions were important throughout the lifetime of the Treaty, which was replaced by the United States and Russia with the New START Treaty in 2010.[43]

START I contained extensive provisions for verification. These included the following:

---

[42] 38 North, 'North Korea's Sixth Nuclear Test: A First Look', 5 September 2017, at: https://www.38north.org/2017/09/punggye090517/.

[43] Nuclear Threat Initiative (NTI), 'Treaty between the United States of America and the Union of Soviet Socialist Republics on Strategic Offensive Reductions (START I)', Last updated 26 October 2011, at: https://www.nti.org/learn/treaties-and-regimes/treaties-between-united-states-america-and-union-soviet-socialist-republics-strategic-offensive-reductions-start-i-start-ii/.

> Transparency measures included a Memorandum of Understanding between the two (initial) parties, which listed the numbers and locations of all strategic delivery vehicles, both deployed and non-deployed, as well the locations and diagrams of all facilities associated with strategic delivery vehicles. Each party was further required to exchange the entire set of data contained in the Memorandum every six months.

> National Technical Means (NTMs), which included satellite monitoring, were supported by a prohibition on actions that would impair the effectiveness of NTMs by the other party.

> On-site inspections were available to verify the accuracy of the data contained in the Memorandum of Understanding. Some of the inspections were at short notice while others were 'planned'. A special verification regime was created for mobile intercontinental ballistic missiles (ICBMs). During the first seven years of the Treaty, the United States conducted 335 inspections while Russia conducted 243.

> Perimeter and portal monitoring of plants producing mobile ICBMs applied only to Russia because the United States had decided not to deploy such missiles. The United States continued its existing monitoring at the Votkinsk plant, which it had begun under the INF Treaty (see below for details of verification for that Treaty).

Finally, the Treaty instituted a *prohibition on encryption of telemetry* transmitted from ballistic missiles during test launches.[44]

The experience of verification in the START I Treaty fed directly into the negotiation of New START. The 2002 Strategic Offensive Reductions Treaty (SORT), more commonly known as the Treaty of Moscow, had obligated each party to reduce and limit strategic nuclear warheads so that by the end of 2012 the number of those warheads did not exceed 2,200 for each party. But the Treaty had no verification provisions in it. Accordingly, the two parties agreed that START I would remain in force during implementation of the Treaty of Moscow.

The Treaty of Moscow remained formally in force until the date the New START Treaty[45] entered into force: 5 February 2011. As of this writing, New

---

[44] Ibid.

[45] Treaty between the United States of America and the Russian Federation on Measures for the Further Reduction and Limitation of Strategic Offensive Arms (New START); signed at Prague, 8 April 2010; entered into force, 5 February 2011; duration extended to 5 February 2026.

START is the only legally binding agreement that imposes formal ceilings on the number of strategic—or indeed any—nuclear weapons possessed by Russia and the United States. New START limits deployed Russian and US long-range nuclear forces to a maximum of 1,550 warheads and 700 delivery vehicles (e.g., ICBMs, submarine-launched ballistic missiles (SLBMs), and heavy bombers). Warheads actually deployed on ICBMs and SLBMs count towards the 1,550 limit while each deployed heavy bomber equipped for nuclear weapons, whether with gravity bombs or cruise missiles, counts as only one warhead, no matter how many warheads it actually carries. The New START Treaty does not place any constraints on the testing, development, or deployment of either current or planned US or Russian missile defence programmes or their long-range conventional strike capabilities.[46]

In the view of the Union of Concerned Scientists, one of the primary accomplishments of the new Treaty was that it streamlined the verification measures from START I, 'without sacrificing any essential information, while adding the most intrusive verification system ever implemented for counting nuclear warheads'.[47] The New START Treaty provided for verification—for the first time—of actual warhead numbers, rather than simply counting delivery vehicles as carrying a pre-determined number of warheads based on maximum loading. While START I's re-entry vehicle inspections only verified that a missile did not exceed the maximum number attributed to that missile type, New START requires each party to specify the number of warheads on each individual missile, which can then be verified by inspections (see below).

This 'major improvement' is said to have greatly increased US confidence in the accuracy of data provided by Russia. Simultaneously, it eliminates the over-counting of deployed warheads that resulted from earlier counting rules. For example, the last data exchange under START I, in July 2009, reported the United States as deploying more than 5,900 warheads, whereas the US Department of Defense claimed that the number was under the 2,200 limit of the Treaty of Moscow.[48]

---

[46] NTI, 'Treaty between the United States of America and the Russian Federation on Measures for the Further Reduction and Limitation of Strategic Offensive Arms (New START)', Last updated 25 February 2021, at: https://www.nti.org/learn/treaties-and-regimes/treaty-between-the-united-states-of-america-and-the-russian-federation-on-measures-for-the-further-reduction-and-limitation-of-strategic-offensive-arms/.

[47] Union of Concerned Scientists, 'Verification of New START', Cambridge, MA, July 2010, at: https://www.ucsusa.org/sites/default/files/2019 09/inspection fact sheet 1.pdf.

[48] Ibid.

The verification measures provided for by the New START Treaty include NTMs (e.g., satellites), on-site inspections, data exchange, and notifications related to strategic offensive arms and facilities. To increase transparency and confidence, the Treaty also provides for the annual exchange of telemetry data on a parity basis for up to five ICBM and SLBM launches per year.

The Treaty allows a total of eighteen on-site inspections each year, divided into two types. Type One inspections focus on sites with deployed and non-deployed strategic systems, while Type Two inspections focus on sites with only non-deployed strategic systems. Each State Party is allowed to conduct ten Type One inspections and eight Type Two inspections annually. In Type One inspections, each party has the right to count the number of re-entry vehicles actually deployed on an ICBM or SLBM. If the inspected Party covers its re-entry vehicles, each must have its own cover. No continuous perimeter and portal monitoring is permitted at missile production facilities, but parties must provide notification within forty-eight hours of any Treaty-limited item leaving a production facility.

The New START Treaty has been a great success in arms control. In contrast to the INF Treaty (see below), there have been no allegations by one party of cheating by the other. On 6 February 2019, US Under Secretary for Arms Control and International Security Andrea L. Thompson delivered a briefing on the future of the Treaty in which she declared that both the United States and Russia had complied with their obligations thereunder. The Treaty allowed a single extension to its mandated expiry on 5 February 2021 of up to five years, but only if both parties so agreed. In January 2021, the incoming Biden administration agreed with the Russian authorities to extend the Treaty's application for the full five years until 5 February 2026.

Verification of stockpile destruction

Ensuring that stockpiles are destroyed in line with treaty obligations is critical to building confidence among States Parties in the full implementation of an arms control or disarmament treaty. A good example of a successful verification process for stockpile destruction—for as long as the system was fully in operation—was contained in the 1987 Intermediate Nuclear Forces Treaty, better known as the INF Treaty.[49]

[49] Treaty between the United States and Soviet Union on the Elimination of Their Intermediate-range and Shorter-range Missiles (INF Treaty); signed at Washington DC, 8

The INF Treaty eliminated all conventional as well as nuclear-armed ground-launched ballistic and cruise missiles with ranges between 500 and 5,500 kilometres, along with their infrastructure. The Treaty, which was initially a bilateral agreement between the Soviet Union and the United States,[50] was the first nuclear arms control agreement to actually reduce the number of retained nuclear weapons, rather than to set ceilings for the number of weapons that could not be exceeded.

In total, the Treaty, which entered into force on 1 June 1988, resulted in the elimination by May 1991 of a total of 2,692 short, medium, and intermediate-range missiles. These comprised 846 US missile systems, including the updated Pershing II missiles, and 1,846 Soviet missile systems, including the Soviet SS-20s.[51]

The Treaty established what was, at the time, the most comprehensive—and intrusive—verification regime in history. On-site inspections included baseline data inspections,[52] inspections of closed facilities, and short-notice inspections of declared sites,[53] as well as inspections to observe the actual destruction of the prohibited missile systems.[54] It also established the first ever continuous monitoring operations at the portal and perimeters of a former missile production facility in each of the two nations to confirm that production of prohibited missiles had indeed ceased.

In January 1988 US President Ronald Reagan signed National Security Directive 296, which instructed US Secretary of Defense Frank Carlucci to establish a new agency—the On-Site Inspection Agency (OSIA)—to

December 1987; entered into force, 1 June 1988; expired (de facto), 2 August 2019, *UNTS* Vol. 1657, Reg. No. 28521.

[50] After the collapse of the Soviet Union, in addition to the Russian Federation as successor state, Belarus, Kazakhstan, and Ukraine also became parties to the INF Treaty.

[51] FAS, 'Intermediate-Range Nuclear Forces [INF]', updated but accessed 1 March 2021, at: https://fas.org/nuke/control/inf/; and Daryl Kimball, 'The Intermediate-Range Nuclear Forces (INF) Treaty at a Glance', Last reviewed August 2019, Fact Sheets & Briefs, at: https://www.armscontrol.org/factsheets/INFtreaty.

[52] The INF Treaty's Inspection Protocol obligated States Parties to inspect and inventory each other's intermediate-range nuclear forces between thirty and ninety days after the Treaty's entry into force. These 'baseline inspections' revealed the size and location of Soviet and US missile systems and supporting infrastructure.

[53] The Treaty allowed the parties to conduct up to twenty short-notice inspections per year at designated sites during the first three years of treaty implementation, and to monitor specified missile-production facilities to guarantee that no new missiles were being produced.

[54] For details, see, e.g., J. P. Harahan, *On-site Inspections under the INF Treaty: A History of the On-Site Inspection Agency and Treaty Implementation, 1988–1991*, Treaty History Series, US Government Printing Office, 1993, text available at: https://fas.org/nuke/control/inf/infbook/tabcon.html.

implement the Treaty's on-site inspection and escorting duties. Thirty days after the INF Treaty's entry into force, OSIA began inspecting 130 Soviet missile sites in Czechoslovakia, East Germany, and the Soviet Union while also escorting Soviet inspection teams at thirty-one sites in Belgium, Germany, Italy, the Netherlands, the United Kingdom, and the United States. Continuous monitoring operations began in both the Soviet Union and the United States in July 1988.

Upon entry into force of the Treaty, the two States Parties listed twelve 'elimination' sites in an official Memorandum of Understanding, designating which missile system would be eliminated at which site.

The United States military was made responsible for removing the INF missiles and launchers from operational status, transporting them to the elimination sites, and conducting the actual eliminations. Four sites were used: three in the continental United States and one in West Germany. The Soviet Union's elimination of its missiles and supporting infrastructure occurred at eight sites. This included two military bases, at Kansk and Chita in the east of the country, where a small number of SS-20 missiles were launched to destruction. The INF Treaty had specifically allowed each party the right to destroy up to 100 missiles through launching by 1 December 1988. At Kapustin Yar, other SS-20 missiles were destroyed though explosive demolition.[55]

The right of the States Parties to conduct on-site inspections under the INF Treaty was, however, time-limited, ending on 31 May 2001 (ten years after the deadline laid down by the Treaty for the completion of all stockpile destruction). The use of surveillance satellites for data collection was, though, allowed to continue. The INF Treaty established a Special Verification Commission (SVC) to act as an implementing body for the Treaty. It was designed both to resolve issues of alleged non-compliance and to agree on measures to improve the Treaty's 'viability and effectiveness'. During the lifetime of the INF Treaty, States Parties were allowed to convene the SVC at any time.

Disputes between the United States and Russia, in particular with regard to US allegations of Russian non-compliance, led to the United States' withdrawal from the Treaty, followed almost immediately by Russian withdrawal. The INF Treaty effectively became defunct on 2 August 2019.

---

[55] Ibid., Chap. 6.

Verification of the prohibition on use

The Open Skies Treaty

The 1992 Open Skies Treaty[56] was cast as a preventive instrument to build confidence between East and West that neither was planning to attack the other. The Treaty allows each of its thirty-four States Parties[57] to conduct short-notice, unarmed reconnaissance flights over the entire territory of any other State Party to collect data on its military forces and activities. While much of the same information can be gathered by satellite, not all of the adhering States have that capability.[58] In addition, aircraft can fly below cloud cover that can obscure photography taken from space.[59] Open Skies is said to be 'the most wide-ranging international effort to date to promote openness and transparency of military forces and their activities'.[60]

Each State Party to the Open Skies Treaty must accept a certain number of overflights each year, referred to as its passive quota, which is related to the size of its territory. A State Party's active quota is the number of flights it may conduct over other States Parties. A State Party's active quota may not exceed its passive quota, and one State Party is precluded from requesting more than half of another State Party's passive quota. In total, more than 1,100 overflights have been conducted in the lifetime of the Treaty. The Treaty establishes ground resolution thresholds for the onboard still and video cameras. The aircraft and its sensors must be formally certified before they can be used for Open Skies in order to confirm that they do not exceed the stipulated resolutions.[61]

In terms of process, an observing State Party must give at least seventy-two hours' notice before arriving in the host country to conduct an

---

[56] Treaty on Open Skies; signed at Helsinki, 24 March 1992; entered into force, 1 January 2002.

[57] Belarus, Belgium, Bosnia and Herzegovina, Bulgaria, Canada, Croatia, Czechia, Denmark, Estonia, Finland, France, Georgia, Germany, Greece, Hungary, Iceland, Italy, Latvia, Lithuania, Luxembourg, the Netherlands, Norway, Poland, Portugal, Romania, Russia, Slovakia, Slovenia, Spain, Sweden, Turkey, Ukraine, the United Kingdom, and the United States.

[58] D. Kimball, 'The Open Skies Treaty at a Glance', Last reviewed November 2020, Fact Sheets & Briefs, Arms Control Association, at: https://www.armscontrol.org/factsheets/openskies.

[59] S. Pifer, 'Is This the End of the Open Skies Treaty?', Blog post, Brookings Institution, Washington DC, 9 March 2020, at: https://www.brookings.edu/blog/order-from-chaos/2020/03/09/is-this-the-end-of-the-open-skies-treaty/.

[60] Organization for Security and Co-operation in Europe (OSCE), 'Open Skies Consultative Commission', undated but accessed 1 March 2021, at: https://www.osce.org/oscc.

[61] Kimball, 'The Open Skies Treaty at a Glance'.

overflight. The host country has twenty-four hours to acknowledge the request and to inform the observing party if it may use its own observation plane or if it must use a plane supplied by the host. At least twenty-four hours before the start of the flight, the observing party will supply its flight plan, which the host has four hours to review. The host may only request changes in flight plans for flight safety or logistical reasons. The observation mission must be completed within ninety-six hours of the observing party's arrival unless otherwise agreed.[62]

The Open Skies Consultative Commission (OSCC) is the implementing body for the Treaty. Consisting of representatives from each of the thirty-four States Parties, the OSCC meets at the headquarters of the Organization for Security and Co-operation in Europe (OSCE) in Vienna. The OSCC, which convenes in monthly plenary meetings, is supported by informal working groups of experts who address technical issues related to sensors, notification formats, aircraft certification, and rules and procedures. The OSCC's main functions are to:

- consider questions relating to compliance with the Treaty;
- seek to resolve ambiguities and differences of interpretation emerging during Treaty implementation;
- consider and decide on applications for accession to the Treaty, and
- review the distribution of flight quotas annually.[63]

The OSCC, which was established by Article X and Annex L of the Treaty, takes formal Decisions by consensus; to date, more than ninety Decisions have been adopted, which are legally binding on the States Parties.[64]

As of this writing, the future of the Open Skies Treaty was in doubt as US President Donald Trump had withdrawn the United States from the Treaty[65] and in January 2021 Russia announced that it would follow suit and withdraw from the Treaty.[66] Whether the Biden administration will rejoin the Treaty[67] and whether this would prompt Russia to reverse its

---

[62] Ibid.

[63] OSCE, 'Open Skies Consultative Commission'.

[64] Ibid.

[65] Pifer, 'Is this the end of the Open Skies Treaty?'

[66] V. Isachenkov, 'Russia Follows US in Withdrawal from Open Skies Treaty', Associated Press, 15 January 2021, at: https://apnews.com/article/russia-leaves-open-skies-treaty-e58019b80ae95e12007265aedfac229b.

[67] US scholars dispute whether President Biden can rejoin the Treaty without the need for renewed Senate consent by supermajority (sixty-seven affirmative votes). The better view is that he can. Thus, Jean Galbraith wrote in early February 2021: 'President Biden has the

decision was unknown as of this writing. Leonid Slutsky, the head of the foreign affairs committee in the lower house of the Russian parliament, said in January 2021 that Russia could review its decision to withdraw if the United States decided to return to the Treaty, but acknowledged that the prospect looked 'utopian'.[68]

Investigating alleged use of a weapon

Within the different arms control and disarmament treaties, a number of mechanisms exist to verify if a weapon has already been used in violation of a State Party's obligations. In the context of the 1992 Chemical Weapons Convention, the OPCW has been given additional powers not only to investigate use but also to determine responsibility. In the past five years chemical weapons have been used on many occasions in Syria, as well as on one occasion in Salisbury in the United Kingdom.[69]

On 8 April 2020, the OPCW released the findings of the first report by its Investigation and Identification Team (IIT). The IIT is responsible for identifying the perpetrators of the use of chemical weapons in Syria where the OPCW's Fact-Finding Mission (FFM) has determined that chemical weapons have been used or were likely to have been used. The IIT's first report set out its mandate, the legal and practical challenges of its work, and the findings of the investigations conducted between June 2019 and March 2020, focusing on incidents in Ltamenah (a town in Hama governorate in the north of Syria), on 24, 25, and 30 March 2017.[70]

authority to rejoin the United States to the treaty in reliance on the Senate's original resolution of advice and consent. Neither Congress nor the Senate has overridden this resolution. What President Trump has unmade unilaterally, President Biden should similarly have the power to remake.' J. Galbraith, 'The President's Authority to Rejoin the Open Skies Treaty', Blog entry, Lawfare, 8 February 2021, at: https://www.lawfareblog.com/presidents-authority-rejoin-open-skies-treaty. For a contrary advice on the Lawfare website, to which Professor Galbraith was responding, see S. Rademaker, 'Are There Shortcuts for the U.S. to Rejoin the Open Skies Treaty?', Blog entry, Lawfare, 15 January 2021, at: https://www.lawfareblog.com/are-there-shortcuts-us-rejoin-open-skies-treaty.

[68] Ibid. See also TASS, 'US Unlikely to Be Back in Open Skies Treaty under Biden Administration—Russian Diplomat', 15 January 2021, at: https://tass.com/world/1245519.

[69] See, e.g., OPCW, 'Incident in Salisbury: Technical Assistance Provided by OPCW Related to Toxic Chemical Incidents in Salisbury and Amesbury', at: https://www.opcw.org/media-centre/featured-topics/incident-salisbury.

[70] OPCW Technical Secretariat, 'OPCW Releases First Report by Investigation and Identification Team. IIT Concludes Units of the Syrian Arab Air Force Used Chemical Weapons in Ltamenah, Syria in March 2017', UN doc. S/1867/2020, The Hague, 8 April 2020, at: https://www.opcw.org/media-centre/news/2020/04/opcw-releases-first-report-investigation-and-identification-team.

The IIT's investigation and analysis included a comprehensive review of all of the information it had obtained, including direct interviews with those who were present in the relevant place at the time of the alleged use; analysis of samples and remnants collected at the sites of the incidents; review of the symptomatology reported by casualties and medical staff; examination of imagery, including satellite images; and extensive consultation of experts. The investigation relied on relevant FFM reports as well as on samples and other material obtained directly by the Technical Secretariat in the territory of Syria.[71]

The challenges faced by the IIT included its inability to access the site of the incidents as well as persons and information within Syria. In its report, the IIT regretted that this access was not granted despite: (a) various requests addressed by the Technical Secretariat to the Syrian authorities; (b) the undertaking by the government to cooperate with the Technical Secretariat under Article VII(7) of the Chemical Weapons Convention; and (c) the obligation on Syria, pursuant to UN Security Council Resolution 2118 (2013), 'to cooperate fully with the OPCW by providing personnel designated by the OPCW with immediate and unfettered access to any and all sites and individuals that the OPCW has grounds to believe to be of importance for the purpose of its mandate'.[72]

The IIT declared that following 'standard practice of international fact-finding bodies and commissions of inquiry',[73] it would

[71] Ibid.

[72] OPCW, 'First Report by the OPCW Investigation and Identification Team Pursuant to Paragraph 10 of Decision C-SS-4/DEC.3 "Addressing the Threat from Chemical Weapons Use" Ltamenah (Syrian Arab Republic) 24, 25, and 30 March 2017', The Hague, at: https://www.opcw.org/sites/default/files/documents/2020/04/s-1867-2020(e).pdf, Executive Summary, para. 7.

[73] See, e.g.: Report of the Independent International Commission of Inquiry on the Syrian Arab Republic, 28 January 2020, UN doc. A/HRC/43/57, para. 3; 'Annex to the Report of the Special Rapporteur on extrajudicial, summary or arbitrary executions: Investigation into the unlawful death of Mr. Jamal Khashoggi', 19 June 2019, UN doc. A/HRC/41/CRP.1, paras 43 and 237; Report of the Detailed Findings of the Independent International Fact-Finding Mission on Myanmar, 17 September 2018, UN doc. A/HRC/39/CRP.2, para. 10; Report of the Commission on Human Rights in South Sudan, 13 March 2018, UN doc. A/HRC/37/71, para. 11; Report of the Commission of Inquiry on Burundi, 11 August 2017, UN doc. A/HRC/36/54, para. 7; Report of the Commission of Inquiry on Human Rights in Eritrea, 9 May 2016, UN doc. A/HRC/32/47, para. 13; Investigation by the Office of the UN High Commissioner for Human Rights on Libya, 15 February 2016, UN doc. A/HRC/31/47, para. 5; Report of the OHCHR Investigation on Sri Lanka (OISL), 16 September 2015, UN doc. A/HRC/30/CRP.2, para. 33; Report of the Commission of Inquiry on Human Rights in the Democratic People's Republic of Korea, 7 February 2014, UN doc. A/HRC/25/63, para. 22; Report of the Independent International Commission of Inquiry on the Syrian Arab Republic, 22 February 2012, UN doc. A/HRC/19/69, para. 10; Report of the International Commission of Inquiry mandated to Establish the Facts and Circumstances of the Events of 28 September 2009 in

only reach conclusions on the identification of perpetrators on the basis of a sufficient and reliable body of information which, consistent with other information, would allow an ordinarily prudent person to reasonably believe that an individual or entity was involved in the use of chemical weapons (i.e., "reasonable grounds") ... Thus, under this degree of certainty, an objective observer would reasonably conclude that a violation was committed.[74]

Using these standards of proof, the report concluded that on 24 March 2017, an Su-22 aircraft of Syria's Air Force dropped a bomb containing sarin in southern Ltamenah, affecting at least sixteen persons. On 25 March 2017 a Syrian Air Force helicopter dropped a cylinder on Ltamenah hospital which released chlorine, affecting at least thirty persons. On 30 March 2017 a Syrian Su-22 military aircraft dropped a bomb containing sarin in southern Ltamenah, affecting at least sixty persons. In his recorded statement to States Parties, OPCW Director-General Fernando Arias declared that the IIT

is not a judicial or quasi-judicial body with the authority to assign individual criminal responsibility, nor does the IIT have the authority to make final findings on non-compliance with the Convention ... It is now up to the Executive Council and the Conference of the States Parties to the Chemical Weapons Convention, the United Nations Secretary-General, and the international community as a whole to take any further action they deem appropriate and necessary.[75]

Both the Government of the Syrian Arab Republic and the Government of the Russian Federation rejected the findings and conclusions of the report.[76]

Guinea (ICIG), 18 September 2009, Annex to UN doc. S/2009/693, para. 215. See also Report of the International Commission of Inquiry on Darfur to the UN Secretary-General Pursuant to Security Council Resolution 1564 of 18 September 2004, 18 September 2004, at 4.

[74] OPCW, 'First Report by the OPCW Investigation and Identification Team', para. 2.18.

[75] OPCW Technical Secretariat, 'OPCW Releases First Report by Investigation and Identification Team. IIT Concludes Units of the Syrian Arab Air Force Used Chemical Weapons in Ltamenah, Syria in March 2017'.

[76] TASS, 'Damascus Rejects OPCW Conclusions on Chemical Weapons Use in Syria's Ltamenah', Moscow, 9 April 2020, at: https://tass.com/world/1142481.

7
The Future of Arms Control and Disarmament

Introduction

This final chapter summarizes some of the trends and lessons that have been learned in arms control and disarmament over the past seventy-five years. It also identifies and summarizes the nature of those weapons and weapons systems currently the subject of discussions and negotiations among States or international experts and those that are on the horizon. This includes autonomous weapons systems, 3D printing, cyber operations, and space-based weapons, each of which poses major problems to the existing arms control and disarmament architecture.

Trends and lessons since 1945

The modern era of disarmament opened with the adoption of the Charter of the United Nations (UN) and the use of the atomic bomb. One offered hope that the scourge of war could be averted in the future; the other had the power to end humankind altogether. The age of extremes had begun.

During the Cold War, which lasted until 1989, arms control was a primary focus, seeking to limit the extent of the arms race between the two superpowers: the United States and the Soviet Union. The adoption of the Partial Test-Ban Treaty in 1963 helped to calm tensions following the Cuban missile crisis. The conclusion of the Anti-Ballistic Missile Treaty in 1971 and the negotiation of the SALT treaties were major achievements for the policy of *détente*.

There were also some significant successes in disarmament, most notably the adoption of the Biological Weapons Convention in 1971 and the Intermediate Nuclear Forces Treaty in 1987. Both treaties eliminated a class of weapon of mass destruction. In addition, the conclusion of the Treaty on the Non-Proliferation of Nuclear Weapons in 1968 helped to limit—but did not prevent—the spread of nuclear weapons beyond the five permanent members of the UN Security Council.

The end of the Cold War was a period of renewed hope. The adoption of the Chemical Weapons Convention in 1992 was the culmination of two decades of work within the United Nations, but this multilateral framework has since come under pressure as consensus has proved highly elusive. The Comprehensive Nuclear-Test-Ban Treaty had to be adopted by a vote in the UN General Assembly in 1996, as did the Arms Trade Treaty in 2013. The refusal by nuclear-armed States to contemplate seriously nuclear disarmament led to the adoption of the Treaty on the Prohibition of Nuclear Weapons in 2017. Polarization has blocked the Conference on Disarmament since 1996, with the remaining nine elements listed on the Decalogue, aside from the achievement of the Chemical Weapons Convention, stuck in an impasse. Comprehensive nuclear disarmament, as stipulated in Article VI of the NPT, appears further away than ever.

Division has also been seen in the international community with respect to conventional arms. Global conventional disarmament treaties, most notably the 1997 Anti-Personnel Mine Ban Convention and the 2008 Convention on Cluster Munitions, were concluded by like-minded States outside UN auspices as agreement on a prohibition proved impossible inside. Discussions on anti-vehicle mines have been abandoned, while ongoing talks on lethal autonomous weapons systems appear to be making little headway. In December 2019 the Arms Control Association reported that States Parties to the Convention on Certain Conventional Weapons (CCW) continued to discuss the danger of lethal autonomous weapons systems, but could not agree to begin a formal process of creating a legal instrument to govern their development and use. This was, the Association noted, the fifth year in which the topic had been addressed by the CCW.[1]

That said, upon the recommendation of the 2019 Group of Governmental Experts on lethal autonomous weapons systems (rather ironically abbreviated to the acronym LAWS), eleven guiding principles were adopted by the 2019 Meeting of States Parties to the CCW.[2] The principles affirm inter

---

[1] Arms Control Association, 'Decision on Autonomous Weapons Talks Eludes CCW', *Arms Control Today*, December 2019, at: https://www.armscontrol.org/act/2019-12/news-briefs/decision-autonomous-weapons-talks-eludes-ccw.

[2] Meeting of the High Contracting Parties to the Convention on Prohibitions or Restrictions on the Use of Certain Conventional Weapons Which May Be Deemed to Be

alia that: international humanitarian law applies to these systems; a human must always be responsible for the decision to use these systems; and States must examine the legality of these new weapons that they are developing or requiring at the design stage.[3] In September 2020, Human Rights Watch again encouraged States to negotiate 'a new legally binding instrument that maintains meaningful human control over the use of force and bans weapons that operate without such control'.[4]

More positive seemed to be the progress on an initiative to limit the use of heavy weapons in populated areas, although recently efforts have been stymied by the global COVID-19 pandemic. As the International Committee of the Red Cross (ICRC) stated in 2019: 'The use of heavy explosive weapons in populated areas directly impacts civilians, leading to death, grave injury, and severe mental trauma to thousands of men, women and children.'[5] In March 2020, Ireland circulated a draft Political Declaration on Strengthening the Protection of Civilians from Humanitarian Harm arising from the Use of Explosive Weapons in Populated Areas.[6] The draft Political Declaration recalls 'the obligations on all States and parties to armed conflict to adhere to International Humanitarian Law when conducting hostilities in populated areas, including the requirements to distinguish between combatants and civilians as well as between military objectives and civilian objects; the prohibitions against indiscriminate and disproportionate attacks and the obligation to take all feasible precautions in attack'.[7]

Excessively Injurious or to Have Indiscriminate Effects, Final Report, UN doc. CCW/MSP/2019/9, 13 December 2019, at: https://undocs.org/CCW/MSP/2019/9, para. 31.

[3] See, e.g., M. Ekelhof and G. P. Paoli, 'The Human Element in Decisions about the Use of Force', UNIDIR, Geneva, 2020, at: https://www.unidir.org/publication/human-element-decisions-about-use-force.

[4] 'Statement on Commonalities, CCW Group of Governmental Experts on Lethal Autonomous Weapons Systems', delivered by Bonnie Docherty, Senior Researcher, Human Rights Watch, 23 September 2020, at: https://www.hrw.org/news/2020/09/23/statement-commonalities-ccw-group-governmental-experts-lethal-autonomous-weapons#.

[5] Statement by Judith Kiconco, Humanitarian Affairs Adviser, Delegation to the African Union of the International Committee of the Red Cross (ICRC), Open Session of The African Union Peace and Security Council on the Protection of Civilians against Use of Explosive Weapons in Populated Areas, Addis Ababa, 17 July 2019, at: https://www.icrc.org/en/document/ewipa-icrc-statement-use-explosive-weapons-populated-areas.

[6] See Irish Ministry of Foreign Affairs, 'Protecting Civilians in Urban Warfare', at: https://www.dfa.ie/our-role-policies/international-priorities/peace-and-security/ewipa-consultations/.

[7] Irish Ministry of Foreign Affairs, Draft Political Declaration on Strengthening the Protection of Civilians from Humanitarian Harm arising from the Use of Explosive Weapons in Populated Areas, March 2020, at: https://www.dfa.ie/media/dfa/ourrolepolicies/peaceandsecurity/ewipa/Draft-Political-Declaration-17032020.pdf, para. 2.3.

Surprisingly, however, the Draft Declaration does not suggest that any weapons either are, or will be, prohibited for use in populated areas. The International Criminal Tribunal for the former Yugoslavia held that artillery-delivered cluster munitions fired into a city (Zagreb) from the limit of their operational range were indiscriminate,[8] as were adapted aerial bombs, also delivered by artillery, into Sarajevo.[9] The UN Commission of Inquiry on the 2014 Gaza conflict reported that most of the projectiles fired by Palestinian armed groups were rockets 'that at best were equipped with only rudimentary guidance systems and in the vast majority of cases had none at all'. The rockets available to armed groups in Gaza at the time 'were unguided and inaccurate'.[10]

Arms control and disarmament and new technologies

To add to these challenges, if they are to remain relevant, disarmament and arms control will need to adapt to rapidly evolving technologies that defy traditional means of verification and control. 3-D printers can be bought at home and can produce conventional weapons. Meanwhile wars are increasingly being fought not just on land, in the air, and at sea, but also in cyberspace, with outer space to come. In cyberspace, offensive cyber operations are threatening an enemy's ability to fight, including, potentially, precluding the capability of nuclear-armed States to launch their nuclear weapons. A 'launch on warning' posture has already led the world to the brink of extinction on a number of occasions in the past. There is no treaty regulating the use of cyberspace for military purposes.

The 1967 Outer Space Treaty boasts all of the five permanent members of the UN Security Council as adherents, but only prevents the stationing of WMD in outer space, including on the Moon. According to Article IV, States Parties 'undertake not to place in orbit around the Earth any objects carrying nuclear weapons or any other kinds of weapons of

---

[8] International Criminal Tribunal for the former Yugoslavia (ICTY), *Prosecutor* v. *Milan Martić*, Judgment (Appeals Chamber) (Case No IT-95-11-A), 8 October 2008, para. 247.

[9] ICTY, *Prosecutor* v. *Dragomir Milošević*, Judgment (Trial Chamber III) (Case No IT-98-29/1-T), 12 December 2007, paras 912, 1001.

[10] Report of the detailed findings of the independent commission of inquiry established pursuant to Human Rights Council resolution S-21/1, UN doc. A/HRC/29/CRP.4, 22 June 2015, para. 97.

mass destruction, install such weapons on celestial bodies, or station such weapons in outer space in any other manner'. Conventional weapons may not be placed on the Moon or other celestial bodies, which must be used only for peaceful purposes, but are otherwise not addressed.

A hypervelocity rod bundle (known familiarly as the 'rod from God') is a non-explosive tungsten cylinder launched downward from orbit and capable of reaching speeds of up to Mach 10 as it descends. The force of the rod's impact is said to be equivalent to a small nuclear explosion, causing devastating shockwaves around the target. As a non-nuclear explosive device, however, its stationing in outer space would not violate the Outer Space Treaty. Kinetic bombardment from space is 'back on the agenda'.[11] In 2014, the United States rejected the draft Treaty on Prevention of the Placement of Weapons in Outer Space and of the Threat or Use of Force Against Outer Space Objects, proposed in the Conference on Disarmament by China and Russia, on the grounds that it was 'fundamentally flawed' for not covering ground-based weapons.[12] According to a US Congressional Research Service report updated in February 2020, 'Conventional prompt global strike (CPGS) weapons may bolster U.S. efforts to deter and defeat adversaries by allowing the United States to attack high-value targets or 'fleeting targets' at the start of or during a conflict'.[13] At the same time, high-speed manoeuvring weapons, such as hypersonic cruise missiles or boost-glide vehicles, 'can combine speed and manoeuvrability between the air and space regimes to produce significant new offensive capability that could pose a complex defensive challenge'.[14]

As of this writing, COVID-19 was still rampaging across the world. While the number of deaths arising from the pandemic so far appears relatively small, dwarfed by the 20 million or more who died from the flu pandemic of 1918, the economic impact has been dramatic. There is, though,

---

[11] Sputnik News, 'US Project Thor Would Fire Tungsten Poles at Targets from Outer Space', *Space Daily*, 12 November 2018, at: https://www.spacedaily.com/reports/US_Project_Thor_would_fire_tungsten_poles_at_targets_from_outer_space_999.html.

[12] Ibid.; and see L. de Gouyon Matignon, 'Treaty on the Prevention of the Placement of Weapons in Outer Space', *Space Legal Issues*, 8 May 2019, at: https://www.spacelegalissues.com/treaty-on-the-prevention-of-the-placement-of-weapons-in-outer-space-the-threat-or-use-of-force-against-outer-space-objects/.

[13] *Conventional Prompt Global Strike and Long-Range Ballistic Missiles: Background and Issues*, Last updated 16 December 2020, US Congressional Research Service, Washington, DC, available at: https://fas.org/sgp/crs/nuke/R41464.pdf, Summary.

[14] National Academy of Sciences, *High-Speed Maneuvering Weapons: A Threat to America's Global Vigilance, Reach, and Power*, Unclassified Summary, Washington, DC, November 2016, p. 4.

no evidence that the long-term economic harm will lead to renewed interest in and commitment to arms control and disarmament. Expenditure on nuclear weapons alone over the next thirty years is expected to exceed US$2 trillion.

Indeed, writing in February 2021, two US security experts declared that New START might be the last nuclear arms control agreement between the Russian Federation and the United States, arguing that there was 'virtually no chance' that another negotiated treaty 'will be waiting to succeed' New START when it expires in February 2026.[15] They arrived at this stance on the basis of the pursuit by both nations of high-precision long-range conventional weapons and cyber and artificial intelligence (AI) capabilities: 'the kind of weapons whose stealthy and destructive potential matters far more than quantity.' New technologies, they observe, are 'blurring the lines between conventional and nuclear weapons', with certain cyber and AI capabilities being 'extremely difficult, if not impossible, to verify'. If the arms control relationship between Russia and the United States is to 'continue and remain meaningful', they conclude, 'both sides will need to come up with new approaches beyond negotiated treaties and intrusive verification regimes'.[16]

---

[15] E. Rumer and R. Sokolsky, 'Why the New START Extension Could Be the End of Arms Control as We Know It', Opinion Editorial, Politico, 7 February 2021, at: https://www.politico.com/news/magazine/2021/02/07/new-start-treaty-framework-cyber-466607.
[16] Ibid.

Index

For the benefit of digital users, indexed terms that span two pages (e.g., 52–53) may, on occasion, appear on only one of those pages.

Note: References marked in bold signify paragraphs of particular importance to the entry in the index.

3D printing 172

Additional Protocols (1977) to the Geneva
    Conventions 36–37, 119
Afghanistan 12, 63, 80, 109–10, 119
African Union 90, 141
aggression 37–38
Al-Qaeda 140
Amiton 153
ammunition 131, 133, 141 *see also*
    Munitions
Antarctic Treaty (1959) 11, 86, 159
Anti-ballistic missile (ABM) Treaty 78–
    79, 84
Anti-Personnel Mine Ban Convention
    (1997) 25–26, 30–32, 33, 37,
    103, **104–18**
  adoption 104, 107
  assisting (prohibited activity) 33, 112–13
  clearance 115–17
  entry into force 107
  negotiation 106–7
  States Parties 104
  stockpile destruction 113–15
    deadline 113–14
  use 31–32
  verification 152
anti-personnel mines 13, 104
  definition 110
  detectable 29, 105, 123
  improvised 110
  remotely delivered 105
anti-vehicle mines 123, 173–74
arbitrary deprivation of life 135–36
armaments *see* arms
armed conflict 4, 27–28

armoured combat vehicles 147
  definition 147
arms
  definition 2
  diversion of 137
  expenditure (*see* arms trade)
arms control
  definition 6–7
arms embargoes 40
arms trade 128–29, 148–49
Arms Trade Treaty (2013) 13, 14, 17, 30,
    128–39, 173
  adoption 17, 129
  Conference of States Parties 138
  entry into force 129
  negotiation 17
  Secretariat 138
  States Parties 129
artillery systems, large-calibre 147
  definition 147
ASEAN 89
assisting or encouraging (prohibited
    activities) 32–33
Association of Southeast Asian Nations
    see ASEAN
atomic bomb 10–11 *see also*
    nuclear weapon
attack helicopters 147
  definition 147
Australia 113
Australia Group 60–62
  Common Control Lists 60–61
  Guidelines for Transfers of Sensitive
    Chemical or Biological Items 60–61
Austria 139, 144
autonomous (weapons systems) 173–74

Axworthy, Lloyd 106
Azerbaijan 58

battle tanks 146
  definition 146
Belarus 71, 82, 140
Belgium 48–49
biological toxins 46, 47–48
biological weapons/warfare 3, 32, 43–
      44, 46–47
Biological Weapons Convention (1971) 11,
      25–26, 32, 38–39, **43–48**, 172–73
  adoption 43–44
  confidence-building measures 55–56
  depositaries 45
  ISU 56
  Meetings of States Parties 57–58
  negotiation 44
  reporting 55–56
  review Conferences 57
  States Parties 45
  stockpile destruction 48
    deadline 48
  verification (lack of) 55, 151–52
  withdrawal 48
Blinken, Antony 21, 83–84
Boko Haram 14–15, 40
Bosnia and Herzegovina 121
brokering 24, 30, 131, 143
Brussels Declaration (1997) 106–7

Cambodia 119
Canada 113
CD *see* Conference on Disarmament
Central African Convention for the Control
      of Small Arms and Light Weapons
      see Kinshasa Convention
Chad 45, 121
chemical weapons 3 *see also*
      toxic chemicals
  definition 50–51
Chemical Weapons Convention (1992) 19,
      22, 25–26, 32, 35, 36, 39–40, **48–54**,
      152, 173
  adoption 48–50
  challenge inspections 153–54
  definition of chemical weapons 50–51
  entry into force 48–49
  general obligations 51
  inspections regime 49–50, 55
  negotiation 48–49

  purposes not prohibited 50–51
  routine inspections 152–53
  Schedule 1 chemicals 46, 60
  Schedule 2 chemicals 153
  Single Small-Scale Facility 153
  States Parties 50
  stockpile destruction 52–53
    deadline 52–53
  threat of use 35
  transfer 52
  use 32
  verification 22
  withdrawal 54
Chile 116–17
China 21, 68–69, 81, 88, 91, 96, 99–100,
      101–2, 128–29, 140
chlorine 53–54
Christmas Island (Kiribati) 75
civilian(s) 36–37, 44, 104, 119, 123, 134, 174
clearance 28, 115–17
cluster munitions 13, 28
  definition 120
Cold War 11, 13, 103, 104, 124, 173
  end of 173
Collective Security Treaty *see* CST
Colombia 110–11, 121–22
combat aircraft 147
  definition 147
command-detonated (munitions) 110
Committee on Disarmament 18–19,
      44, 45, 69
companies/corporations 25, 26, 39
Comprehensive Nuclear-Test-Ban Treaty
      see CTBT
Conference on Disarmament 18–20, 21,
      48–49, 111
Congo, Democratic Republic of 140
control 115–16 *see also* jurisdiction
Control Arms (NGO campaign) 130
conventional weapon(s) **103–27**
  definition 3–5
Convention on Certain Conventional
      Weapons 2, 36–37, 103, 105,
      122–24, 173
  Amended Protocol II on Mines
      (1996) 29, 30, 31, 37, 105
  Protocol I on Non-Detectable Fragments
      (1980) 123
  Protocol II on Mines (1980) 2, 105
  Protocol III on Incendiary Weapons
      (1980) 123

Protocol IV on Blinding Laser Weapons
      (1995) 13, 31, 105–6, 123–24
Protocol V on explosive remnants of war
      (2003) 124
Convention on Cluster Munitions
      (2008) 25–26, 30–31, 37,
      103, **119–22**
   adoption 119
   clearance (of cluster munition
         remnants) 121–22
   entry into force 119
   negotiation 119
   States Parties 119
   stockpile destruction 120–21
   verification 152
Cook Islands 87
cooperation and assistance,
      international 118
Coordinating Committee for Multilateral
      Export Controls 143
Costa Rica 86–87
Covenant of the League of Nations 9–10
COVID-19 (virus) 96, 138
crimes against humanity 37–38, 133, 134
CST 91–92
CTBT 17, 27–28, 63–64, 77, 159–61, 173
   Comprehensive Nuclear Test-Ban
         Treaty Organization
         (CTBTO) 77, 159–60
   entry into force 77
Cuban missile crisis 172
customary international law 51–52
cyber operations 4–5, 101, 172
Cyprus 20
Czechia 33, 51–52, 113
Czechoslovakia, invasion of 11–12

Decalogue 19 *see also* Conference on
      Disarmament
détente, policy of 172
detonators 30
development 24, 26–27, 110–11
   definition 26–27
Diego Garcia 91
disarmament
   definition 5
   general and complete 5–6
disarmament, demobilisation, and
      reintegration (DDR) 14–15
drone 101, 147
dual-use (items) 2

ECOWAS Convention on Small Arms and
      Light Weapons (2006) 141
Egypt 140
Einstein, Albert 65
enforced disappearance 135–36
environmental (remediation) 24, 95–96
Eritrea 117, 140
European Court of Human Rights
      Finogenov case 4
European Union 128
   Common Position 128, **140**
expanding bullets 8–9
exploding bullets 7–8
export 135 *see also* transfer

fentanyl 4
Finaud, Marc 20
First World War 9–10
fissile material cut-off treaty (possibility
      of) 19–20
France 48–49, 68–69, 87, 88, 91, 105

Gaza 175
Geneva Conventions (1949) 134–35
Geneva Protocol (1925) 36, 43–44, 58
genocide 37–38, 133–34
Georgia 125
Germany 48–49, 53–54
Goldblat, Jozef 6–7
good faith, duty of 39
Gorbachev, Mikhail 150, 161
Greece 114–15
Ground Zero 63
Gulf War (1990) 49, 156

Hague, The 9–10 *see also* Hague Peace
      Conference
Hague Declaration (IV, 2) on Asphyxiating or
      Deleterious Gases (1899) 8–9, 48–49
Hague Peace Conference 7–8, 9, 43–
      44, 48–49
Haiti 45
Hiroshima (bombing) 10–11, 63, 67
hypersonic 100
   cruise missile 100
   glide vehicle 100
hypervelocity rod bundle 176

ICBM 78, 93, 100
ICRC *see* International Committee of the
      Red Cross

Implementation Support Unit (ISU) 23
importation 47
India 15–16, 68–69, 71, 109–10, 148–49
INF Treaty 12–13, 63–64, **80–81**, 172–73
  expiry 81
  impact 80–81
  negotiation 12–13
  On-Site Inspection Agency 165–66
  verification regime 164–66
  withdrawal 12–13, 20–21, 64, 81
injurious, excessively (weapon) *see*
        superfluous injury
innocent passage, right of 88
inspection *see* verification
intercontinental ballistic missile *see* ICBM
Intermediate Nuclear Forces Treaty *see*
        INF Treaty
International Atomic Energy Agency
        (IAEA) 27, 63–64, 71–72, 89, 90–91,
        95, 97–98, 151, 154–58
  Additional Protocol 72, 95, **157–58**
  Comprehensive Safeguards
        Agreement 72, 95, 155–57
  Director General 98, 157
  Rafael Mariano Grossi 98, 157
  Small Quantities Protocol 72
International Campaign to Ban Landmines
        (ICBL) 109
International Committee of the Red Cross
        (ICRC) 44, 174
International Court of Justice 34–
        35, 129–30
  Advisory Opinion on the legality
        of the threat or use of nuclear
        weapons 34–35
  Nicaragua case 129–30
International Criminal Court 37–38
international criminal law 24, 34–35,
        37–39, 135, 174, 175 *see also*
        aggression; crimes against humanity;
        genocide; war crimes
International Criminal Tribunal for the
        former Yugoslavia 175
international humanitarian law 7, 13, 24,
        26, **36–37**, 44, 108, 174
  grave breaches 135
  serious violations 135–36
international human rights law 13
  serious violation of 135–36
international peace and security 3
interpretative declaration 33

Iran 14, 15–16, 20, 38–39, 45–46, 60–61, 72,
        97–98, 129, 140, 158 *see also* JCPOA
Iraq 60–61, 72, 109–10, 119, 140 *see
        also* Osirak; Tuwaitha Nuclear
        Research Centre
Ireland 119, 174
Islamic State 14–15, 109–10
Israel 68–69, 71, 119, 156

Japan 99–100
JCPOA (Iran nuclear deal) 15–16, 20–21,
        72, 97–98, 158
Joint Comprehensive Plan of Action (2015)
        see JCPOA
Joyner, Daniel 27
jurisdiction 39, 115–16
jus ad bellum 7–8, 24, **34–35**, 93

Kapustin Yar 166
Kazakhstan 68, 71, 75, 82, 91–92 *see also*
        Semipalatinsk
Kierulf, John 5
kinetic bombardment 132
kinetic impact projectiles 132–33
Kinshasa Convention (2010) **141–42**
Korda, Matt 69
Korea, Democratic People's Republic of 14,
        16, 68–69, 71, 73, 75, 98–99, 129,
        140, 156–57, 160–61
  Chairman Kim 99
Korea, Republic of 99–100
Korean peninsula 99, 107, 109
Kristensen, Hans M. 69
Kyrgyzstan 91–92

Lake Chad Basin 14–15
landmine 2
Landmine Monitor 110–11, 152 *see
        also* ICBL
Laos 119
launch on warning (posture) 101–2
Lavrov, Sergey 20–21
law of armed conflict *see* international
        humanitarian law
law of neutrality 7–8
law of war *see* international
        humanitarian law
League of Nations 9–10
Lebanon 119, 140
Libya 72, 140
Los Alamos (facility) 66

Manhattan Project 66–67
Marshall Islands 75
micro-disarmament 14–15
Mine Action Review 116–17, 152
MIRVs 12, 84
missile *see also* hypersonic
    Novator 9M729 80–81
    Pershing II 165
    SS-20 (Soviet) 165
missiles and missile launchers 148
    definition 148
Missile Technology Control Regime
        (MCTR) 144–46
    annex 144–45
    Guidelines for Sensitive Missile-Relevant
        Transfers 145
Moldova 125
Mongolia 91
Montenegro 113
Moon 92–93
Moon Treaty (1979) 158–59
Mozambique 58, 117
multiple independently targeted re-entry
        vehicles *see* MIRVs
Munitions *see* ammunition
mustard gas 48–49, 53
Myanmar 109, 140

Nagasaki (bombing) 10–11, 67
Natanz 97
National implementation (of treaties) 39–40
NATO 5, 112–13, 124–25
Nepal 116
Netherlands, the 87
New START Treaty (2010) 21, 63–64,
        78, 82–84
    expiry 83–84
    extension 21, 164
    verification regime 162–64
New Zealand 71
Nigeria 109–10
Non-Aligned Movement (NAM) 5–6
non-proliferation 7
    definition 7
    horizontal 7
    vertical 7
non-State actor 7, 25, 32–33, 36–37, 69, 95,
        109–11, 141
North Atlantic Treaty Organization
        see NATO
Norway 119

Novaya Zemlya 75
Novichok 52–53, 60
NPT 5–6, 11–12, 19–20, 27, 29, 31, 63–64,
        69–71, 74, 96, 98, 172–73
    non-nuclear-weapon State 27, 29, 31
    nuclear-weapon State 7, 31, 69, 71–72
    Review Conference (2020) 96
    States Parties 71
    withdrawal 98
nuclear disarmament 11, 70–71
nuclear energy, peaceful use of 70
nuclear explosive devices *see* nuclear weapon
nuclear fission 63, 65, 66
nuclear material 71–72
    accountancy 155–56
Nuclear Suppliers Group 73–74
    Non-Proliferation Principle 73
Nuclear Threat Initiative (NTI) 89, 101–2
nuclear weapons **63–102**
    definition of 70
    development 27, 68–69
    gun-type 66
    implosion 66
    testing 16, 27–28, 66, 68–69, 75, 76

OAS 86–87
OPCW *see* Organization for the Prohibition
        of Chemical Weapons
Open Skies Consultative Commission
        (OSCC) 168
Open Skies Treaty (1992) 20–21, 103, **125–
        26** *see also* Open Skies Consultative
        Commission
    verification 167–69
    withdrawal 168–69
Organization for the Prohibition of
        Chemical Weapons 22, 23, 35, 59–
        60, 152, 169–71
    Director-General 23, 35
    Fact-Finding Mission for Syria 22, 59–60
    inspections regime 152
    inspectorate 152
    Investigation and Identification Team
        (IIT) 169–71
OPCW–UN Joint Investigative Mechanism
        (JIM) 22, 59–60
Organization for Security and Co-operation
        in Europe (OSCE) 103, 127
Organization of American States *see* OAS
Osirak 156
Outer Space Treaty (1967) 11, **92–93**

Pakistan 15–16, 21, 68–69, 71, 109–10
Partial Nuclear-Test-Ban Treaty (1963) 11,
         27–28, 76–77, 158–59
parts and components 2, 52, 131–32
peaceful purposes *see also* purposes not
         prohibited
plutonium 66
poison 8–9
Poland 113
Porton Down 153
prisoners of war 134–35
production 28–29, 110–11
    definition 28–29
    facilities, destruction of 39–40

radioactive fallout 75
radiological weapons 3
    definition 3
reconnaissance 145, 147
Regional Nuclear-Free Zones 85–93
riot control agent 3–4, 32, 51 *see also*
         tear gas
rocket *see* missile
Russia 20–21, 45, 47, 52–53, 64, 71, 82,
         88, 91, 93, 100, 101, 125, 128, 148–
         49, 171
Russian
    President Dmitry Medvedev 82
    President Vladimir Putin 79, 80–81
    President Boris Yeltsin 46–47, 84
    Special Forces 4

Sadaam Hussein 49, 156
Sahrawi Arab Democratic Republic 90
Sakharov, Andrei 76
Salisbury (use of chemical weapons) 60, 169
SALT (talks/treaties) 11–12, 79–80
SALW *see* small arms and light weapons
Sarin 53, 153, 171
Saudi Arabia 20, 148–49
Second World War 8–9
Selebi, Jacob 107
Semipalatinsk (test site) 68, 75
Serbia 113
Singapore 99–100
SIPRI 148–49
    Arms Transfers Database 148–49
slavery 9
small arms and light weapons 14–15, 132–
         33, 148
    2001 Programme of Action 16–17

Somalia 140
South Africa 68–69
South Sudan 71, 109, 140
Soviet Union 6–7, 45, 46–47, 68, 165–66 *see
         also* Russia; Warsaw Pact
    Premier Alexei Kosygin 78
    Premier Leonid Brezhnev 80
    Red Army 46–47, 68
space-based weapons 172
Spain 91
St Petersburg Declaration (1868) 7–8
Stalingrad 46–47
START I Treaty 82
    verification 161–62
START II Treaty 84
START III Treaty 84
State responsibility 33, 34
Stockholm International Peace Research
         Institute *see* SIPRI
stockpile
    definition 29
    destruction 29
        deadline 29–30
stockpiling 24, 29, 30
strontium 76
submunitions *see also* cluster munitions
    unexploded 28
Sun, the 63
superfluous injury 8–9
Sweden 119
Syria 14, 22, 58, 59, 109–10, 129, 140, 169–71
    Ltamenah 169
Szilárd, Leó 65

Taiwan 116
Tajikistan 91–92
Taliban 140
tear gas 32, 36 *see also* riot control agent
terrorism 130, 135
testing 27–28
Thailand 89
Thompson, Andrea L. 164
torture 133, 135–36
toxic chemicals 4, 50, 53
transfer 24, 30, 36–37, 47–48, 52, 105–6,
         111–12 *see also* Arms Trade
         Treaty; export
    definition 24, 30, 111–12, 131, 141
transit 52
transnational organised crime 135
trans-shipment 24, 131

Treaty of Bangkok (1995) **89**
Treaty of Pelindaba (1996) **90–91**
Treaty of Rarotonga (1985) **87–88**
Treaty of Semipalatinsk (2006) **91–92**
Treaty of Tlatelolco (1967) **86–87**
Treaty of Versailles (1919) 9–10
Treaty on the Non-Proliferation of Nuclear
    Weapons *see* NPT
Treaty on the Prohibition of Nuclear
    Weapons (2017) 17, 25–26, 27–28,
    37, 63–64, **94–96**
  Adoption 94
Tunisia 110–11
Turkey 20, 109
Turkmenistan 75, 91
Tuwaitha Nuclear Research Centre 156

Ukraine 71, 82, 109–10, 114–15
Union of Concerned Scientists 163
United Arab Emirates 20
United Kingdom 44, 48–49, 68–69, 75, 87,
    88, 91, 93, 113, 116–17
United Nations (UN)
  Charter 10, 14–15, 34
  Convention on Certain Conventional
      Weapons 36–37, 103, 122–24, 173
      (*see also* Convention on Certain
      Conventional Weapons)
  Conventional Armaments
      Commission 3–4
  Disarmament Commission 16–17
  General Assembly 10–11, 14, 16–17, 48–
      49, 85, 129, 173
    Resolution 1(I) 10–11
    Resolution 1652 (XVI) 90
    Resolution 1962 (XVIII) 92
    Resolution 2222 (XXI) 92
    Resolution 3472B (XXX) 85
    Resolution 3477 (XXX) 87
    Resolution 45/56A 90
    Resolution 45/57 58
    Resolution 61/89 130
    Resolution 71/258 94
    Resolution 74/56 18
    Resolution S-10/2 18–19
    Special Sessions on
        disarmament 6, 16–18
  Office for Disarmament Affairs
      (UNODA) 56
  Register of Conventional Arms
      (UNROCA) 131–32, **146–48**

  Secretary-General 15, 54, 90, 104–
      5, 128–29
  Secretary-General's Mechanism
      58–59
  Security Council 14–15, 25, 40, 54, 98–
      99, 151–52, 156–57
    1540 Committee 41–42
    Al-Qaida Sanctions Committee 40
    Al-Qaida Sanctions List 40
    Resolution 620 58
    Resolution 1172 15–16
    Resolution 1540 25, **41–42**
    Resolution 1696 15–16
    Resolution 1977 41–42
    Resolution 2083 40
    Resolution 2209 53–54
    Resolution 2231 15–16, 97
    Resolution 2235 22
    Resolution 2319 22
    Resolution 2356 98–99
    Resolution 2375 16, 156–57
United States 6–7, 27, 45, 47, 52–53, 55,
    63, 64, 75, 82, 87, 88, 89, 91, 93, 96,
    99–100, 103, 107, 109, 119, 125, 128,
    148–49, 151–52, 158, 165–66
  Central Intelligence Agency 97, 99
  Congressional Research Service 176
  Department of Defense 3, 4–5, 53, 93
  President Barack Obama 82
  President Bill Clinton 84
  President Dwight D.
      Eisenhower 125–26
  President George H. W. Bush 13, 84,
      125–26, 161
  President George W. Bush 79, 84
  President Jimmy Carter 80
  President Joe Biden 21, 83
  President Lyndon Johnson 11–12, 78
  President Richard Nixon 11–12, 46, 79
  President Ronald Reagan 12–13, 150
  President Franklin D. Roosevelt 65
  President Donald Trump 99, 168–69
uranium 66, 158
use 24–25, 31–32, 37, 108–9
  definition 31–32, 108
  in populated areas of heavy
      weapons 174
Uzbekistan 75, 81, 91

vaccine 47–48
Venezuela 140

verification **150–71**
victim
    assistance 117–18, 122
Vienna Convention on the Law of Treaties
    (1969) 39
Vienna Document (2011) 103, **127**
Vietnam 119
Vietnam War 119
VX 153

war crime(s) 37–38, 133, 134–36
Warsaw Pact 103, 124–26
warships 148
    definition 147
Wassenaar Arrangement 143–44
    List of Dual-Use Goods and
        Technologies 143
    Munitions List 143

weapon of mass destruction 3, 10–11,
    93, 144–45
    definition 3
weapons *see also* biological weapons;
    chemical weapons; conventional
    weapon; nuclear weapons;
    radiological weapons
    definition 2
Western Sahara *see also* Sahrawi Arab
    Democratic Republic
WMD *see* weapon of mass destruction

Yemen 108–10, 140
    President Ali Abdullah Saleh 108–9
Ypres 53–54

Zangger Committee 74
Zimbabwe 140